The Gates of Gaza: Critical Voices from Israel on Oc
and the War with Hamas

De Gruyter
Disruptions

Volume 4

The Gates of Gaza:
Critical Voices from Israel on October 7 and the War with Hamas

Edited by Lihi Ben Shitrit

DE GRUYTER

ISBN (Paperback) 978-3-11-143497-1
ISBN (Hardcover) 978-3-11-144735-3
e-ISBN (PDF) 978-3-11-143504-6
e-ISBN (EPUB) 978-3-11-143532-9
ISSN 2748-9086

Library of Congress Control Number: 2024933846

Bibliographic information published by the Deutsche Nationalbibliothek
The Deutsche Nationalbibliothek lists this publication in the Deutsche Nationalbibliografie;
detailed bibliographic data are available on the Internet at http://dnb.dnb.de.

© 2024 Walter de Gruyter GmbH, Berlin/Boston
Cover image: Olga Sidelnikova/iStock/Getty Images Plus
Printing and binding: CPI books GmbH, Leck

www.degruyter.com

In memory of Vivian Silver, who never stopped waging peace.

Acknowledgments

Deepest gratitude to the contributors to this collection, who agreed to write, translate, or republish their work for this volume. Thank you also to the book's superb editorial team: Julia Brauch and Verena Deutsch at De Gruyter, and Sara Magness for her copyediting.

As some of the pieces have been previously published, the authors would like to acknowledge the original outlets as follows: Shaul Arieli and Eva Illouz, *Haaretz*; Eran Tzidkiyahu and Yaniv Ronen, *The Forum for Regional Thinking*; Idan Landau, Landau's blog *Don't Die Stupid*; Ghadir Hani, *Walla*; Orly Noy and Noam Shuster-Eliassi, *+972 Magazine*; Omer Bartov and Nicholas Kristof, *The New York Times*.

Table of Contents

I. Introduction

Lihi Ben Shitrit
Chapter 1: The Gates of Gaza
October 31, 2023 —— 3

II. How Did We Get Here?

Shaul Arieli
Chapter 2: Thirty Years Since the Oslo Accord: You Can't Cross a Ravine in Two Jumps
September 21, 2023 —— 13

Eva Illouz
Chapter 3: Can Israel Wake Up from Its Worst Nightmare and Do the Right Thing?
October 17, 2023 —— 21

Idan Landau
Chapter 4: The State's Betrayal of Its Citizens
October 16, 2023 —— 25

Shaul Arieli
Chapter 5: The Failure Is the Result of Netanyahu's False Reality
October 19, 2023 —— 41

Yaniv Ronen
Chapter 6: What Is Hamas? Facts and Analysis
October 18, 2023 —— 47

III. Notes from the War

Yofi Tirosh
Chapter 7: A War Chronology
November 17, 2023 —— **53**

Assaf David
Chapter 8: Flashes from the Life That Was
October 14, 2023 —— **65**

Ameer Fakhoury
Chapter 9: I'll Write While I Can Still Breathe
October 16, 2023 —— **69**

Ghadir Hani
Chapter 10: The Arab Community Is Still in Shock from Hamas's Massacre
November 6, 2023 —— **71**

Eran Tzidkiyahu
Chapter 11: Comments on the Current Moment
October 18, 2023 —— **73**

Orit Kamir
Chapter 12: Fighting on Two Fronts: Between Hamas's Atrocities and Israel's Extremist Government
November 28, 2023, and January 11, 2024 —— **83**

Orly Noy
Chapter 13: Listen to Israeli Survivors: They Don't Want Revenge
October 25, 2023 —— **91**

Noam Shuster-Eliassi
Chapter 14: Picking Up the Pieces of Our Grief
October 20, 2023 —— **95**

Jessica Ausinheiler
Chapter 15: Child Loss: A Mother's Reflection
December 12, 2023 —— **99**

Meirav Jones
Chapter 16: From the River to the Sea
  December 14, 2023 —— **103**

Tal Correm
Chapter 17: The Imperative of Thinking in Dark Times
  December 16, 2023 —— **107**

Anwar Mhajne
Chapter 18: Silencing Dissent: Suppression Tactics in Israel Since October 7
  November 15, 2023 —— **111**

IV. Going Forward: Questions of Morality and Hope

David Kretzmer
Chapter 19: Reflections on International Law
  December 11, 2023 —— **123**

Omer Bartov
Chapter 20: What I Believe as a Historian of Genocide
  November 10, 2023 —— **139**

Rawia Aburabia
Chapter 21: On the Need for Moral Clarity and Political Complexity
  December 21, 2023 —— **143**

Hannah Safran
Chapter 22: If Not Now, When? Time for a Feminist Peace Vision
  December 3, 2023 —— **147**

Tanya Zion-Waldoks and Galit Cohen-Kedem
Chapter 23: On Hope I: In Search of Generational Hope
  November 2023 —— **151**

Avi Shilon
Chapter 24: On Hope II: Hope in Days of Despair
  November 30, 2023 —— **163**

Hagar Kotef and Merav Amir
Chapter 25: On Hope III: Terms of (Dis)engagement—Critique and Solidarity After October 7
    November, 2023 —— **169**

V. Epilogue

Ali Al-Awar
Chapter 26: A View from Gaza
    November 4, 2023 —— **185**

Nicholas Kristof
Chapter 27: Do We Treat Palestinians as Lesser Victims?
    October 21, 2023 —— **189**

References —— **193**

I. Introduction

Lihi Ben Shitrit
Chapter 1: The Gates of Gaza

October 31, 2023

Lihi Ben Shitrit, PhD, is the director of the Taub Center for Israel Studies and the Henry Taub Associate Professor of Israel Studies at the Skirball Department of Hebrew and Judaic Studies at NYU. She is also an associate professor at the School of Public and International Affairs, University of Georgia. She is the author of *Righteous Transgressions: Women's Activism on the Israeli and Palestinian Religious Right* (Princeton University Press, 2015) and *Women and the Holy City: The Struggle over Jerusalem's Sacred Space* (Cambridge University Press, 2020). She holds a PhD, MPhil, and MA in political science from Yale University and a B.A. in Near Eastern Studies from Princeton University.

On October 7, 2023 hundreds of armed terrorists of the Palestinian Islamic Resistance Movement—Hamas—crossed the border from the Gaza Strip into southern Israel and committed the largest and most brutal massacre of Israeli civilians in the history of the state. They occupied villages and towns, shot any person they saw, went house to house and executed entire families. They burned fathers, mothers, and children alive. They beheaded some of the dead. They searched for those hiding—under tables, in safe rooms, even in chemical bathrooms outdoors—and shot them. They shot children of all ages. They arrived at a music festival and murdered the young people there. They sexually abused people dead and alive. They paraded the undressed body of a young woman in front of cheering crowds. They shoved another woman, her pants covered in blood, into a moving jeep with countless armed men. They mutilated some of those they killed. In their wake they left over 1,200 dead, and they captured 240 people, including babies, children, women, men, and the elderly, and transported them into underground tunnels in the Gaza Strip to a fate yet unknown.

October 7 was made from the stuff of nightmares, the most disturbing and sadistic horror. Some videos taken by the terrorists show their joy and ecstasy at others' pain. They must have been in an altered state. It is hard to believe such cruelty could exist. It is hard to find words to describe their mix of brutality, sadism, gore, and joy at the terror of the victims. I watched some of those videos; it was a mistake, no one should watch them. They were physically sickening. I lay in bed and wailed quietly like a wounded animal, paralyzed, trying to take those images out of my head, to turn back time to before all of this happened.

The scale of the sadism of these events is unfathomable. It doesn't fit easily with our understanding of political violence. It was men shedding their humanity. It was what collective trauma specialist Nathaniel Laor called a terrorism disaster: "a man-made event that sharply and intensively targets people, whole populations,

https://doi.org/10.1515/9783111435046-002

and nations, with the aim to shatter their basic assumptions about human nature and social norms; which seeks to sow death, horror, and extreme insecurity by exhibiting untamed madness that reduces life to merely material randomness."[1] And as we Israelis watched it—or just heard and read about it, because the traditional media mercifully spared us the worst of the images and videos—that's what happened to us. Our basic assumptions about human nature and social norms were shaken. We saw evil and we were its targets. Many of us, maybe all of us, were overtaken by pain, fear, and anger.

What do you do with these feelings? What is the possible response? Politicians and military men immediately started saying what they thought most Israelis wanted to hear. They thought Israelis wanted the most baritone voices, cracking at the effort to go both very deep and very loud, to reassure them that:

> The IDF [Israel Defense Force] will immediately deploy its full force to destroy Hamas's capabilities. We will strike them until complete destruction and seek revenge for the black day they brought upon Israel and its citizens. As [the poet] Bialik said, "The revenge for the blood of a small child, the devil has not yet created" … All the places where Hamas operates, their evil city, all the places where Hamas hides, acts from, we will turn into heaps of rubble. I say to the residents of Gaza, leave now, because we will act everywhere and with full force.
> (Prime Minister Benjamin Netanyahu, October 7, 2023)[2]

> I ordered a complete siege of Gaza. We are fighting human animals and we act accordingly … There will be no electricity, there will be no food, there will be no fuel [in Gaza]. Everything closed.
> (Defense Minister Yoav Galant, October 9, 2023)[3]

> The stress is on damage, not accuracy.
> (IDF spokesperson, on Israel's aerial bombing of Gaza, October 10, 2023)[4]

> We must create an unprecedented humanitarian disaster in Gaza. The ultimate weapon—targeting the water system. Only the movement of tens of thousands and the outcry of the international community will create the leverage for Gaza to be either without Hamas or without people. We are in an existential war.
> (Former head of Israel's National Security Council, Gen. Giora Eiland, October 11, 2023)[5]

They decided Israelis wanted strongmen to exact righteous revenge that will destroy evil. Many hearing their words forgot that these men have publicly vowed to inflict pain in the past. They have retaliated devastatingly after Hamas attacks

---

[1] Achitov (2023). All translations from Hebrew and Arabic are the authors'.
[2] Aichner (2023).
[3] Zaytun (2023).
[4] B'Tselem (2023a).
[5] Kan Reshet Bet (2023).

before, but that never seemed to deliver the security they promised. Many rightly called the 7th of October 9/11 to the magnitude of ten, or thirty. In proportional terms, given Israel's population size, that was an accurate description. They conveniently left out, though, what happened after September 11, 2001 as the US embarked on a war to overthrow the Taliban. They did not mention that after twenty years of that war and after countless American and Afghan lives lost—the Taliban was now back in power in Afghanistan.

What was different in this round of engagement with Hamas, compared to those of the past, was the magnitude and brutality of the terrorists' attack and the humiliation of the military's top brass and the government. Israel found itself in an explosive situation, with politicians fretting about their future—when citizens will inevitably hold them accountable for not preventing the entirely preventable disaster of October 7—and a wholly traumatized and reeling population. All this against a backdrop of months of unprecedented mass demonstrations against the government's attempt at a judicial overhaul, which many Israelis saw as an attack on the country's democracy.

And so, the military campaign to destroy Hamas and wipe it off the face of the earth began. As of this writing, on October 31, 2023, more than 1.4 million Gazans have been displaced by the war—that's more than half of Gaza's entire population. The UN reports that nearly half of all homes in Gaza have been destroyed or damaged. Those displaced will not have a home to return to. According to Gaza's health ministry, over 8,000 people have been killed; of them more than 3,000 are children. [update as of January 8, 2024: the numbers have surged to over 22,000 casualties, close to 70% of them being women and children, with 9,000 child casualties;[6] up to 1.9 million people have been displaced[7]]. When you see on the news the scenes from Gaza, of families losing everything and everyone, including their children, your heart is crushed as though under the buildings that have been turned to rubble. You cannot breathe.

Israeli news channels rarely show these sights. They don't report on the names and faces of the countless dead in Gaza. Some in Israel justify these deaths as collateral damage. They remind us that these deaths are not intentional. Yet the IDF announced that its "stress is on damage, not accuracy." Even if Gazan civilians and children are not the main targets, their lives just don't matter in this military campaign. Inside Israel, over 130,000 Israelis had to leave their homes to seek shelter from rockets. More Israelis die or are injured by rocket attacks. Hezbollah in Lebanon is threatening to enter the fray, and the Houthis in Yemen launch Iranian-

---

6 Kottasová et al. (2024).
7 UNRWA (2024).

supplied rockets in Israel's direction. The IDF is beginning ground incursions into the Gaza Strip.

While this is unfolding, the Israeli government has yet to explain how it will return all the captured Israeli hostages home. It has failed to articulate any exit strategy from Gaza, any clear redlines for the number of civilian casualties and refugees caused by its retaliation on Hamas, or any realistic long-term plan.

It is unclear what most Israelis think; they are still processing. It is safe to guess that while they initially rallied around the war, Israelis will soon become as split on the causes, consequences, and course of action of this war as they were split politically before the war. As events progress, opinions will shift.

But there are many critical voices in Israel who have been speaking clearly. They have warned about the folly and failings of "military solutions." They have raised questions about morality, legality, and even just strategy and common sense. Revenge and bluster are not a strategy, they argued. Before October 7 and the war, they were prophetic, many of them have warned of the unsustainability of a reality of occupation, siege, and denial of human, civil, and political rights to Palestinians, and have told us, repeatedly, that Israelis were not safe as long as Palestinians were not safe. Their perspective and analysis are needed now more than ever.

This collection is a record of these voices. It provides a chronicle of the reactions of critical intellectuals and scholars to unfolding events. I asked authors to contribute from their writing—both published and unpublished—to this critical conversation. All the pieces here have been written in the span of a few days to a few months from October 7 and comprise an archive of a particular discourse taking shape in Israel at this historical juncture.

The authors write from different perspectives and positions; they disagree with each other on many things. Some consider themselves liberal Zionists, others position themselves as non- or post-Zionists, anti-Zionists, or prefer not to be labeled at all. Some work within the paradigm of national self-determination, others within the paradigm of settler-colonialism, and yet others request of us, and themselves, to complicate, deepen, or re-think our paradigms. If I venture to say what I think they have in common, it is, first, that they are still grappling with the horror of Hamas's acts on October 7, as any person should. Second, while in the grip of the horror, they also remember that an eye for an eye leaves us all blind,[8] that we will have to live with our Palestinian neighbors after this war, and that we lose our humanity when we say that "we have no choice" but to treat hundreds of thousands of civilians in Gaza as collateral damage.

---

8 An expression commonly attributed to M.K. Gandhi, see Shapiro (2006) p. 269–270.

They remember that the planners and perpetrators of the October 7 crimes justified their actions as "fighting for freedom," and that some of their extreme cheerleaders in the West justified these crimes as anti-colonialism. "So a few Israeli children were murdered," these cheerleaders imply, mothers shot, people beheaded with a hose, babies and grandparents kidnapped into tunnels underground. But it was all for a "righteous struggle." It was to keep Palestinian children safe, to fight an enemy that wants to erase Palestine from the map and deny Palestinians their right to self-determination. This logic must be rejected. None of these reasons could ever justify the acts of October 7. And, in the same way, no righteous struggle, no fight to keep Israeli children safe, to battle an enemy who wants to erase Israel from the map and deny Jews their right to self-determination, could justify killing thousands of children.

***

This collection is divided into four parts. The first section, titled "How Did We Get Here?" provides critical analysis of the history, political conditions, and policies that led to the October 7 attack. In the first piece, Shaul Arieli reviews the thirty years that have passed since the signing of the Oslo Accord (the piece was written on September 21, 2023 less than 3 weeks before the October 7 attack). It elucidates the squandered opportunities to resolve the Israeli-Palestinian conflict, and argues that, "In the long term, the missed opportunities of the Oslo process may come to be seen as a disaster for Israel comparable to the Palestinian Nakba of 1948." The following contributions in this section analyze a shorter timeframe, namely the period of right-wing rule under Benjamin Netanyahu in the past decade, leading up to the fateful October of 2023.

The second section, "Notes from the War," presents immediate reactions by authors as they witnessed the atrocious and traumatic attack of October 7, the build-up toward a war in Gaza, and the first two months of the war until the current moment in which the Israeli retaliation in Gaza has proceeded with unbearable destruction of life. The pieces are written in various registers. Some authors chronicle unmediated reactions and emotions in themselves and their communities that October 7 generated. Others reflect on the political and military response, while others address the public discourses that have surrounded the unfolding events, at home and abroad.

The third section, "Going Forward: Questions of Morality and Hope," analyzes current and future developments with an eye toward imagining a postwar future in Israel and Palestine in the aftermath of the unfolding catastrophe. Some of the pieces take on the legal, moral, and political implications of the war, while others, at my request, try to find glimmers of hope for a better future. Finally, while all pieces were written by Israeli citizens—mostly in Israel and some abroad—the Epilogue introduces two outsider perspectives. The first is by Ali Al-Awar, a Palestinian scholar with decades of peace-work commitment, who shares with us the view from Gaza, where his family resides and where it had suffered impossible loss. Second, the journalist Nicholas Kristof, who is neither Israeli nor lives in Israel. Together they allow both the readers and the authors a moment of external reflection, and extend an invitation for a wider conversation.

Two additional final notes: Each chapter in this book lists the day in which it was written, spanning a few days to a few months from October 7, 2023. The numbers of Israeli and Palestinian casualties mentioned in each piece reflect the data on the date of writing. Each chapter also reflects a point in time as the war progressed, and constitutes a critical intervention at each point in this journey that, had it been heeded, would have kept the number of causalities much lower, and would have changed the course of the conflict. Tragically, none of these interventions were heeded. A second note, an essential complementary book to this one would collect Palestinian voices from the West Bank and Gaza on the themes of October 7 and the war in Gaza. The focus of this volume, however, is critical voices from Israel—both Jewish Israelis and Palestinian citizens of Israel—on the current war. As a Jewish Israeli scholar, it is not my place to curate a Palestinian collection. As much as Israelis like myself might empathize with and ally ourselves to the pain Palestinians currently experience, we must make space for Palestinians to make their own voices heard, on their own terms.

***

After October 7 some Israelis found urgent relevance in Moshe Dayan's 1956 eulogy at the funeral of Roi Rotberg—a member of Kibbutz Nachal Oz who was murdered by Palestinian infiltrators from Gaza.[9] Nachal Oz was one of the kibbutzim that suffered a shattering death toll on October 7. As others have noted,[10] there are parts of the eulogy that speak profoundly to some, and parts that are terrifying to others:

> The young Roi who left Tel Aviv to build his home at the gates of Gaza to be a wall for us, was blinded by the light in his heart and he did not see the flash of the sword. The yearning for peace deafened his ears and he did not hear the voice of murder waiting in ambush. The gates of Gaza weighed too heavily on his shoulders and overcame him.

---

9 Dayan (1956).
10 Rabinovich (2023, pp. 180–181), Dubnov (2024).

This was true of the members of Nachal Oz on October 7, many of whom supported peace with the Palestinians and the establishment of a Palestinian state, and opposed Israel's policies of occupation. Dayan's prescriptions for the future, however, alarmingly resonate with those who now support devastating military action in Gaza:

> Beyond the furrow of the border, a sea of hatred and desire for revenge is swelling, awaiting the day when serenity will dull our path, for the day when we will heed the ambassadors of malevolent hypocrisy who call upon us to lay down our arms.
>
> We will make our reckoning with ourselves today; we are a generation that settles the land and without the steel helmet and the canon's maw, we will not be able to plant a tree and build a home. Let us not be deterred from seeing the loathing that is inflaming and filling the lives of the hundreds of thousands of Arabs who live around us. Let us not avert our eyes lest our arms weaken.
>
> This is the fate of our generation. This is our life's choice—to be prepared and armed, strong and determined, lest the sword be stricken from our fist and our lives cut down.

But those who subscribe to this outlook do not seem to grasp that when an action fails to achieve its stated results for decades upon decades, a new path must be taken. They also neglect to heed Dayan's eerie acknowledgment:

> Let us not cast the blame on the murderers today. Why should we complain of their burning hatred for us? For eight years [since 1948] they have been sitting in the refugee camps in Gaza, and before their eyes we have been transforming the lands and the villages, where they and their fathers dwelt, into our estate.

Those eight years have turned into seventy-five years. The Palestinian dream of a safe home and self-determination and the Jewish dream of a safe haven and self-determination continue to compete. There are those who say one can happen only at the expense of the other and so both peoples are forever destined to live by their swords. They argue everyone must pick a side, either with us or against us. The authors in this collection of essays hope otherwise.

II. How Did We Get Here?

Shaul Arieli

Chapter 2: Thirty Years Since the Oslo Accord: You Can't Cross a Ravine in Two Jumps

September 21, 2023

> Col. (reserve) **Shaul Arieli**, PhD, is an expert on the Israeli–Palestinian conflict. He was the Commander of the Northern Brigade in Gaza, Head of the Interim Agreement Administration under the Rabin, Peres, and Netanyahu governments, Deputy Military Secretary to the Minister of Defense, and Head of the Peace Administration in PM Barak's government. Arieli teaches at the Reichman University in Herzliya and the Hebrew University of Jerusalem. He is a board member of Commanders for Israel's Security (CIS) and a leading member of the Geneva Initiative. He is considered one of Israel's leading experts on the Israeli–Palestinian conflict, the borders of Israel, and the separation barrier. Arieli has published ten books and many academic articles and newspaper opinion pieces.

This month marks the thirtieth anniversary of the signing of the Oslo Accord—the Declaration of Principles on Interim Self-Government Arrangements—between Israel and the PLO [Palestinian Liberation Organization]. The agreement delineated a road map for resolving the Israeli–Palestinian conflict without defining what the permanent arrangement would look like. The thirty years that have passed show that the agreement failed to address the gaps between the divergent perceptions and goals of the two sides, and may be likened to an attempt to cross a ravine in two jumps. During the implementation of the agreement, after the initial jump, the signatories fell into the jaws of those on both sides who opposed the agreement and insisted "it's all mine."

The following are some of the milestones that have shaped the enormous complexity of the Israeli–Palestinian conflict and the gulf between each side's perceptions:

- The Balfour Declaration of 1917 and the Mandate of 1922 served as the opening shots in the conflict. These documents formalized international recognition of the right of the Jewish people, living outside their land, to a national home in their homeland, while denying this right to the country's Arab inhabitants.
- The international recognition of the right of the country's Arabs to self-determination in 1937–47, culminating in the UN Partition Resolution 181, which allocated 45% of Mandatory Palestine for a Palestinian state. The Zionist movement accepted the partition resolution as the only way to establish a democratic state with a Jewish majority. The Arabs, who represented a majority of the population and owned 90% of the land, rejected it and fought to pre-

https://doi.org/10.1515/9783111435046-003

vent its implementation. At the end of the war they emerged as a disadvantaged minority in Israel and as refugees in the neighboring Arab countries (with the exception of Jordan, where they are citizens).
- Resolution 242 of the UN Security Council, adopted in November 1967 after the Six-Day War, adopted a new formula for compromise: Israel would hold 78% of the area of Mandatory Palestine and return the territories it occupied in 1967 in return for peace agreements.
- In 1974 the Palestinians began to internalize the need for compromise and accordingly adopted the Phased Plan. In 1988, after Jordan nullified its annexation of the West Bank and the PLO was again recognized as the sole representative of the Palestinian people, the PLO recognized Partition Resolution 181 (which mentions a Jewish state) and Resolution 242, implying acceptance of a Palestinian state in 22% of the territory of "historical Palestine."

The Oslo Accord outlined a gradual process that was intended to lead in three years and three stages (the Gaza–Jericho Agreement, the Interim Agreement, and additional arrangements) to a starting point creating the conditions for negotiations toward a permanent agreement. The entire area of the Gaza Strip and West Bank—with the exception of East Jerusalem, the settlements, and military sites (which would be discussed in the negotiations for a permanent agreement)—would be transferred to the responsibility of an elected Palestinian Authority. Israeli Prime Minister Yitzhak Rabin insisted on this gradual framework as part of his perception of the peace process: "I prefer interim agreements, with a test period between each stage, to an attempt to move forward in a single step to a comprehensive agreement."

Rabin imposed this approach on the Palestinians, although he was aware that the reality of the Jewish settlements in 1993 was different from that in 1978 when the Autonomy Agreement was signed at Camp David. At a government meeting on August 30, 1993, Rabin declared: "The whole idea of autonomy, the interim agreement, is a complex one. It was invented when there were virtually no Jewish settlements in the Territories, so that the whole matter was much simpler. Jewish settlement, particularly in densely populated areas, has complicated life—that was its political goal. This was political settlement, not security settlement, without any contribution to security."[1]

Five factors motivated Rabin to adhere to his gradual approach. The first was the success of this approach as implemented in the peace process with Egypt: a troop separation agreement in 1974, an interim agreement in 1975, a framework

---

1 Aderet (2023).

agreement in 1978, and a permanent agreement in 1979. The second was the reliance on the Autonomy Agreement signed by Menachem Begin at Camp David in 1978, which was almost identical to the 1993 Declaration of Principles.

The third factor was concern regarding the ability of the PLO to adhere to the agreement, as Foreign Minister Shimon Peres noted: "The Palestinians have reached the bottom of the barrel; their position today is terrible. I must say that it is possible that the whole business of the PLO may disintegrate." The fourth factor was the desire to postpone the need to cope with removing settlements, after the Palestinians agreed that these would remain during the interim period. The fifth was the issue of Jerusalem.

Two Similar Peoples

Both Rabin and Peres ignored the insistence of each side on maintaining its own narrative. Yasser Arafat's deputy, Abu Iyad, wrote: "The two peoples were made similar by the suffering each had endured—the Israelis by Nazism, the Palestinians by colonialism—similar also in their determination to attain their objectives whatever the price, similar in their intransigence which far exceeds that of their leaders."[2]

The gradual approach gave the opponents of compromise on both sides—Hamas and the messianic-nationalist stream in Israel—time to recover from the blow of the agreement, which was only made public when it was signed. They were able to thwart the main changes to which each side had committed itself, and by so doing to undermine the trust needed in order to implement a long process toward compromise. Ehud Barak—IDF chief of staff at the time—and Rabin were aware of this risk. At the same 1993 meeting, Barak commented: "I would just note that there will be extremist elements in Palestinian society that will have an active interest in trying to torpedo this agreement and its maturation." Rabin interrupted him: "The same in Israeli society." Rabin attempted to shape the reality on the ground ahead of the negotiations toward a permanent agreement through numerous steps, including Government Decision 360 (1992), which froze the construction of new settlements, the reallocation of budgets from Judea and Samaria [the West Bank] to Israel proper, and a prohibition against the construction of infrastructures strengthening the connection between the settlements in the various "blocks."

---

[2] Abu Iyad (1981) p. 208.

Rabin's assassination in 1995 by a Jewish extremist and the election of Benjamin Netanyahu as prime minister reversed these trends and sparked processes that eroded the territorial commitment to the Palestinians. After transferring Hebron and implementing a minor step toward the Palestinians, Netanyahu froze the ongoing transfer of land to the Palestinian Authority, and proudly boasted of this. The messianic nationalists, under a series of leaders—from Yitzhak Levy and Effi Eitam through Naftali Bennett and on to Bezalel Smotrich and Itamar Ben-Gvir—received budgets and security support from all the governments headed by Netanyahu, enabling them to sabotage the peace process. They managed to increase the number of Israelis living in the West Bank fourfold, including the founding of 170 illegal outposts and farms (forty of which have already received retroactive approval), the construction of a network of bypass roads serving isolated settlements, the expulsion of Palestinians from their land, attacks on Palestinians, and the demolition of their homes. These actions seriously eroded trust in Israel among the Palestinians.

On the other side, Hamas, seeing its dream of an Islamic Palestine from the Jordan River to the Mediterranean Sea vanishing in front of its eyes, continued to use terror against Israel and the PA, impairing the main benefit the Israelis had anticipated—security. Arafat failed to meet his commitment to pursue an uncompromising struggle against terror, thereby fueling Israeli fears and eroding the level of mutual trust to a level that even Mahmoud Abbas, the current Palestinian president and a loyal exponent of the peace process, has to date failed to repair. Numerous opinion polls show a dramatic fall in support for the two-state solution among Israeli Jews, from 60% to around one-third, although the majority still support separation, including unilaterally. The Palestinian public shares the despair at any possibility of a solution; many Palestinians, particularly the younger generation, prefer a solution of a single state with equality for all.

The negotiations toward a permanent agreement eventually began after a delay of two years. Only 38% of the territory of the West Bank and Gaza Strip was transferred to the Palestinians; on the other side, Israel was badly shaken by terror attacks. The challenge was how to bridge the gaps between the perceptions of the two sides regarding the permanent agreement and the question of which conflict the process sought to address—that of 1917, 1948, or 1967. The enormous gulf was already evident in the mutual recognition between Israel and the PLO. The PLO granted Israel full territorial payment (recognition of Israel in the 1967 borders), thereby leaving Israel with 78% of the area of Mandatory Palestine. In return, the PLO sought solutions to the problems created by a century of conflict: the Palestinian right to self-determination in Mandatory Palestine, a Palestinian capital in Jerusalem, the borders, and the refugees.

Israel presented 1967 as the starting point for the conflict, and the territories occupied in that year as the content of the conflict. It did not offer the PLO reciprocal payment, confining itself to recognizing the organization as the legitimate representative of the Palestinian people. This position, based on Israel's strength, was reflected in Rabin's refusal to utter the words "Palestinian state," referring instead to "an entity that is less than a state."

In his speech to the Knesset on October 4, 1995, in the session that ratified the Interim Agreement, Rabin offered a portrait of the permanent agreement that did not envision a fully independent Palestinian state; from the Palestinian perspective this was ridiculous. Ehud Barak, elected prime minister in 1999, followed suit, defining the goal of the negotiations as "a just division of the territories of Judea and Samaria." In other words, a compromise would be reached on the basis of the 1967 post-war borders, rather than from the true starting point: the Balfour Declaration.

Barak's Failure

From the PLO's perspective, its recognition of the Partition Resolution and of UN Resolutions 242 and 338 gave the Palestinian people a legitimate place in the international community, from which it had excluded itself since 1917 by its refusal to accept international decisions. This recognition implied the implementation of the UN resolutions: an Israeli withdrawal to the 1967 borders in return for peace agreements. Accordingly, when it accepted the gradual process imposed on it, the PLO assumed that the process would end in the establishment of a Palestinian state in the 1967 borders (with land swaps).

In the negotiations that began in the second half of 1999, Barak chose not to continue to pay the price for a gradual process. He argued that the two sides should not deal with "installments" but should proceed to a permanent agreement in two stages: a framework agreement outlining the ultimate reality, followed by a detailed agreement; this was agreed in the protocol signed at Sharm el-Sheikh in May 1999. However, Barak failed to recognize that for the messianic nationalist settlers in Israel, even the smallest success is one guided by divine intervention. He adopted a lenient approach toward the facts they created on the ground—more and more settlements—which, as noted, eroded Palestinian trust in the process.

Under Barak the number of apartments constructed in the settlements soared. In 1999, he even agreed to the "whitewashing" of illegal outposts that had flourished under Netanyahu's first government. Barak's failure to understand the Palestinian position and the limits of their flexibility reached its peak at Camp David in 2000. His most generous offer was supposed to send Arafat back to the Palestinian people with a proposal that would secure just 84% of the area of the West Bank and Gaza Strip, demilitarized and without heavy weapons, as well as a further 7% in the Jordan Valley to be held by Israel under a temporary lease—without access to the border with Jordan, without a capital in Al-Quds (East Jerusalem), with Israeli sovereignty on the Temple Mount, and without any possibility for the return of Palestinian refugees. In other words, Barak's offer was detached from the international resolutions and from the Palestinian narrative and their perception of compromise. The offer created the conditions for the outbreak of the Second Intifada, following Ariel Sharon's visit to the Temple Mount, and entrenched the mantra that "there is no partner."

It was only fifteen years after the signing of the Oslo Accord that Israel, under prime minister Ehud Olmert, fell into line with the international resolutions. During the Annapolis process in 2007–8, Olmert and Abbas reached agreement on the parameters for negotiations. Both leaders made significant process, but were unable to close all the gaps before Olmert resigned after he was indicted for corruption.

The opponents of compromise on both sides had taken advantage of the preceding fifteen years to erode trust between the two sides and resume the mutual bloodshed. In 2005 Israel withdrew unilaterally from the Gaza Strip and in 2007 Hamas seized control of the area by force, creating the division between the West Bank and Gaza Strip. Netanyahu's return to the prime minister's office in 2009 dealt a death blow to the peace process and the two-state solution. President Trump's "Vision for Peace" (2020), which was conceived and dictated by Netanyahu, presented a cynical and absurd reworking of the two-state concept.

With strong backing from the US administrations, Israel missed the opportunity to convert the Oslo Accord into the final chord of its conflict with the Palestinians from a position of strength, and in the best possible conditions it could achieve. Rabin was wrong to impose the principle of a gradual solution on the peace process: the most complicated and intricate issues in the century-long conflict required a solution in a single, sharp cut. This was the spirit of the 1947 Partition Plan, whose initiators recognized that it offered the "most practical" solution given the unbridgeable gulf between the narratives of the two sides. As then-Minister of Police Moshe Shahal warned at the abovementioned 1993 government meeting: "It would be better to head for a permanent solution and implement it in stages ... Autonomy in itself creates an impossible reality for implementation."

The Palestinians have paid a heavy price for their mistakes over the years—the Second Intifada and the failure to fight Hamas terror. Today, the absence of a peace process and Israel's refusal to compromise may force the PLO, whose political approach has failed, to make way for Hamas or to adopt Hamas's policy of armed resistance.

Nevertheless, the Oslo process secured unprecedented achievements for both sides. From the Israeli side, the formation of the Palestinian Authority relieved it of responsibility for direct management of the daily lives of millions of Palestinians. Jordan's relinquishing of its role as the representative of the Palestinians paved the way for the peace treaty between Israel and Jordan. The establishment of diplomatic relations with Arab states later permitted the signing of the Abraham Accords. The process encouraged dramatic economic growth in Israel. For the Palestinians, the establishment of the Palestinian Authority in democratic elections created the foundation for a "state in the making" and led to the recognition by the UN of Palestine with observer status; it also led to the recognition by Israel of the PLO as the sole representative of the Palestinian people.

In the long term, the missed opportunities of the Oslo process may come to be seen as a disaster for Israel comparable to the Palestinian Nakba of 1948. Israel has behaved and continues to behave from a position of power, seeking to gain more than it is entitled to in accordance with the international resolutions. It has ignored and continues to ignore the risk that it may fail in this approach and pay a very heavy price. Right now, the price has reached a peak with Netanyahu's judicial coup—the sacrificing of the State of Israel as a democratic state on the altar of the West Bank and the entrenchment of apartheid.

In the first stage, the apartheid regime is pushing Israel into the role of a global pariah. Ultimately, it will transform Israel into an Arab state with a Haredi and messianic Jewish minority. Israel currently faces a diplomatic opportunity in the form of a possible agreement with Saudi Arabia. Including significant steps in this agreement, particularly in the territorial dimension, that can restore the path to separation between two states may save Israel from the abyss it is hurtling toward.

Eva Illouz
Chapter 3: Can Israel Wake Up from Its Worst Nightmare and Do the Right Thing?

October 17, 2023

>**Eva Illouz**, PhD, is a professor of sociology at the Hebrew University of Jerusalem and the School for Advanced Studies in the Social Sciences in Paris. She was the first woman president of Bezalel Academy of Art and Design. In 2022, Illouz was ranked as the eighth most influential woman in sociology worldwide. She has published many books, her most recent being *The Emotional Life of Populism: How Fear, Disgust, Resentment, and Love Undermine Democracy* (2023).

Horror movies elicit a unique kind of terror we never experience in ordinary life. They activate unconscious fears, making us experience a form of terror that is total, primal, and overwhelming. Horror movies have developed into various subgenres; one is that of the criminal psychopath who has broken into the house, but the heroine doesn't know where he is and only feels his presence. Danger is imminent but unseen. He's on a rampage but evades even the smartest surveillance (see *A Stranger in the House*). In another subgenre, the categories become reversed. The weak (e.g., a child) becomes all-powerful (e.g., possessed by the devil in *The Exorcist*) and the strong (e.g., the parents) becomes powerless or blind to what's happening. Another example of inversion can be a joyful party that becomes a site of carnage. A third category draws from the horror of nightmares, when we dream that someone is going to kill us but we're paralyzed and can't run away. The paralysis itself elicits terror (see *Gerald's Game*). A fourth and final subgenre of horror movies focuses on gore: torn limbs or beheaded faces, as well as the psychopathic face that enjoys it (*Suspiria*).

In recent days, Israelis have experienced all four categories of undiluted terror. An enemy they thought was weak infiltrated the quiet of their yards, kitchens, and bedrooms, launching a rampage of extraordinary gore and cruelty. The invincible Israeli security apparatus, which is supposed to defend us, evaporated into thin air, as in the stuff of nightmares. The army and the police didn't arrive in time to stop the massacres. For the longest time, the army was on its way.

The massacre that happened in Israel isn't like other massacres. Waking up to an enemy breaching the privacy of our homes and the prolonged paralysis of the entire system tapped into a primal and visceral terror. This is, after all, what terrorism is about: disrupting and breaking a society through terror. Hamas has proved to be far more masterful than ISIS in its capacity to produce a multidimensional form of terror. The magnitude and depth of the trauma will probably change

Israel's political and military culture irreversibly. There will never be a return to the Israel of before October 7, 2023.

But another form of horror has no narrative genre: the gradual realization that the unfathomable collapse of the entire security apparatus isn't a one-time accident but the outcome of a deep and widespread systemic failure. We now realize that our house has been built on quicksand that is slowly swallowing us whole.

This systemic failure has three layers. Let's start with the most straightforward: the government under which this massive collapse happened. I don't need to repeat the list of criminals—on trial or convicted—who serve in this government. Criminals have one property that sets them apart from normative people: they are indifferent to the law. The law is a system of rules that has authority because it represents the common good. Criminals' desire for power, money, or land takes precedence over the well-being of others and the common good.

It's hard to count this government's many ways of criminality. On July 24, before the vote on the reasonableness standard that would weaken the Supreme Court, Benjamin Netanyahu refused to meet with the army's chief of staff, Herzl Halevi, who wanted to brief the prime minister on the worsening security situation. Egypt's foreign minister also warned Netanyahu that Hamas was preparing something (though the Prime Minister's Office denies this). In recent months, countless former heads of the Shin Bet security service, the Mossad, and the defense establishment reiterated that the judicial coup planned by the government posed a security threat. But the criminals ignored the warnings and charged ahead.

I wish I could say the criminal acts stopped there. Netanyahu's appearance in front of the cameras to declare the state of war was actually scary: his robotic tone lacked basic humanity and empathy. No decent or simply normal human being would be able to sleep or continue serving after 1,200 civilians and soldiers had been so brutally murdered.

Not only would they be unable to sleep, not only would they be ashamed to exist, as any normal person would (remember Menachem Begin's depression as the death toll mounted during the First Lebanon War). They would also be incapable of giving us the indecent spectacle of narcissistic political infighting over the forming of an emergency government. The criminality of Netanyahu's government, which ignored all the security warnings in order to retain power and grab more, is too painful to discuss further.

The second layer of the systemic failure is to be found in the army, and the political conception that has guided military strategy (military strategies are always guided by an implicit political interpretation of the world). For decades, Netanyahu sold us the thesis that Hamas was worth pampering against the Palestinian Authority (to prevent the possibility of a two-state solution), that the conflict could be managed as a low-intensity military conflict with occasional flare-ups, that the subduing of Hamas could be bought with Qatari money, that Hamas was a pragmatic movement and not a millenarist one, and that the Middle East could be reshaped by erasing the Palestinian problem from the map of the "new Middle East."

Technology, high-tech wizardry, and massive business deals were supposed to buttress this sweet dream. This security doctrine has just showed its hollowness and even idiocy. But it has had a massive effect: it has transformed the army into an occupation army, trained to control civilians rather than guard the borders. The soldiers of the strongest army in the Middle East had great difficulties fighting Hamas terrorists, suffering a hair-raising number of casualties. Chief of Staff Halevi lives in the settlement of Kfar Ha'oranim, a fact that caps the long process by which the army shifted its identity and now contains so many settlers and religious people.

We can ask ourselves: why were such a disproportionate number of soldiers moved from the southern border with Gaza to the West Bank under Halevi's watch? Is there a relationship between a settlers' government and the concentration of military resources in "their" area? Who gave the order to allow an abnormally large number of soldiers to return home for the religious holiday? By definition, a security system that collapsed so effortlessly, so thoroughly, is suffering a deep dysfunction. And this is likely due to the existence of a heavy ideological fog where its brain should be.

The third layer is the most disturbing: the collapse of the state during this harrowing event. Hundreds of people would have been saved if the police and the army had arrived earlier. The senior French-Israeli journalist Danièle Kriegel reported that soldiers couldn't move around easily because trains don't run on Shabbat. I don't need to remind readers why there are no trains on Shabbat. But why weren't there buses to transport the troops? They could have arrived at 8 a.m. and started operations at 9 a.m. Instead, their arrival took eight to ten hours or so.

I write these words and can't believe them myself. Where were the soldiers? And why were the soldiers given outdated equipment? Why were thousands of houses deprived of adequate shelter? The army was so utterly unable to manage the crisis that many families learned the fate of their loved ones through the gruesome videos posted by Hamas. The army was incapable of coordinating the response to the crisis. Civil society provided the evacuees with food, clothing, and shelter. The opposition protesters who the day before were treated as traitors stepped in and saved their community by substituting for the absent state.

What are the reasons for this absence? This is the resounding proof that something in the State of Israel is dysfunctional. The most likely hypothesis is that an unfathomable amount of resources that have gone to the settlements and the ultra-Orthodox were crucially needed elsewhere, not only for the well-being of hard-working Israelis but for their very security. The state has increasingly redirected its financial and organizational resources to interest groups. We now understand that the problem of the arrangement with the ultra-Orthodox and the West Bank isn't only economic—it concerns the entire country's security. On October 7, the clear flaws in Israel's social contract exploded in our face. Israelis have been tolerant of this social contract, and compliant, because they were assured of their security. We can no longer make this assumption. The social contract no longer exists.

In the months to come, we will need to contemplate many questions. Have these events proved or disproved the left's position that only a political solution can end the conflict? Can we still count on the army and the rest of the security apparatus? How do we reconstruct Israeli society with our Arab brothers and sisters who stood by us without blinking? But most urgent will be the need to rethink the very foundations of the Israeli social contract. We now have the proof that Israel cannot ensure its security while assigning disproportionate resources to messianics and the ultra-Orthodox. Israel must now choose its path.

Idan Landau
Chapter 4: The State's Betrayal of Its Citizens

October 16, 2023

Idan Landau, PhD, is a professor of linguistics in the Department of Linguistics at Tel Aviv University (TAU). Alongside his many academic books and articles, he has a popular current affairs blog in Hebrew called Don't Die Stupid. He earned his MA in linguistics from Tel Aviv University, and PhD in linguistics from MIT.

Introduction

As I write these words, tens of thousands of soldiers stand at the gates of Gaza, awaiting the command "Forward!" My hands tremble, my breathing is irregular. I cannot imagine any good outcome. The kidnapped Israelis have already been declared "collateral damage,"[1] and my heart aches at our leadership's indifference to their fate. My heart aches at the number of casualties in Gaza—at this moment, 2,750 casualties, with about half of them being women and children [update as of March, 2024: the numbers have surged to over 30,000 casualties, close to 70% of them being women and children; with 12,300 child casualties].[2] And my heart refuses to imagine what is yet to unfold.

This is not the time to write, I told myself throughout the first week of the war, while collecting materials, comparing, formulating, writing, erasing, and editing. It is not the time to read. This is the time of blood crying out from the earth, the time of revenge, the time of eyes blinded by the heartbreak. So why am I writing? For whom?

I have no answers. Not to persuade. Words no longer persuade anyone in this land. It took me some time to realize this, and when I did, I decided to stop writing about the conflict and politics. I noticed I was repeating myself, quoting myself, and it became embarrassing.

Yet while I remained silent, the system, the "propaganda machine," continued to churn out columns all the time. The amount of fake news[3] was beyond what one could handle, and the battleground shifted to the swift clashes of Twitter, where

---

1 Haaretz Update (2023).
2 Gaza Health Ministry (2024).
3 Goichman (2023).

https://doi.org/10.1515/9783111435046-005

the deluge seemed to overwhelm any capacity to stop and think, to rethink, to check facts, to draw conclusions.

On October 7, almost in parallel to the Hamas attack, a persistent wave of conspiracy theories flooded the internet. Its immediate effect, as planned, was to divert attention from the main culprits in the collapse of the defense and social security networks in Israel. The magnitude of the crisis was so immense that an equally powerful wave of disinformation and propaganda was needed to deflect criticism, upend political discourse, and leave everyone confused and disoriented. In a period of profound grief and shock, that wasn't difficult to do.

I needed to write a chronicle as thoroughly documented as possible, with archival depth and historical context beyond the two-dimensional image seen on screens, where everything appeared as a drama controlled by unseen and arbitrary forces, deviating from all logic.

I tried to find logic, precisely when the dance of demons around me screamed in my ears that there was none. And I knew that every passing day would bring another wave of disinformation. Every day would bring more casualties and injuries. The troubled soul does not linger on facts, on what led to what, on causal chains. And there will be those who help conceal the reality that preceded the disaster, pointing fingers at convenient culprits, "traitors," they will say. This essay is here to bear witness: this is how things were, how they came to this point. And it wasn't accidental.

Failure 1: The IDF Terminates Security for the Gaza Envelope Communities

Where to begin? Perhaps in September 2013, when the IDF decided to discontinue security arrangements for twenty-two communities in the north and south of Israel. The announcement read, "The IDF has decided to cancel the deployment of soldiers securing communities on the northern and southern borders. Security for settlements in the West Bank will continue as usual."[4] The Minister of Defense at the time was Moshe Ya'alon, a champion of West Bank settlements. *Security for the settlements continues, while security for the Gaza Envelope communities is canceled.* A sign of things to come. Yair Fergon, head of the Netiv Ha'asara local council, said, "It is inconceivable to leave the communities in the Gaza Envelope [Israeli towns and villages around the Gaza border] defenseless and rely on residents to protect themselves. The abandoning of the Gaza Envelope communities

---

4 Harel et al. (2013).

is a real threat to life. We still do not live in an era of peace, and we cannot wait for the next disaster. I am sure there was an error in the decision-makers' judgment."[5]

Not an error, a policy.

In August 2014, Operation Protective Edge in Gaza ended, and the IDF restored security to the communities. For how long? Only for four and a half months. During the operation, an extensive tunnel system leading from Gaza to Israeli territory was exposed. The IDF focused on neutralizing the tunnels, convincing itself (but not the residents of the Envelope) that this was sufficient to protect the communities. In December, the decision was made to cancel military protection for all communities beyond one kilometer from the border.[6] Local council heads protested the decision; the "smart fence," a high-tech system, was still in the planning stages. All that separated them from Hamas was a concrete wall. The crisis of trust between local council leaders in the Envelope and the security establishment, which began before Operation Protective Edge,[7] intensified and grew. Meir Kozlovsky, head of the security team of the Sha'ar Hanegev Regional Council, said at the time, "Even if they knew about the tunnels, in the end, they decided not to deal with them, and we became the human shield. They were not ready; no special forces were stationed here, and the terrorists could have surprised us. We saw the capabilities of Hamas fighters, and one can only assume that it could have ended in a national disaster, a larger failure than Yom Kippur."[8] Indeed, yes.

Read these words again and again. The residents of the Envelope knew. Their representatives knew. They warned. But all the warnings shattered against the wall of IDF hubris.

In January 2015, IDF security forces left the communities of the Envelope again.[9] A resident of Kibbutz Ein Hashlosha wondered, "Before the operation, we didn't know how bad the situation was, so we didn't see the importance of soldiers securing the kibbutzim in real-time. But after everything that happened in the summer, we don't understand how they take the soldiers from here." A protest march by Envelope residents toward the border was stopped by the IDF;[10] the same Ynet photographer who documented the march in 2015, as well as the infiltration of Hamas fighters on October 7, 2023, Roee Idan, was killed shortly after documenting the attack.

---

5 Harel et al. (2013).
6 Sidler (2014).
7 Shtekerman and Lutzky (2014).
8 Shtekerman and Lutzky (2014).
9 Sidler (2015).
10 Tzuri (2015a).

Two more striking statements from those days of civil struggle that tragically failed: first, residents' representatives came to the Foreign Affairs and Defense Committee in the Knesset [the Israeli parliament] to try to convey the urgency of retaining a security presence in their communities. During the discussion, Knesset member Moti Yogev from the far-right Jewish Home party told an Envelope resident, "You supported the Gaza disengagement—tough luck." [11] Yogev is a resident of the violent West Bank settlement of Dolev, which, through seizure orders on private Palestinian land, continues to expand in every direction. In return, it receives a private bypass road from the state to shorten the commute to Jerusalem. Yogev knows that he can say and do whatever he wants without consequences; after all, he belongs to the chosen sector—the settlers.

A second statement from those days is equally resonant. It came from Brigadier General Itai Virov, commander of the Gaza Division, in a closed-door conversation with residents of Nachal Oz in an attempt to appease their anger over the cancellation of security. In a rare moment of candor, Virov said:

> It's good that we didn't defeat Hamas. I see what's happening today in the Sinai. It's good that these [ISIS] savages stay in Sinai and deal with the Egyptian army, and we'll deal with those in front of us [Hamas]. In the end, after the war, we wanted to see Hamas remain in the same place [in power]. The collapse of the [Gaza] Strip could lead us to worse places. The alternatives to Hamas rule and military rule in Gaza are even worse.[12]

So, in 2014, there was already a strategic understanding within the IDF that Hamas is preferable to ISIS. Already in the 1980s and 1990s Israel encouraged the Mujama al-Islami, which was founded by Sheikh Ahmed Yassin and later gave rise to Hamas, as a counter to the PLO. Dr. Mahmoud al-Zahar, one of the militant leaders of the movement, even visited the office of then Defense Minister Yitzhak Rabin.[13] This perception became entwined later with the preference of right-wing governments to deal with the zealots of Hamas rather than the moderates of the Palestinian Authority (Netanyahu: "If you want to thwart the establishment of a Palestinian state you must support strengthening Hamas and transferring money to Hamas; it is part of our strategy";[14] Smotrich: "Hamas is an asset").[15]

But Virov's more piercing statement in the same closed-door conversation was this:

---

[11] Bender (2015).
[12] Tzuri (2015b).
[13] Eldar (2023).
[14] Weitz (2023).
[15] https://www.youtube.com/watch?v=pB16PMEPuiM.

The senior officer admitted, however, that there is no real deterrent capability against the residents of Gaza. "Deterrence in this neighborhood is arrogance, to say nothing of great arrogance," said Virov. "Gaza is a great tragedy. It has no prospects for resources. It has nothing. It is even more complex. If there is no ability to deter, I say explicitly—this war is not a deterrent war. Dozens of thousands of homes with their roofs plastered to their floors and dozens of [destroyed] streets where vehicles cannot pass—it is not certain that all these will deter the Gazans.[16]

Like Moshe Dayan in his eulogy for Roi Rotberg [see Chapter 1 in this volume], so did Itai Virov understand that there is something deep-rooted in our war with Gaza. Something that has no easy military solution. Virov also dared to say things that only radical-left people (for example, me) repeat and say: there is no military deterrence in the south. On the other hand, Virov does not have the courage of Dayan, who took full responsibility for the abandonment of Israel's southern residents to a life of terror and mourning. Virov mumbled something later about a "deterrence system" as a consolation prize after real deterrence has been abandoned.

This makes the abandonment of the Gaza Envelope communities even more criminal. Because in truth, even regular army units could not have stopped the onslaught of Hamas fighters on October 7. Hence the appalling conclusion: Israel cannot truly guarantee the peace of the residents of the Gaza Envelope as long as it is locked into a military strategy against Gaza.

Failure 2: Technology Will Protect Us from Any Threat

"Autonomous 'Jaguar' ATVs that patrol and shoot remotely, 'Tzur' drones performing reconnaissance near the double fence, sophisticated sensors collecting acoustic intelligence, and an intimidating obstacle dozens of kilometers long, above and below the ground."[17] The military commentator of *Yedioth Ahronoth*, Alex Fishman, who usually writes with restraint, waxed poetic when he shared with his readers the scope of the project that was supposed, once and for all, to prevent infiltrations from Gaza. His amazement was of a familiar kind, called "techno-fetishism": astonishment at technological innovations per se, not necessarily because their effectiveness has been proven, or their superiority over non-technological solutions has been demonstrated, or someone has bothered to check that they do not pose new and unexpected problems and are not fraught with vulnerabili-

---

16 Tzuri (2015b).
17 Fishman (2021).

ties, which create difficulties that may outweigh the benefit gained through these innovations.

The entire IDF aligns itself with the spirit of the time and undergoes digitization/cyberization constantly. Five years ago, I described extensively dozens of such projects that were integrated into the IDF, and analyzed the reasons for their flourishing: economic reasons (contracts worth millions of shekels for arms and electronic equipment companies), and mainly, strategic reasons—granting maneuvering space for prolonged military operations with minimal risk to soldiers, who are kept at a distance from the buzzing battlefield through technological control. All this turns peace, or even just words of peace for the sake of calming things down, into an unprofitable matter.[18]

Well, all this cost us 3.5 billion shekels, and on October 7, it collapsed like dust: Hamas's cheap drones and hand gliders mocked the best engineers of Israel's advanced military industry. Will the lesson be learned? I'm doubtful. In fact, I am convinced that at this very moment engineers are diligently working on an "anti-drone defense system," one that will protect us from drones and gliders. Expect to hear the word "laser" resonating loudly in the coming months. Another three to four billion shekels, dozens of contracts enriching the industry, a festive propaganda film—and poof, we are ready for war. The previous one. The one that was.

What is missile defense if not an expression of the lack of deterrence? In another post from the same period, I wrote:

> Who needs to defend themselves more and more? Those who fail to deter their enemy from attacking. Israel boasts of its technological superiority in the battlefield, a superiority that has been harnessed in the past decade especially for huge projects of defense and interception, monitoring and neutralization. But it is clear that the growing need for these projects is a precise measure of the level of national anxiety: deterrence does not work, so we need defense and neutralization. There is an inverse relationship between the effectiveness of deterrence and the effectiveness of defense. Deterrence relies on convincing the enemy that any violent action on his part will be met with a sharp and much more painful response that will not pay off for him. In contrast, defense and neutralization are more "defeatist" strategies. They assume from the outset that the enemy is not deterred and therefore we must defend against his attack.[19]

---

18 https://idanlandau.com/2018/06/14/no-price-for-war-no-reason-for-peace/.
19 https://idanlandau.com/2018/02/08/deterrence-collapsed-shielding-frenzy/.

Failure 3: The Battalions Guard the Troublemakers in Judea and Samaria

The main points are already known by now. Twenty-three IDF battalions are deployed in the West Bank. Fifty reserve battalions were called up for reserve duty in the West Bank this year. Each illegal settlement outpost receives a security unit. And that's just routine. On October 5, two days before the Hamas attack, the settlers again organized an "ascent" to Joseph's Tomb in Nablus. Each such ascent is accompanied by comprehensive IDF security[20] and inevitable clashes with the Palestinian residents of Nablus, whose city is completely paralyzed. There are always wounded, sometimes even fatalities.[21] The settlers are not interested in the price. Over 3,000[22] worshippers visited Joseph's Tomb on October 5, and the IDF sent three battalions to secure them.[23]

And of course, on the same day, October 5, the festive Sukkot celebrations of MK Tzvi Sukot took place on the main road of Hawara,[24] with its Palestinian residents closed and locked in their homes, and a gigantic force of twenty-six battalions (according to Brigadier General Amos Yadlin) sent to secure Sukot's friends and the entire region that became explosive.[25]

The Egyptian intelligence informant who passed on the information about "something big" about to happen in Gaza ten days before the October 7 attack, recounted that the head of Egyptian intelligence was "stunned by the indifference" shown by Israel.[26] The Israeli response was that the IDF and security forces were "absorbed" in dealing with the cities in Judea and Samaria [West Bank], from which terrorism is operated against Israel.

No wonder there were hardly any soldiers left in the Gaza Envelope.

Failure 4: The Jewish Flood on Al-Aqsa

"A new record: 5,323 Jews ascended to the Temple Mount on Sukkot,"[27] declared the headlines bombastically on October 6, like a trombone orchestra on the *Titanic*

---

20 Sheizaf and Haj Yehya (2023).
21 Khoury et al. (2023).
22 Lepkovitch (2023).
23 Harel (2023).
24 Baruch, H. (2023).
25 Gorali (2023).
26 Peri (2023).
27 Segal (2023a).

minutes before it sank. While the pilgrims devoted themselves to the holiday as usual, spitting on Christians in the Old City,[28] the Jordanian Foreign Ministry issued an official complaint to Israel.[29] The breach of the status quo on the Temple Mount/Al-Aqsa Mosque further fueled the youth uprising at the Gaza border, who declared, "All our capabilities will be used for the sake of Al-Aqsa Mosque."[30]

At first glance, these are warnings we've heard countless times from Hamas, which never resulted in any such attack afterward. Nevertheless, those closely following the dynamics, like Nir Hasson, cautioned on October 2: "Beyond the festive scenes from Jerusalem, there is an explosive reality that may burst at any moment."[31] The spitting on Christians, the violence of border police toward Muslim women, the removal of young Palestinians from the Mount to ensure Jewish prayer—all these were signs of an impending storm.[32] Together, they were the fuse that ignited "Operation Al-Aqsa," a more accurate name for the current war than "Swords of Iron."

There is no doubt that Hamas planned the operation months before. Yet there is also no doubt that they were waiting for the right moment—a Jewish provocation on the Temple Mount—to justify their actions. As always, extremists on both sides play into each other's hands; ultimately, they are on the same side.

Enlightened people on both sides will raise their voices, rightfully, against the claim that organizing prayer services on the Temple Mount is a legitimate cause for declaring war. How good it would be to live in an ideal world where freedom of worship for all religions is self-evident, requiring no debate or protection by armed police. Unfortunately, the tumultuous world of the Temple Mount is far from ideal. Well known to all sides for almost three decades is that the least explosive, most peaceful situation for everyone is the status quo. This status quo developed over the years through negotiations between the Israeli police, the Jerusalem municipality, and the Muslim Waqf. However, since the 1990s, Israel has significantly expanded the number of Jewish worshippers permitted on the Temple Mount, even on Muslim holidays, while simultaneously restricting Muslim entry. These moves were unilaterally implemented by right-wing governments, led by figures like Ariel Sharon and Ehud Olmert.

Israel's handling of the Temple Mount parallels its approach to the Gaza Strip: moving from a period of negotiation, albeit technical and practical rather than on a diplomatic level, to a period of forceful and unilateral dictation by Israel about

---

28 Hason (2023a).
29 Halabi et al. (2023).
30 Cohen and Halabi (2023).
31 Hason (2023b).
32 Hason (2023c).

how things will be managed (what will enter Gaza and when, who will ascend to the Temple Mount/Al-Aqsa Mosque and when).

Of course, the one who holds the power can always dictate. Gradually, they may convince themselves that this approach works—not listening to the complaints and forgetting that there are human beings on the other side with needs similar to their own. One can carry on like this for quite some time. There is just one problem: when you stop listening to the other side, you also miss the accumulating resentment and anger boiling beneath the surface, until the breaking point, which always catches you off guard.

Failure 5: The Lie of Military Deterrence

At this point, one can add a series of military failures: the intelligence failure, the operational failure, the logistical failure, and so on. These are already being exposed in the Israeli media and will likely capture much attention in the coming months. However, I will delve into a much more fundamental failure. Focusing on military failures assumes that any approach to Gaza should be military, but the failure I will discuss challenges this assumption. The likelihood of encountering open discussions on this in the Israeli media is minimal.

My starting point should be self-evident, and yet experience teaches that it cannot be stressed enough: there is no military deterrence in the south. There is no military deterrence in the south. There is no military deterrence in the south.

Oh, how much have I written about Gaza—every operation, escalation, invasion, siege, and war crime. Read the commentator Amir Oren,[33] Brigadier General Itai Virov mentioned above, Brigadier General Dov Tamari, who fundamentally question the concept of Israel's military deterrence;[34] and many more experts could be quoted. Here are some words written by Dr. Mati Steinberg, a scholar of Palestinian nationalism and Islamic fundamentalism, after Operation Guardian of the Walls in Gaza in 2021:

> In the shaping of Hamas's deterrence by Israel, two factors are connected: In the Gaza Strip, Hamas has reached a point where "it has nothing to lose." At this point, which is psychological and not mathematical, the material damage and losses of lives cease to cause an increase of pain. The increase in the damage reaches a threshold and is no longer proportional to the growth of feeling of pain. It is a point of indifference to pain (according to the research of Kahneman and Tversky). There is no point in improving the economy or promising such

---

33 Oren (2014).
34 Tamari (2018).

an improvement to create a sense that there is something to lose as long as the population is subject to occupation or subjugated to foreign dictates—"Man does not live by bread alone." In the absence of an additional option that provides an answer to the national-communal need in the form of autonomy and sovereignty, there is no deterrence. To this is added the second factor of "what is there to gain" at the strategic level ... The combination of "nothing to lose" with "something to gain" significantly depletes Israeli deterrence.[35]

Observe above: when an Israeli commentator puts himself, personally, in the place of the Palestinian side and considers their "feeling of pain," he may come to different conclusions than those imposed on us in a standardized and cyclical manner from the mouths of generic security experts in TV studios.

How many IDF operations have there been in Gaza against Hamas in recent years? I counted twelve: First Rain (2005), Summer Rains (2006), Hot Winter (2008), Cast Lead (2008–9), Pillar of Defense (2012), Cloud Pillar (2012), Protective Edge (2014), Black Belt (2019), Guardian of the Walls (2021), Dawn Uprising (2022), Shield and Arrow (2023), Iron Swords (2023). In addition to these, one should add the violent clashes at the border in 2018–21 ("The Great March of Return"), which claimed the lives of 316 Palestinians and left around 20,000 injured in Gaza. How many Gazans did Israel kill altogether? According to B'Tselem data, since 2000, Israel has killed almost 8,000 residents of Gaza, half of them at least not involved in hostilities.[36] These were the data before the current war.

Did the loss of the lives of 8,000 Palestinians in any way deter the planners of Operation Al-Aqsa Flood from launching their deadly October 7 attack? Did dozens of thousands of injuries and hundreds of thousands of destroyed homes over the years make them reconsider before the lethal attack? Did Hamas fighters know they would not return alive, and if so, did it diminish their determination?

These are rhetorical questions. Read the recent Gisha report[37] on life in Gaza, a horrifying daily reality for over 2 million people with only a few hours of electricity per day, a lack of clean drinking water, unemployment of over 80%, a place that the UN predicted would not be fit for human habitation by 2020.[38]

Israelis have a ready answer to all these challenges: they elected Hamas, it's their problem. A very easy answer that once again diverts the discussion (whether they chose or did not choose, they are in a situation where they have nothing to lose). Israelis elected Netanyahu and Smotrich and Ben-Gvir; do we deserve them? Maybe some of us do, but certainly not a significant portion of us who

---

35 Stinberg (2021).
36 https://statistics.btselem.org/he/all-fatalities/by-date-of-incident/pal-by-israel-sec/gaza-strip?section=overall&tab=overview (last accessed: Feb. 2, 2024).
37 https://features.gisha.org/gaza_up_close_he/.
38 McCloskey (2020).

did not vote for them. This is even clearer under Hamas's repressive regime, which brutally silences any opposition. The common Israeli complaint "Why do they support Hamas?" reflects ignorance and lack of understanding (at best) of civil society's reality under a tyrannical regime. Given that Israelis are already in the early stages of such a regime, it might be time to reassess this charge we make against the Gazans. We and they have more in common than we think.

Regardless, a significant part of the suffering in Gaza is a direct result of the blockade, restrictions on goods entering Gaza, on the fishing industry, the policy of "separation" between Gaza and the West Bank, disruption of healthcare systems, and prevention of medical treatments.

Once again, Israelis conveniently label each of these as "security measures." What they fail to grasp is that as long as Israel continues to view every aspect of life in Gaza through the lens of security—every exit request, every export or import license, every agricultural field near the border—Gazans will continue to experience their lives as trapped in a giant prison. The world will continue to see Gaza as the "largest open prison in the world," and the claim that "we left Gaza, gave them autonomy, and they attacked us in return" will be dismissed as the manipulative nonsense it is.

A look at social media reveals the solution favored by quite a few Israelis: to erase Gaza completely. Now is the time, now is the great opportunity to implement a longstanding fantasy, now, finally, deliver the final blow. It's almost poetic, this combination of arrogance and absurdity. Because every IDF operation in Gaza since the rise of Hamas has tested the world's tolerance for the piles of bodies accumulating in the streets of Jabaliya and Shujaiya. Look back and see: the European Union pressures, the Security Council pressures, diplomats talk about the 'ticking clock,'[39] and finally, Washington signals the ultimate red light,[40] and the IDF retreats. Another genocide fantasy is buried. This time things seem different only because of the starting point—Israel has truly suffered a terrible and shocking blow that silences any criticism. More will die this time. But soon the scenes from October 7 will be replaced by the devastated neighborhoods of Gaza, and the blame game will continue on both sides. We won't be able to destroy Gaza.

Gaza is here; it is not going anywhere. Even after Israel kills thousands of its residents, over 2 million people will remain there. And, unfortunately, a large portion of them are devout Muslims who support Hamas. Hamas is no longer a house of cards that can be toppled with an airy breeze. Hamas is civil infrastructure, an education system, a worldview, a bureaucratic mechanism, all fully integrated into

---

39 Ravid (2014).
40 Ben Hurin (2009).

the fabric of Gaza's life. It cannot be toppled any more than one can extract a person's nervous system and leave them alive.[41] Only in the delusions of security enthusiasts, who repeat the same nonsense over and over through twelve bloody operations, can Israel "topple Hamas."

I read again, with a slight tremor, the sentence "It cannot be toppled any more than one can extract a person's nervous system and leave them alive." Indeed, perhaps it is possible to extract a person's nervous system and, in the process, kill them. If toppling Hamas means an action on the scale of genocide in the Gaza Strip, then it is an attainable goal. But I cannot even contemplate it, even though there are already experts who believe that Israel is heading in that direction.[42] If we accept this, this essay and the millions of words poured out on Gaza will be erased by history. Everything will become meaningless.

Another feature of the lie that Hamas can be toppled: the lie is propagated by both the right and left in Israel, by both Bibists and anti-Bibists. Among the pack of crooks that led us to infinite bloodshed against Gaza, Netanyahu and Ehud Barak, Yoav Galant and Ehud Olmert, Moshe Ya'alon and Tzipi Livni, Yair Lapid and Benny Gantz, all sat side by side. They all sat in cabinets that perpetuated the cursed mantra that Hamas only understands force, and blocked any other option. And in the current political quagmire in Israel, it is very difficult to formulate a position that so blatantly undermines both Netanyahu and his opponents (because who will be left?).

Who Is Responsible for the Betrayal?

The failures, remember? Cancelling security for the Gaza Envelope communities despite the residents' pleas, undermining the status quo on the Temple Mount/Al-Aqsa, the absolute absence of public infrastructure and social security networks, the collapse of the deterrence lie. All these are failures of the state; its betrayal of its citizens. Who is responsible for this?

There are two answers. One, the empirical and accurate answer, will go back and examine who made the decisions and when. The picture that emerges is alarming: everything is rotten. The fish rots from the head, but the rot permeates all its organs. The entire security system was a full partner in this colossal deception (whether knowingly or unknowingly, self-deception or just public deception, is not important now in terms of responsibility). The entire political system, not just

---

41 Bar'el (2023).
42 Raz, S. (2023).

Netanyahu's coalition, cooperated and even nurtured the groundless complacency in the face of a vast array of issues: what safeguarded our personal security; the agreements related to the status quo on the Temple Mount; the support systems for the home front; the commitment of the authorities to the lives of citizens, as well as the commitment to the lives of citizens who fall into captivity; and how much our state really invests in preserving life versus perpetuating violence.

These are difficult questions, and the answers are unbearable for the majority of Israelis. They are unbearable because they imply indirect involvement of almost every one of us in the failure. It's not "them." It's not just Bibi's gang. It's the entire chain of political and military leadership over (at least) the past two decades, during which the policy of blockade and military operations against Gaza has been shaped. And if it's the entire chain of leadership, it's also everyone who voted for them and thought that voting for them would keep us alive and build support systems for life here. And it's everyone who sees themselves as loyal to an army that is essentially investing most of its efforts in the wrong direction: the settlements' defense army, the unmanned pyrotechnical army, the army with the stupid "smart fence."

We all swallowed these lies with gusto; we all passed them on. That rot, deception, coercion, and complacency go so deep that they are embedded in the central institutions of the state, not concentrated in an individual or a single decision. They stain us as well, and this is difficult to bear. We saw the survivors of Kfar Azza and Be'eri on TV, crying not only for their loved ones but also for an entire world of faith and security that had collapsed and died within a few hours. Absolute disorientation in relation to what they, and we, thought to be true.

The difficulty only begins here. Because from this answer, the empirical and precise answer, far-reaching conclusions emerge. The state's systems must undergo a fundamental change. The political representatives of all parties—right, center, left Zionist—all who have been members of the governments of recent years, all who are partners in these colossal failures that have lasted so many years. These representatives must go. Not change their haircut or their suit, not run again for the Knesset on a rebranded platform; just go.

The Return of the Repressed: Shadow Lands

In Naomi Klein's latest book *Doppelganger*, one of the central themes is "Shadow Lands."[43] These are a part of our reality that, from the perspective of those who

---

[43] Klein (2023).

live in relative comfort in the Western world, are always in the shadows, outside our field of vision. Suffering and distress are a constant presence there, but that hardly reaches our eyes and consciousness, thanks to a sophisticated system of censorship, reinforcement, division of labor, and political and economic arrangements that ensure that what exists in the Shadow Lands stays there.

Gaza is our shadow land. The repressed place, the open wound that the gaze avoids but that pierces our consciousness, assaults our memory, and refuses to fade away. In Gaza, all the crimes of the Israeli occupation are recorded, and those who want to delve again into the chain of mistakes, the remorse, the concealments and revelations, are invited to read the comprehensive interviews conducted by Yizhar Be'er with the IDF's Gaza and Southern Command officers in the last decade on the blog *Holy Cows*.[44] Everything is written there. Our lopsided recent history.

Does anyone truly believe that this reality is sustainable? That these immense gaps between the Israeli standard of living and the Palestinian standard just across the border can be ignored, blurred, or obscured? That this division will pass peacefully? On one side of the border, people dance freely at a nature party, on top of the world. Just a stone's throw away, thousands huddle at the bottom of the world, in wretched refugee camps, half the day without electricity, struggling with infectious diseases due to a lack of clean water, disconnected for years from a brother or sister in the West Bank, with no coming and no going, only the constant buzzing of drones above and missile strikes that destroy half the neighborhood every two or three years.

Yes, Moshe Dayan believed it's possible to live like that. "To be prepared and armed, strong and determined, lest the sword be stricken from our fist and our lives cut down,"[45] he declared in 1956. A terrible and ominous mistake—the sword is not slipping from our grasp, and yet our lives are being cut down again and again, with our own iron swords. A mistake imposed on generations of Israelis, in their waking and sleep, getting under their skin so that they cannot even imagine a different state—one in which they are not clenched into a fist.

I write these words against the backdrop of a flood of calls for genocide in Gaza. An open letter from dozens of religious Zionists calls on the IDF "not to consider the civilian population of the enemy."[46] The return to Gaza has been the sweet dream of the right since the Gaza disengagement in 2005, and its messianic followers jumped on the bandwagon with joy. After the repeal of the disengage-

---

[44] https://parotk.com/?s=עזה (last accessed: Feb. 2, 2024).
[45] Dayan (1956).
[46] Amar (2023).

ment law in the northern West Bank, the far-right MK Orit Struk turned her gaze to the south: "Unfortunately, the return to Gaza will also be accompanied by many casualties, just as the evacuation of Gaza [from Jewish settlers in 2005] was accompanied by many casualties. But there is no doubt that in the end, it is part of the Land of Israel, and a day will come when we return to it."[47] In the first week of the war, MK Amit Halevi of Likud outlined a detailed plan for a mass slaughter, following which hundreds of thousands of Gazans would be transferred to Egypt, and Jews will be settled in their place.[48] MK Simcha Rothman declared that the goal of the war is to ensure "our children can walk freely in the streets of Gaza."[49]

A simple Google search on the phrase "erase Gaza" in Hebrew brings up hundreds of results from the past week—from journalists, mayors, and others. Large signs with the inscriptions "Destroy Gaza" and "The victory picture: 0 residents in Gaza" were hung on the Ayalon highways. Genocide talk has become mainstream.

---

[47] Baruch, U. (2023).
[48] Segal (2023b).
[49] https://twitter.com/yuval_ganor/status/1712744796073148578 (last accessed: Feb. 2, 2024).

Shaul Arieli
Chapter 5: The Failure Is the Result of Netanyahu's False Reality

October 19, 2023

> Col. (reserve) **Shaul Arieli**, PhD, is an expert on the Israeli–Palestinian conflict. He was the Commander of the Northern Brigade in Gaza, Head of the Interim Agreement Administration under the Rabin, Peres, and Netanyahu governments, Deputy Military Secretary to the Minister of Defense, and Head of the Peace Administration in PM Barak's government. Arieli teaches at the Reichman University in Herzliya and the Hebrew University of Jerusalem. He is a board member of Commanders for Israel's Security (CIS) and a leading member of the Geneva Initiative. He is considered one of Israel's leading experts on the Israeli–Palestinian conflict, the borders of Israel, and the separation barrier. Arieli has published ten books and many academic articles and newspaper opinion pieces.

Each of the different groups that comprise Israeli society has its own distinct perception of reality. In contrast to the past, it is not just a matter of different interpretations of an agreed reality, but rather disagreement about the facts themselves and the presentation of alternative "facts" that create a false reality. Benjamin Netanyahu and his associates have created a fake reality in the minds of half the Israeli public in order to justify their policies and vision, which have led, among other outcomes, to the failure of October 7 around the Gaza border.

Throughout most of modern Zionist history, the three groups within the Jewish people—secular Zionists, religious messianics, and Haredim (ultra-Orthodox)—have agreed in principle about the facts. Their disagreements revolved around the different interpretation of these facts by each group, in keeping with its vision. Secular Zionists regarded the Balfour Declaration, the UN Partition Resolution of 1947, the establishment of Israel, the 1948 War of Independence, and the 1967 Six-Day War as milestones in the success of the Jewish people in securing international recognition for their right to self-determination in their homeland; and for the aspiration to become a nation like any other, part and parcel of the international community.

Religious messianics saw these same events as evidence of the revealed "End Times" and the beginning of redemption, ultimately leading to the establishment of the Kingdom of David and a return to Temple days. Conversely, Haredim regarded the events as violations of the "Three Oaths" that prohibit organized migration by Jews to the Land of Israel and hence a desecration of the messianic ideal.

Over time, the gulf between these three groups widened, resulting in each moving in almost-parallel realities. This process was due in part to the failure of the peace process between Israel and the PLO, which had sought to secure a permanent agreement, and to Netanyahu's policy of refusing to resume negotiations toward such an agreement, which was supposed to ensure a separation between Israelis and Palestinians. This policy eroded the feasibility of the secular-Zionist vision: maintaining a democratic state with Jewish national characteristics as a member of the family of nations. The path was now ostensibly clear for the religious messianics and their new allies—the "Hardal" or Haredi-nationalist stream—to realize the dream of "inheriting the land" in keeping with the doctrine of conquest and settlement presented in the Book of Joshua. But in actual reality—which was ignored by Netanyahu and his government—the Palestinians, the international community, and a majority of the Israeli public refused to cooperate with this goal.

In order to adjust reality to his policy, Netanyahu began to act through various channels—conventional media and social media, the education system, government ministers, and coalition Members of Knesset—to inculcate a fake reality in the minds of the Israeli public consistent with his policies and his personal and political aspirations. In other words, instead of basing his policy on a professional and responsible examination of reality in terms of the feasibility of the messianic-nationalist vision, he chose to inculcate among the public a sense of false reality based on a collection of lies, in order to justify his irresponsible and opportunistic policies.

Lies and incitement laid the foundation for this fake reality. His refrains have become familiar: "the leftists have forgotten what it means to be Jews; the protestors against the government are anarchists and traitors; the Arabs are flooding to the polling stations; the Supreme Court is endangering state security; Mahmoud Abbas supports terror; Hamas serves our interests," and so forth.

In the diplomatic and security sphere, Netanyahu aimed to frighten the public and convince Israelis that they will always be left to stand alone. And so Iran became the "Nazi dictatorship" and ISIS and Hezbollah the proof that in "every generation people seek to annihilate us," as the Passover song goes. According to his approach, the peace initiative of the Arab League from 2002 is impractical, [the PA president] Mahmoud Abbas adheres to the "phased plan" for the destruction of Israel, while Hamas should be nurtured and strengthened. It was vital for Netanyahu to maintain the division among the Palestinians, which undermines Abbas's legitimacy and authority as the only possible partner for ending the conflict. Similarly, he nurtured the illusion that this division removes the Palestinians in Gaza from the demographic equation, thereby facilitating the annexation of the West Bank.

This ghetto policy sparked and fueled processes in the domestic and social sphere. Netanyahu demanded that even his opponents display "unity" and support the nation's political leaders. He demanded total support from the judiciary for his antidemocratic laws and for actions that violate international law. And he expected that the media would always be supportive, and that the public would readily pay with their lives when violence erupted.

By nurturing this false reality, Netanyahu sought to ensure that opposition to his rule would disappear, in the absence of any possibility of changing the government. He chose his ministers carefully to this end, sending them off to erode the pillars of democracy. His appointed justice ministers Ayelet Shaked, Amir Ohana, and Yariv Levin undermined the status of the Supreme Court; his education ministers Naftali Bennett and Yoav Kish targeted the field of education; Miri Regev focused on culture and sport; Yuli Edelstein worked in the Knesset; Bezalel Smotrich in the fields of finance and defense; Itamar Ben-Gvir in public security, and so forth.

When the reality on the ground refused to cooperate, the strategy shifted to a parade of meaningless platitudes: from "economic peace" to "conflict management" or "conflict reduction"—anything to maintain the fake consciousness that brought Netanyahu back to the prime minister's office again and again over fourteen years, while the leaders of the messianic-nationalist and Haredi parties served as his viziers. His behavior toward the Palestinian Authority in the West Bank and his decisions during the various military operations against Hamas in Gaza, and during the processes leading to these confrontations, exposed his simple political goal: to return as quickly as possible to his comfort zone—a situation he mistakenly calls the "status quo" that allowed him to remain in power.

The fake "status quo" that has formed the foundation for Netanyahu's policies over the past few years does not reflect the reality of security and diplomatic balance and stability. On the contrary, it manifests the prime minister's profound fear of any diplomatic initiative that might end the recurring rounds of escalation under his rule, including the terrible price we are now paying. Netanyahu's "status quo" is a euphemism for conceptual stalemate on the Israeli side, preserving the conditions that allowed Hamas to spark a series of confrontations culminating in the horrors and war crimes of October 7.

Thus the status quo protected Netanyahu's position as prime minister while enabling the messianic nationalists to implement his policy and theirs: the expansion of the settlements, construction of illegal outposts, Jewish terror, expanding the Jewish presence in East Jerusalem, opposing true negotiations with Mahmoud Abbas, nurturing the division between Hamas and the Palestinian Authority, and maintaining the siege of Gaza. All this came at the price of eroding Israel's democracy, its image, and its international standing; damaging social cohesion and solidarity; and enabling the strengthening of Hamas and the weakening of the Palestinian Authority.

Even after October 7, Netanyahu and his government have refused to wake up and abandon their fake reality. Voices can be heard in messianic-nationalist circles that adhere to the teaching of Rabbi Zvi Yehuda Kook, the spiritual father of the settler vanguard Gush Emunim, who claimed that the Holocaust was caused by the Jews' refusal to recognize the signs of the "revealed End of Days." Kook thundered: "God's people adhered so much to the impurity of the land of the nations [i.e., to exile] that it had to be cut and torn away from exile through the bloodshed that comes with the End."[1] An article by far-right Professor Yoel Elitzur argues that the massacre perpetrated by Hamas is part of God's plan for the Israelis who "bring disasters upon the Jewish people and thwart the divine plan."[2] He associates the massacre with secularism and the failure to advance the idea of a "Greater Israel."

Netanyahu personally ignored numerous warnings from senior figures in the defense establishment, denied that he had received alerts, and continued to push his judicial reform, weakening Israel's resilience. Detachment from reality is the only way to explain the transfer of most of the forces in the Gaza border to the West Bank just before Simchat Torah and October 7; the dismantling of the rapid response squads in the Gaza Envelope; and conversely—the allocation of forces to protect illegal outposts and a sukkah in the Palestinian town of Hawara; the allocation of billions of shekels to Haredi students at the expense of the purchase of equipment for reservists; the incitement by Ben-Gvir against Arab citizens of Israel in the heart of an Arab town struck by Hamas; and attempts to place the blame for the current failure on chiefs of staff who retired a decade ago and on newsreaders and the leaders of the opposition protest movement.

Even more seriously, the detachment from reality in the Netanyahu government and the appointment of unqualified ministers for personal motives, contrary to proper governance, explain the government's inability to manage the campaign or define a diplomatic purpose behind a military operation that will levy a heavy cost on Israeli society.

In his book *The Bar Kokhba Syndrome: Risk and Realism in International Relations* (1982), Yehoshafat Harkabi[3] offers an analysis of the failure of the Bar Kokhba Revolt in the second century CE that can help us understand the detachment from reality that characterizes Netanyahu and his government. The book argues that great political vision calls for a transformation of reality, yet vision has to be grounded in reality in order to be realized. When a vision is completely detach-

---

1 Kook (1981).
2 Cohen, I. (2023).
3 Harkabi (1983).

ed from the conditions of reality, it becomes mere fantasy, and often a dangerous one. In other words, a vision based on a fake reality will ultimately fail to change the existing reality and will crash to the ground, taking its faithfuls with it, and leading society and state to disaster.

It has now become clear that Netanyahu's policy allowed Hamas to undermine the imaginary status quo and to lead to the collapse of all of Netanyahu's false strategies. With this in mind, and given the current events, which make a mockery of his incitement against advocates of democracy and of the canonical secular-Zionist vision, will the Israeli public find the maturity to reject the fake reality? Will they finally have had enough of a man whose entire philosophy is confined to his own political survival, and who allowed extremists to lead Israel? Will they demand that Netanyahu resign, and choose a new leader in the next elections—one who will prioritize the national interest by resolving the conflict with the Palestinians and the Arab world, while defending Israel's security and its international standing?

Yaniv Ronen
Chapter 6: What Is Hamas? Facts and Analysis

October 18, 2023

> **Yaniv Ronen**, PhD, is a historian and a research fellow at the Forum for Regional Thinking. Ronen has served as a senior researcher at the Research and Information Center of the Knesset (the Israeli parliament).

Facts

Hamas: an acronym in Arabic for "the Islamic Resistance Movement"—Harakat al-Muqawamah al-Islamiyyah. *Hamas* is also a word meaning enthusiasm, zeal, or strength.

Hamas is the Palestinian incarnation of the Muslim Brotherhood movement founded in Egypt in 1928 by Hassan al-Banna. Initially, the Egyptian Brotherhood focused on educating Muslims and aimed to establish an Islamic government. The movement sprang branches in many Muslim countries across the Middle East and North Africa. Its first branch in Palestine was established in Jerusalem in 1945.

During Israel's 1948 War of Independence, the Muslim Brotherhood sent a force to fight, which was stationed in Gaza and Hebron. After the war, some of the fighters from the movement remained in these places and intensified their activities. One prominent activist of the Muslim Brotherhood movement in Gaza was Ahmed Yassin, born in the village of al-Jura (the ruins of which are located in Ashkelon Park) west of the town of Majdal, which later became the city of Ashkelon. Yassin attained influence as a religious leader, but over time he felt that the framework of the Muslim Brotherhood did not adequately meet the needs of Gaza's residents. In 1973, he established an organization called "The Islamic Association" (Al-Mujama Al-Islami). In 1978, this association obtained official recognition by the Israeli military government. High-ranking officials in the Israeli security establishment saw the Islamic Association as a positive phenomenon and strengthened it to serve as a counterbalance to the PLO, which was Israel's main and bitter enemy at the time.

Israel permitted the Islamic Association to register as an Ottoman association according to the Associations Law, enabling it to legally raise money. The organization's leader, Moussa Abu Marzouk, expanded its activities and established charity

https://doi.org/10.1515/9783111435046-007

organizations in various countries that transferred donations to the Association. The Islamic Association operated in various fields, including education, charity, and medical care. Gradually, it gained a foothold in all the mosques in the Gaza Strip. This was the situation until the outbreak of the First Intifada in December 1987.

The outbreak of the First Intifada—the Palestinian popular uprising—took the Association by surprise. The fighting headquarters, formed by activists from Fatah, led the Palestinian struggle and posed a political challenge to the Association. The Association's leaders could not remain as bystanders to the intifada, and so they established the Islamic Resistance Movement, Hamas, as they joined the Palestinian national struggle.

In August 1988, Hamas published its Covenant in which it emphasized its commitment to the establishment of an Islamic state throughout historical Palestine. The Covenant also designated the duty of jihad against Israel as a personal obligation for every Muslim. It outlined the movement's connections with the Muslim Brotherhood and detailed its relationship with the PLO. The Covenant also included explicitly anti-Semitic passages, blaming Jews for various global issues.

Soon after, Hamas established several terrorist cells. Among them, the Izz ad-Din al-Qassam Brigades stood out and became the official military wing of the movement. The military wing was named after Sheikh Izz ad-Din al-Qassam, a religious figure originally from Syria who rebelled against the French rule there, escaped a death sentence, and settled in Haifa. Al-Qassam gained prominence as a charismatic preacher and attracted a following of devotees. In 1930, he established a group called the Black Hand, which began carrying out attacks against the British and Jews in Mandatory Palestine. He was eventually killed by the British in late 1935 in Samaria. His death played a significant role in igniting the Great Arab Revolt of 1936.

Following Hamas's kidnapping and murder of the Jewish police officer Nissim Toledano in 1992, Israel decided to deport about 400 Hamas activists to Lebanon. According to the decision of the Israeli Supreme Court, the deportation was limited to a specified period. Upon the arrest and deportation of many Hamas activists, Hamas established its Political Bureau outside the occupied Palestinian territories. This bureau became the leadership for external affairs and adopted a more militant stance, often conflicting with the domestic leadership.

With the return of the deportees to the occupied territories, activists were in possession of new knowledge gained from Hezbollah regarding the assembly and operation of highly powerful explosive devices and recruiting suicide bombers for their operations. The first suicide bombing occurred in Afula (forty days after a Jewish doctor, Baruch Goldstein, massacred Muslim worshippers in Hebron's Tomb of the Patriarchs), marking the beginning of a series of suicide bombings and indiscriminate killings of Israeli civilians, and undermining the implementation of the Oslo Peace Accord signed in 1993. The violence also undermined the legitimacy of the Palestinian National Authority, established through the Oslo agreements.

During the Second Intifada that erupted in September 2000, the military wing of Hamas led the terror activities and executed numerous severe suicide bombings within Israeli cities. After a suicide bomber attacked the Park Hotel in Netanya in April 2002, Israel launched Operation Defensive Shield in the West Bank and Gaza. Hamas operatives, who had honed their military capabilities during the Second Intifada, began firing short-range, rudimentary Qassam rockets from the Gaza Strip.

In 2004, Israel assassinated two prominent Hamas leaders, Sheikh Ahmed Yassin and Abdel Aziz al-Rantisi. In the wake of these assassinations, Hamas decided to halt suicide bombings in 2005. This cessation of attacks was aimed at allowing for Palestinian elections, which were on the horizon.

Israel's withdrawal from the Gaza Strip in 2005 as part of the disengagement plan bolstered Hamas, which was now perceived by Palestinians as the only force capable of achieving concessions from Israel. The movement's growing prestige was reflected in its success in the 2006 Palestinian Legislative Council elections, where it ran under the Change and Reform Party. Following the failure of negotiations with Fatah and a short-lived unity government, Hamas seized control of the Gaza Strip in 2007, expelling and in some cases killing Fatah members. In response, Israel imposed a blockade on the Gaza Strip that has continued to this day.

Hamas used its hold on Gaza to enhance its military and terrorist capabilities, including the launching of Qassam rockets. Since the summer of 2006, Gaza under Hamas's rule has seen a cycle of intermittent hostilities with Israel. Israel initiated multiple military operations, such as Operation Summer Rains (2006), Operation Cast Lead (2008), Operation Pillar of Defense (2012), Operation Protective Edge (2014), Operation Guardian of the Walls (2021), and Operation Dawn's Light (2022), as well as Shield and Arrow (2023). The last two operations specifically targeted the Islamic Jihad organization.

In 2017, Hamas revised its charter. It announced its disassociation from the Muslim Brotherhood to appease Egypt and Saudi Arabia, which had declared the Brotherhood a terrorist organization. As part of this charter change, anti-Semitic clauses were removed, and an effort was made to distinguish between Judaism and Zionism. It emphasized that anti-Semitism is a reprehensible phenomenon associated with residents of European lands, not Arabs or Islam. Since 2018, Hamas has been receiving funding directly from Qatar with Israeli approval, following the Palestinian Authority's cessation of salary payments to government employees in Gaza.

Analysis

Prominent researcher of Hamas, Professor Shaul Mishal, is correct in his description of Hamas as a multifaceted movement. While its well-known terrorist-military aspect and its recent adoption of new forms of war crimes and crimes against humanity is one facet, Hamas also has a significant civilian component. This civilian aspect of Hamas is dedicated to activities in education, welfare, healthcare, policing, and religious indoctrination. For this reason, the movement has deep ties to Palestinian civil society and enjoys stable support from around 40 % of the population in the occupied territories. In Gaza, Hamas has essentially become a quasi-state entity, controlling all aspects of civilian life.

Hamas's civilian activities, combined with a network of charity organizations operating under its umbrella for years, provide the movement with an almost unlimited human resource capacity. Consequently, Hamas continues to rapidly generate new leaders even after the assassination of its senior figures.

It is possible to topple Hamas's rule, but this would require a full occupation of the Gaza Strip, followed by the dismantling of the organization's civilian bodies and functions. Afterward, an alternative civilian infrastructure would need to be introduced. If this is not done, Gaza could descend into a terrible chaos that might breed worse organizations. One need only examine the Iraqi case, where the US disbanded the state mechanisms built by Saddam Hussein without implanting an adequate new civilian and political alternative. The result of that action was the rise of the notorious organization ISIS.

For the past twenty years, Israel's policy toward Hamas has swung between attempts to crush and eradicate the organization and efforts to buy its cooperation. Both approaches have failed. Since the days of the Islamic Association, Israel has tried to use Islamists as tools against the secular Palestinian leadership, such as Fatah and the Palestinian Authority. In the 1980s, Israel and the West had not yet fully understood the lethal potential of political Islam. The United States initially empowered the Mujahideen in Afghanistan to fight the Soviets, unaware of the future emergence of Al-Qaeda from within the Mujahideen. Not learning from the American experience, Israel in the early 2000s allowed the Qassam Brigades to build a guerrilla and terror army with Qatari money, as a means for Israel to avoid negotiations with the Palestinian Authority.

Experience shows that Hamas is capable of adapting and changing. Just as the Islamic Association managed to give birth to Hamas, and Hamas established its military, political, and civilian wings, and as it shifted its core charter and political stance to suit the current needs, Hamas could also alter its course in the future based on political contingency.

III. Notes from the War

Yofi Tirosh
Chapter 7: A War Chronology

November 17, 2023

Yofi Tirosh, SJD, is a feminist legal scholar and a nationally recognized award-winning human rights activist. Tirosh is an associate professor and Vice Dean at the Tel Aviv University Faculty of Law, former Dean of the Sapir Academic College School of Law, and a senior research fellow at the Shalom Hartman Institute in Jerusalem. Tirosh is an expert in antidiscrimination law and in law and culture, and her recent work focuses on the tension between gender equality and religion. Before writing her doctorate at the University of Michigan Law School, she received her LLB from the Hebrew University and clerked at Israel's Supreme Court.

During the months of the protest in Israel against the judicial overhaul, I created a WhatsApp broadcast list of friends and colleagues abroad, to whom I sent my interviews, op-eds, and webinars on what is happening here. On Saturday, October 7, 2023, at 2:15 p.m., I sent a link to my post on Facebook. It said:

We're in Israel's 9/11, with everything this means.
The unbelievable loss of lives, the hostages, the terrible images that await us for months to come, from Israel and from Gaza, the shock and the horror.
I'm afraid this will produce extreme nationalism, abuse of emergency powers, oppression, polarization, and silence of criticism.
I hope we can emerge from this.

These are some of the messages from the days that followed.

Sunday, October 8, 10:33 p.m.

Dear friends, thank you for your caring and concerned messages. I am unable to answer them individually. Sharing a short update after a very long second day of this inconceivable war.

The situation is beyond words. Simply horrific. So many people we know, former students, neighbors from my childhood in the moshav (the village in the south where I grew up), colleagues from Sapir College, are either dead, wounded, captive in Gaza, or simply absent, and there is no contact with them. The numbers keep rising.

As you know, the reality in Israel is always very complex, moving from one emergency to the next, but I simply do not have categories available to me, a vocabulary, for making sense of the events. Names and stories keep surfacing.

https://doi.org/10.1515/9783111435046-008

Hamas terrorists are still out here in the south. There are still families under siege, hiding in their homes. There are families who decided on shivas without funerals because they cannot be conducted because of the fire.

Meanwhile, the most horrible government in our history is not functioning, and Netanyahu is sticking to his narrow political calculations, refusing to let in responsible and experienced partners to his coalition who demand, rightfully, that he removes the messianic Jewish supremacists [from his government] because he doesn't want to be left alone and lose his seat after this all ends.

The chaos in the leadership makes me so angry. It is unbelievable that after ten months of determined protest that pointed to the dangers and the destruction, this government hasn't fallen.

As vice dean, I have been working all day to support our students in the south, to reorganize classes and exams to remote format, to adjust to the understandable cancellations of international visiting professors, and more. Trying to stay strong to support my various communities. Shalom from Tel Aviv.

Tuesday, October 10, 10:06 p.m.

Dear friends, I am writing this update from Tel Aviv at the end of Tuesday, the fourth day of the war. One of the terrorist organizations announced that at 9 p.m. they would start bombing us again. So I have been writing this in my study, at the edge of my seat, prepared to run to the safe room on the other side of the apartment with Zohar. We always feel ambivalent about the cats that remain outside because it is impossible to make them enter the room within a few seconds. We heard bombs and rockets all day long, the walls of our building shaking, mostly from afar. Twice the sirens were in our immediate area, and we rushed to the safe room. When Zohar went out grocery shopping, I insisted on making him promise me that if there was a siren, he would enter the nearest building.

There are talks about a northern front that might open. The government is still astonishing in its failure to agree with the opposition on an emergency government, which will enable some more experienced and responsible leaders to partake in running this immense crisis.

The scale of the horror keeps unfolding. The increasing numbers of casualties receive faces and names. Our upstairs neighbor, a soldier whom we know from childhood and watched grow up into a man, is severely wounded from the fighting and is in critical condition.[1] First Sergeant Omri Belkin, who was supposed to begin his first year of law school at my law faculty in Tel Aviv University, was killed in combat on Saturday. His family received the notice only on Monday. "His peers from his military unit will not be able to attend the funeral." His father was a renowned commander in an elite unit. My friend Vivian Silver, who immigrated from Canada many years ago and is an amazing activist on Bedouin women's rights, peace, and coexistence, and who was part of my daily online yoga class for years, is probably in Hamas captivity. (Her home in a southern village is burned down and also wired with bombs probably, so they are not absolutely sure yet. Her last text message was "They're coming. I am hiding behind the closet.") I just know that if she is alive, she is providing reassurance and structure to her fellows in captivity.

The news keeps pouring in. Entire families have been wiped out. Kibbutz communities lost scores of their members, and it is doubtful that they will be able to rebuild the kibbutz. Dozens of bodies of babies were found today. The word is that their heads were slashed, but I am not sure if it is just one of those vicious rumors that are part of the psychological warfare that is also happening in the cyber dimension [update: the reports of dozens of babies murdered later proved to be unfounded].

The main elevator in the law school building is paralyzed, because the contractor who was renovating it has been recruited. The next contractor on the University's list is a Palestinian from the occupied territories, and the security forces do not approve him at this time. So even if we resume studies, we will have an accessibility challenge for disabled students and faculty. The international visiting professors who were supposed to teach at the school in the coming weeks were kind enough to agree to move their classes to Zoom, and we are adjusting the curriculum to fit the differences in time zones. But questions linger—how will it be possible to teach and study antidiscrimination law, for example, when so much is changing and the questions are so big?

There is so much more, but I will end this message here. Thank you for your care and friendship. Shalom from Tel Aviv.

Friday, October 13, 11:52 p.m.

Dear friends: Since my last message, I have struggled with how to compose my next message because there are so many dimensions to what is happening. I realize the

---

[1] Adam is now back home. It will be a long recovery, but he is out of danger.

impacts of the events here have become very palpable on your side of the ocean. I am so sorry. I decided that rather than attempting (and failing) to encompass many aspects, I will send a daily report on one aspect of my day.

This morning Zohar and I went to the shiva of Sergeant Major Chen Nahmias, a sniper in the special unit to combat terrorism. Chen was the brother-in-law of my friend and colleague Yifat Bitton, a tort law and antidiscrimination scholar. Chen, forty-three years old, a father of four whose oldest daughter is nine and a half years old, was in the first forces to arrive in the city of Sderot, where Hamas invaded, at 7:30 a.m. on Saturday. His unit met fire they hadn't expected. He was the only one in his jeep to get killed, despite the shield vest he wore.

Chen's mother lost her first husband in the Yom Kippur War, on October 8, 1973. A widow with three children, she remarried and gave birth to Chen, whom she lost on October 7, 2023. Chen married a woman who grew up without a father; he also died in that war. In the chaos, Chen's body was not traced until Monday. One painful story out of so many. Shabat shalom from Tel Aviv.

Saturday, October 14, 10:08 p.m.

This morning, we decided to go to the beach. I told Zohar that I needed some time with my back to the city, to reality, gazing at the horizon, getting some of the feeling that the sight of the ocean gives, of quiet and blueness and peace. Our regular sandy café in south Tel Aviv, Banana Beach, was closed, like all others. Expecting this, we brought our camping coffee kit and cooked Arabic coffee, which was comforting. When we returned back home, just before I entered the shower, there was a siren, followed by very loud falls. As I am writing this update, another siren sent us to the safe room.

Because of the relative quiet of the Shabbat, there is room for the new reality to begin sinking in. I am trying to prepare myself for the images of torture of hostages that we are likely to receive, but I don't know how. How can one prepare for this? Every night just before I fall asleep, uncontrolled emotions and images flood me.

This time last week, we already understood that we were in a state of unprecedented emergency, but we hadn't realized the scale of casualties and atrocities. Many in the south were still hiding from Hamas terrorists in their homes or lying on the ground quietly in orchids and fields near the party site. So much has changed during this week.

I do not want to go into a geopolitical analysis and into the futile game of balancing or comparing. Just to say that I regret that Israel's leadership, to the extent that there is one (and there hardly is) seems to be responding viscerally rather than effectively. I am longing for less honor and more dignity. Shalom from Tel Aviv.

Monday, October 16, 9:41 p.m.

It's night here, and the first headline I saw this morning still overshadows the many other news and events that this day summoned. During his meeting with the representatives of the captives' families, in which the families demanded that Prime Minister Netanyahu prioritize returning the hostages home, Netanyahu staged a dramatic entrance of families from his side of the political spectrum, religious settlers, who expressed admiring support and a willingness to pay any price. The heartless cynicism is killing me. But I am worried more than I am enraged. This is clearly an incapacitated politician, not a leader. How can he be trusted to do the right thing for the country in the hard decisions that await him? I am relieved that the infantry operation entering Gaza hasn't started yet. Shalom from Tel Aviv.

Tuesday, October 17, 11:15 p.m.

The names of the murdered and missing since October 7, and the newly killed and injured from this week's fighting, keep coming. Unbelievable stories. So much loss in my surroundings. Just this past hour, news about the bombarded hospital in Gaza. The versions battle is endless, but people whose judgment and sources I trust say this is an accident by Islamic Jihad, and I found a small consolation in this.

Here in Tel Aviv, the strong boom noises of missiles—falling or being targeted while in the air nearby—have become routine. Several times daily, our windows are shaking. It is amazing how quickly one adapts to the new reality.

Yesterday I wrote about Netanyahu's ugly manipulation in the meeting with the hostages' families. Today it was discovered that things are even worse than they seemed: the religious man who was presented as a family member of the hostages is not related to the hostages. He heads an organization advocating the exoneration of settlers indicted in crimes against Palestinians.

I am relieved that Biden is on his way here. Many here feel that the US administration rightfully recognizes that Netanyahu is unfit to lead at this time.

But I also got a haircut today; a small blessing. Shalom from Tel Aviv.

Wednesday, October 18, 8:55 p.m.

Every evening around 8 p.m., missiles on Tel Aviv and sirens send us to the safe room, followed by a loud explosion noise. Judging by our conversations, Zohar and I feel perhaps the closest to the palpability of death than we have ever felt. We planned yesterday to set up our permissions on social media and email accounts so that if one of us died, the other could access the information. This issue comes up now with the many bereaved spouses and families. We didn't get around to it.

The most significant event of the day for me was President Biden's speech. Most of all, he demonstrated leadership and humanness, which we have been lacking here for so many years that we have forgotten what they can look like. His genuine empathy for what it feels like to lose dear ones. "The scent when you open the closet door. The morning coffee you shared together." He is the only public figure in Israel that talks about the hostages. They seem to have been completely forgotten by Israel's government. It is inconceivable. No one from the government has even called the families yet.

Then, this message from Biden: "The Palestinian people are suffering greatly as well. We mourn the loss of innocent Palestinian lives … The people of Gaza need food, water, medicine, shelter … You are a Jewish state, but you're also a democracy. And like the United States, you don't live by the rules of terrorists … What sets us apart from the terrorists is we believe in the fundamental dignity of every human life—Israeli, Palestinian, Arab, Jew, Muslim, Christian—everyone. You can't give up what makes you who you are. If you give that up, then the terrorists win. And we can never let them win."[2]

I realize we can easily be cynical about America's horrible track record of disrespecting the human lives of innocent civilians around the world to reach its strategic goals. But still, I can't tell you how this message is essential in the atmosphere in Israel today. Recall the post-9/11 atmosphere of nationalism and heightened patriotism and xenophobia. This is what it's like here. And Biden was wise to contextualize this with the persecution history of the Jewish people. Shalom from Tel Aviv.

---

2 White House (2023a).

Thursday, October 19, 10:39 p.m.

A few days after all this began, I realized there was no choice, and I must keep a list. As insensitive as this may sound, I had to keep track of all the affected people in my social and professional circles. In the past few days, I have been most preoccupied, emotionally and in conversations, with the sheer raw fear of parents and spouses of soldiers or reservists sitting there next to the border for several days now, waiting for the command to enter. Many of these young people can call home only every few days. The inescapable knowing that their children or partners are soon going to face actual danger to their lives. I don't know how they do it. Shalom from Tel Aviv.

Friday, October 20, 6:56 p.m.

The familiar historical pattern of rapid narrowing of free speech in times of emergency is hitting us hard here, and in academia especially. The current government has targeted academia through attacks and legislative proposals to silence "unpatriotic" speech and deny tenure from faculty with "unfitting" opinions.

Since last Saturday, the personal witch-hunt has escalated. Today, a prominent constitutional law expert who "changed sides" to the "radical center" during the past ten months posted a personal attack on international law scholars, my colleagues at Tel Aviv University, effectively blaming them for harming Israeli security because of their stances on humanitarian law in wartimes, and calling on law schools to nominate faculty with opinions that can contribute to Israel's security. I, too, was (falsely) accused of supporting BDS.

I know you are busy with such questions on your campuses, and I am grateful for your engagement and commitment to a truthful and conscientious discussion. Shabbat Shalom from Tel Aviv.

Wednesday, October 25, 11:04 p.m.

Zohar returned from volunteering in the Negev tired but satisfied. He brought beautiful lettuce heads that he picked himself and were given to him by the grateful farmer, a guy our age, who started crying when he expressed his gratitude to the volunteers at the end of the workday. Tomorrow, Zohar will join another group of farm volunteers, this time with Brothers in Farms, the initiative of the reservist protesters who morphed overnight from Brothers in Arms.

An hour ago, heavy missiles on cities just south of Tel Aviv. A residential building in Rishon Le-Tzion was hit directly, luckily with only lightly wounded, and similar-scale casualties in the city of Petah Tikva.

Again, I find myself grateful to President Biden. This time for speaking up today against the settlers' murderous violence, which has escalated since the war began. The gap [between the US leadership and our lack of leadership] is unbearable. On the one hand, impressive determination and efficiency in taking advantage of the war to achieve extremist goals in the occupied territories and deepen the de facto annexation, deportations, and trigger-happy killings of Palestinians with no constraints; huge budget transfers to the coalition's base that go under the radar because the attention is on the war. On the other hand, disgraceful government dysfunction on every level—financial, psychological, welfare, logistical—almost three weeks into the war, and nearly every emergency need is still in the hands of civilian networks of dedicated and conscientious people. This is a costly and stark demonstration of what this government was busy with in the past ten months. Nepotistic nominations of unqualified men (yes, I mean men), corruption, destruction of the civil service, and sheer contempt to administrative law. This morning, Israel's citizens learned that the Netanyahus moved late last night to another home, a billionaire friend's villa, because it has a bunker against nuclear and biological weapons. I hope they don't arrest me for saying this (and they do arrest more and more people for much more mundane speech): I don't think that these are the causes of death that Netanyahu should be worried about right now.

I am going to make Zohar another hearty sandwich for tomorrow's intense physical labor. Shalom from Tel Aviv.

Saturday, October 28, 11:58 p.m.

Two sirens went off today in our area, one at 2 p.m. when we were taking a nap, the other at 6:30 p.m., when we were just about to leave for Jerusalem to have dinner with Zohar's sister. Much fewer bombs than in Gaza. Much more than there should be, anywhere. We decided to take the risk and drive anyway. We are back safely.

On the way, the highway electric signs say, "Together we will win." The togetherness feels artificial. And what does "win" mean? Flags are everywhere, too. From being an emblem of the protest against autocracy, Israel's flag changed its meaning so quickly. Shalom from Tel Aviv.

Monday, October 30, 10:11 p.m.

During the many months of protest against the populist antidemocratic regime, I developed a unique friendship with a reservist who serves on an air force commando unit. Aviv, about my age, is a master in acupuncture, supporting women's health and reproduction. He contacted me about half a year ago, asking that I explain to him and his friend about the role of the ultra-right influential think tank, the Kohelet Forum, in facilitating the judicial overhaul. We never really met, but we established a friendship and a bond due to constant collaboration on various protest initiatives and exchanging views and words of encouragement. When he wants to consult on particularly sensitive protest activities, he won't talk on the regular phone line but via an audio WhatsApp call, which is more secure. Like all of us, since October 7, Aviv has channeled his efforts and skills to help in this country's crisis. A few days ago, he went with three friends from his unit to perform an emotionally and physically complex assignment: retrieving personal items from the cars of those who were at the bloody party. They found wallets and personal items that can help with the identification of bodies, and other objects that should be returned to the families for memory's sake. In his post describing that day, Aviv mentions finding toys, books, glasses, makeup, and baby food. His post is also critical of the malfunction of the government, who left these cars behind without canvassing them or guarding them; many of them were already looted. It shouldn't have been he and his friends performing this delicate and essential task. It should have been the state. But it is missing in action. Shalom from Tel Aviv.

Fig. 1: Near the site of the Reim Party massacre Photo Credit: Aviv Messinger.

Fig. 2: Near the site of the Reim Party massacre. Photo Credit: Aviv Messinger.

Tuesday, October 31, 10:31 p.m.

The dead keep piling up. More civilians in Gaza. More soldiers. And empty words that fail to frame things; to give them meaning. Finish with Hamas. What does that even mean?

Today, I cried for the first time since the war began. It wasn't a deep cry. A short weep that came unplanned, as tears tend to. The trigger wasn't even bad news, which has been arriving hourly. It was a video clip on the heroism of women in this war. Fighters, leaders. And still excluded from the decision-making tables, simply excluded and ignored. International human rights and women's rights bodies ignore the gendered atrocities that were done to women, and probably (and horrifically) are still being done now.

Zohar is perhaps the only person with the magic force of dragging me away from work and activism to take some time and get air. Today, we went to a try-out class in fly-fit yoga, where you hang, stretch, and roll on long, elastic, colorful hammocks that hang from the ceiling. I wondered whether it was appropriate to describe this joy of body and playfulness, to pause on a normal and positive moment amidst the immense pain. I decided that it was the moral thing to do, indeed. Shalom from Tel Aviv.

Thursday, November 2, 10:37 p.m.

A new instruction in yoga class: "Some people feel uncomfortable closing their eyes these days. That is OK, you may keep them open." Shalom from Tel Aviv.

Tuesday, November 7, 11:13 p.m.

A month ago today. The memorial ceremony on the Tel Aviv University campus was simple and straightforward. No clichés, no dramatic effects. Also, no students except for a student representative. About a third of our students are in reserve duty. Electrical engineering professor Meir Ariel spoke, describing his son, Dan, the youngest and least bookish of his children, who was at that party on that cursed Saturday. Dan and two friends were shot and wounded. They hid from Hamas for many hours, bleeding. When they heard Hamas's killers coming near them, Dan's friend whispered to Dan, "Pretend you're dead," and lay over him. But the murderers spotted a movement and killed Dan. They had no ammunition left, so they ended his life with their bare hands. One of the three friends was saved, and the third was kidnapped. Meir and his family looked for Dan for three days. Every anonymous body arriving at a hospital for identification raised hope for some certainty. On Tuesday morning came that knock on their door. "You know the pattern of this story," said the father laconically. Since then, he said, he has returned to campus and resumed his research and class preparation. "Fifty minutes work, ten minutes crying. That is the formula." Shalom from Tel Aviv.

Tuesday, November 14, 6:57 a.m.

Vivian is not in captivity. She was murdered in her home in Kibbutz Be'eri. Her burned body was finally identified. On November 3, 2022, I was fortunate to offer Vivian a ride from Beer Sheva to Tel Aviv. We attended a New Israel Fund event that celebrated forty activists who make Israel a better place, for which we were both selected. She was to spend the night in Tel Aviv in order to go the next morning to help Palestinians in their olive picking and protect them from settler violence. During our ride, Vivian asked for my help with connecting to lawyers who may be able to assist in the efforts to return the bodies of Palestinians who were killed by armed forces in Israel to their families.

One must pause here. This is too much. But pause how? What kind of pause is appropriate? Sarcasm? Bitterness? Hope? I do not know. I am trying to confine my feelings to sadness and cherishing the generous humanness of this woman.

Also searching for a word for that need to revise part of my understanding and experience of the past weeks. Is there a verb for this? For more than a month, I have been imagining Vivian in captivity every night. It wasn't by choice. It was what surfaced in my soul when my mind released control just before falling asleep. In an update from the first week of the war, I wrote, I just know that if she is alive, she is providing reassurance and structure to her fellows in captivity." Shalom from Tel Aviv.

Wednesday, November 15, 11:13 p.m.

There was this problem during the pandemic of how to open an email. A reference to "these turbulent times" usually did the job. I spend hours writing and rewriting the opening sentence of collective emails to students. There is also the problem of how to open a conversation. "How's it going" is inappropriate. And if it comes out of my mouth out of habit and the other person says "Okay," or "Fine," I feel they are disingenuous. Sometimes I even feel angry. When asked how it's going, I reply, "Bearable." I really mean "just barely." Shalom from Tel Aviv.

Friday, November 17, 2:07 p.m.

About 250,000 Israelis are evacuated from their homes near the southern border with Gaza and the northern border with Lebanon. They are in hotels, hostels, and Airbnbs throughout the country. The *balagan* [chaos] and disfunction by the governmental ministries in managing this crisis is still being mitigated by Israel's civil society. Since many from the south left in great haste on October 7 or 8, they do not have the most basic personal items. Noa Mondshein, the owner of a private custom-fit bra store in Jaffa, offered to send bras to the evacuees. She received lists with names and sizes. Noa gift-wrapped each bra and added a personal note to the woman receiving it. This was in mid-October. This morning, Zohar and I went to the store to express our gratitude by shopping for a new bra for me. We were astonished to find Noa still picking and gift-wrapping bras to send to evacuees. Shabbat Shalom from Tel Aviv.

Assaf David
Chapter 8: Flashes from the Life That Was

October 14, 2023

Assaf David, PhD, is the co-founder of the Forum for Regional Thinking, its academic director, and the editor of its website. He is also the director of the Israel in the Middle East cluster at the Van Leer Jerusalem Institute. He teaches political science at the Hebrew University of Jerusalem and has taught in the Department of Middle East Studies and the Department of Politics and Government at the Ben-Gurion University of the Negev. David's areas of research focus on Jordan, relations between army and society in the Middle East, Arab public discourse, Israel's place in the Middle East, and the Middle East as an academic discipline in Israel.

> "for there was not a house where there was not one dead" (Exodus 12:30)

Tragedy upon tragedy upon tragedy. Anger upon anger upon anger. The news of the horrifying acts in the Valley of Slaughter [the site of Hamas's attack on October 7] —at parties, in moshavim and kibbutzim. The cruelty that extinguished the last minutes of their lives. What the hostages in Gaza—men, the elderly, women, and children, innocent infants—experience in these very moments. My body is paralyzed, my mind feels mad. I refuse to watch the videos, look at pictures, or listen to the voices from the void, in an attempt to preserve my sanity. But my soul is stained, distressed, and darkened in a terrifying way every day, every hour. This is a tragedy that will never be erased. It frightens me to think of what it will do to us, what it has already done to us.

Yoel Ben-Porat, the commander of Unit 8200 during the Yom Kippur War, who warned in advance of the outbreak of the war and was ignored, lost his sanity over it. He believed that the thousands of dead and injured, the worst trauma Israel had ever suffered—until last week—rested on his shoulders and conscience. The current trauma is even heavier. It doesn't invoke 1973 for us, but the Holocaust, and this time within our own state. A state devastated by its own leadership, but it nevertheless exists and endures; with an army weakened by right-wing populism and humiliated by Hamas, yet still strong and formidable; and with feelings of revenge that have no bounds. Now the fire will consume everything around us. Tragedy upon tragedy. Our anger at them and their anger at us, and our anger at them, again and again, without end.

I remember, especially in recent years, tough and bitter conversations. During the days in lectures to groups and in the evenings and late into the nights with friends and comrades, partners on the journey. An emotional processing of the dark significance that arose from our analysis, the certain knowledge we all had

—from the state's leadership (while there still was a leadership), its institutions, its army, security services, and intelligence, to civil society organizations and the people who think and act in the field—that we are sitting on a vast and seething fuel reservoir [the Occupation of the Palestinians]. Some of us were trying to completely empty that reservoir and some of us were trying to at least reduce its size and heat. But many others were throwing into it one burning match after another; some out of apathy and some intentionally and for personal gain. And in the face of all this, the absolute majority in the country was simply not aware of the reservoir's existence and believed they could continue their lives as usual. The fuel reservoir continued to grow, its temperature rising.

And those among us who were trying to empty the reservoir, small and weak, lacking voice and influence, looked with palpable fear at the clouds from hell that would envelop us and them. We cried out, warned, and pleaded before those residing in the silent hermitage of the government, in the army, in academia, in the general public. How many texts, initiatives, projects, and interviews we—women and men, academics, activists, and civil society organizations—offered.

At a safe distance from us but out of similar concern and worry, many from the military-intelligence establishment, including generals, senior officers, and heads of agencies and security services, issued their warnings. All of us had become aware of the march of radical-right pyromaniacs and irresponsible populists [Israeli radical-right politicians and settlers], many of whom were smelting religion and nationalism into an enormous flamethrower, with which they sprayed fire at the reservoir with incomprehensible arrogance and contempt.

How many personal posts I wrote that elicited horror and tears—both mine and from those who read them—about the disaster that will befall us due to our arrogance, negligence, and failures: our weakening of the moderate voices in Palestinian society and politics while strengthening extremist forces to the very edge of human reason. Initially, we wrote as a warning, but later we gave up and rushed to seek shelter. Those posts emerged from late-night conversations with friends who were breaking down in tears, deeply aware that the flood was approaching, taking on a dark form of rage, vengeance, and madness that we couldn't contain. It will harm us, our families, left-wing people and right-wing people, the elderly, women, and children.

We were frightened of what we were saying to ourselves in closed rooms and couldn't think, speak, or write until we summoned some courage. "Pray to God, pray very hard, so you can escape the fire when it burns." "The terrible days are coming soon," I wrote just two months ago. From all around me, friends wrote equally chilling messages. Many of those who identified with us back then are now calling for Gaza to be wiped out, in light of the horrifying events in the south. Tragedy upon tragedy upon tragedy, anger upon anger upon anger.

How can one not lose their mind?

There will come a time to talk about Hamas and ISIS, about Gaza and the West Bank, about the cruelty of slave rebellions, about the loss of humanity among us and among them, about what preceded what, about the benefits that may now grow from the Abraham Accords. There will come a time to expand on the causes, to analyze the present and think about the future. To hold those responsible accountable. For now, I will only say what Israeli Jews refuse to accept at the moment, but will have to come to terms with in a month or a year from now: there will be no life, and there will be no quality of life, for Jews between the river and the sea as long as there is no life and no quality of life for Palestinians between the river and the sea. This is how it was and how it will be until the end of days.

Our citizens and our children are perishing, imprisoned by Hamas. Guiltless Gazans pay the price for Hamas's rule and its horrors. Halt the war machine, release the captives, allow us to mourn and weep, leave room to think wisely and correctly about how to dismantle Hamas and reduce the number of its supporters.

A final word to my Palestinian friends and partners, especially in the territories and Gaza. For so many years, we talked about the inhumanity of Israelis toward Palestinians, in the face of a disinterested and callous world. These days, we talk about the inhumanity of Palestinians toward Israelis. Given the magnitude of the horrors and their severity, we simply cannot do otherwise. It's not just because of the world's indifference, but because of ourselves. "For the hurt of the daughter of my people I am hurt; I am black; astonishment has taken hold on me. Is there no balm in Gilead; is there no physician there? why then is not the health of the daughter of my people recovered? Oh that my head were waters, and mine eyes a fountain of tears, that I might weep day and night for the slain of the daughter of my people" (Jeremiah 8:21–9:1).

Ameer Fakhoury
Chapter 9: I'll Write While I Can Still Breathe

October 16, 2023

> **Ameer Fakhoury**, PhD, is a postdoctoral fellow at the Polonsky Academy of the Van Leer Research Institute in Jerusalem. He is a jurist and a political and cultural sociologist. He holds a bachelor's degree in law from the Hebrew University and a master's degree in peace studies and conflict resolution from the University of Haifa. Fakhoury wrote his doctorate at the University of Haifa on the socio-mental syntax of Christian Arabs in Israel. His current research focuses on two main topics: symbolic struggles among the Palestinian middle class in Israel; and struggles over the boundaries of the political community in Israel, from a comparative perspective. Fakhoury is co-director of the Nissan project for joint society research, whose mission is to establish shared society as an independent field. He is also co-director of the "Partnership-Based Peace" think tank operating at the Van Leer Institute. In civil society, Fakhoury is one of the leaders of the "Peace Based on Partnership" movement, and the former director of the community of human rights lawyers at the School for Peace in Wahat Al-Salam, and its former research unit director.

Murdering innocent civilians is a despicable war crime. It is a violation of the basic legal and ethical prohibition not to intentionally harm noncombatants. The killing of families and all the horrors being revealed before our eyes are moral abominations: not just a war crime, but a direct attack on humanity. This position needs to be written and declared loudly, clearly, confidently, and lucidly. No context (apartheid, mass imprisonment, occupation, settler-colonialism, or war crimes) justifies or can ever justify cruel and indiscriminate mass murder. A vicious attack on human morals and humanity.

Members of the Arab-Palestinian nation need to say this because and not despite the fact that they belong to that nation. Members of the Arab-Palestinian nation need to say this because of and not despite their justified interest in freedom, honor, and independence.

Human morality is indivisible. Opposition to the massacre that took place on that terrible Shabbat needs to be accompanied by no less determined opposition to crimes being planned and carried out in the Gaza Strip ("Finally there's no electricity in Gaza," said a senior journalist), as well as crimes that have been carried out elsewhere against the Palestinian people. It's impossible to hold human morality in one hand and beat it with the other.

Ignoring the context of violence is not only immoral, but also reveals a lack of political insight, because it doesn't allow us to develop a politics that will prevent further violence in the future. It doesn't allow us to deal with the violence and to replace it with the politics (in the broadest sense possible) of talking and reconciliation. The bloodshed and the hundred-year war will be ended through peace, justice, and reconciliation between the peoples—this is a nearly universal rule. Whoever doesn't invest in this, each according to their ability and circumstances, whoever doesn't make this part of their daily routine, contributes by default to the continued bloodletting. It's no longer possible to ignore this fact or to try to "live with the conflict."

Palestinian Arabs with Israeli citizenship are showing responsibility, political insight, ethics, and human, complex and even exceptional political understanding —as one would expect from the special place they occupy (listen to and/or read, for instance, Ayman Odeh, Hanin Majadli, Samer Swaid, Raef Zraik, Marzuq al-Halabi, and Thabet Abu Rass, among many others). They should not be content with that. Through their leadership, they need to strive for a more effective role in shaping a vision of peace, reconciliation, and justice between the two peoples and in convincing the two peoples that this is achievable. They must strive to lead during these dark moments in order to save the two peoples—out of ethical responsibility, civic obligation, and a binational understanding of the complexity of this land.

The joint binational [Jewish–Arab] initiatives now emerging and blooming from Israeli civil society are a beacon of light, an example and a model, and they provide space to breathe. They are a creation and continuation of a shared civil society and an island of partnership and sanity. They are a glimpse at one of the possible futures here, and the only one that is sustainable. They should be widened to offer a beacon that shines over the entire homeland and region. Anyone who still isn't invested in these efforts—now is the time.

If we survive the catastrophe and there is space for politics afterwards, there will be a struggle over how to understand what happened and draw conclusions from it. Hatred and violence, continued apartheid and expulsion will receive a tailwind. Even genocide will be suggested (every bridge over the Ayalon Highway currently features the sign "Eradicate Gaza"). Only a vision of national and human partnership based on a shared fate and justice for all can defeat these ideas. This has never been the intuitive conclusion, neither here nor anywhere else in the world. The community of justice, peace, and reconciliation must explain and convince and, most importantly, practically realize this while showing understanding and empathy for those who are afraid, angry, and frustrated. This was always the right thing to do, and it will become more urgent than ever the day after the war.

Ghadir Hani

Chapter 10: The Arab Community Is Still in Shock from Hamas's Massacre

November 6, 2023

> **Ghadir Hani** is a social activist in the field of shared life and peace. She is one of the leaders of Standing Together, a movement that interlinks the work for peace and the end of the occupation, equality and anti-racism, and social justice struggles. She is on the board of Women Waging Peace, and is the director of the Habima Al-Manbar interfaith dialogue initiative. She has been involved in numerous initiatives, including A Different Voice—an organization for a dignified life on both sides of the Gaza border—Hagar for Jewish–Arab education, women's activism in the Negev, and many others. She is the recipient of the prestigious Sami Michael Award for Just and Equal Society.

Friends, I ask that you share my words. It's hard for all of us to find words these days, and it's even harder for me as an Arab citizen in Israel. Tomorrow we will count a month since that damned morning, that morning when the sky fell. Even today, time does not dull the pain. On the contrary, what we couldn't digest in the first days—the extent of the horrors, the shocking murder of families, the abuse— all of these are heightened by personal stories with names and faces, causing us all to tear up, cry, remain speechless, incapable of expressing the depth of pain. The brutal war continues to hit us all, with more and more dead and wounded in body and soul. All of us, even those who are not physically injured, are injured. In one moment, our lives became a whirlwind of blood, rage, fear, and terror.

The Arab public in Israel, a group to which I belong, found itself speechless in the face of the horror. For me, the knowledge that the people of Hamas—my people, Palestinians—deliberately chose to murder and abuse Israeli civilians (and not only Israelis), among them the elderly, women, and children, is unfathomable and unforgivable. I will shout everywhere and with all my voice: whoever is capable of harming the innocent, whoever is capable of perpetrating such atrocities, is not a human being. I am ashamed that those murderers belong to my people.

A lot has happened since the cursed Shabbat. So many ripples to the circles of pain and destruction. I am painfully aware that many in the Jewish-Israeli public have no compassion for the citizens of Gaza. I also know the arguments—Hamas was elected with a majority of votes, etc. It saddens me greatly that the suffering of the civilian population in the Gaza Strip, whose lives have not been livable for so many years, is perceived with indifference and sometimes even with glee among many in the Jewish-Israeli public.

I hear around me, also in relation to the Arab citizens of Israel, horrible statements of revenge on the Arabs wherever they are. I am not afraid to say, even if they [the Israeli police] come to question me, that I feel the pain of the civilians of Gaza. A human heart can unfortunately contain a lot of pain. The thousands of children who were killed in the bombings in Gaza are just that: children—with dreams, who played and lived in hardship that not many people even comprehend; their small palms buried in the rubble flood me with tears. Humanity is becoming extinct in our region, but we must not lose our humanity. Those children in Jabaliya, Khan Yunis or Gaza—their death is a terrible tragedy.

We too, the Arab public in Israel, are still in shock. As we have always been used to, in times of security tension, silence is the natural act. The silence stems first of all from fear, lest they see us as the enemy. The obvious must be said out loud—the Arab public in Israel is shocked by the actions of Hamas. The Arab public in Israel is shocked by the endless number of dead in Gaza. The Arab public in Israel is afraid that it will pay a heavy price for the terrible Hamas attack, and the feelings of revenge from many in the Jewish-Israeli public—and therefore, in the absence of a public space that can contain the complexity, many in the Arab public remain silent.

But there are those who are not silent and who dare to speak. Many of them speak with courage in condemning the attack and discussing the importance of the solidarity of the Arab population in Israel with their Jewish neighbors. Their position is the position of the majority of the Arab public. It is not for nothing that in Kfar Qasim, Batira, Bir HaDaj, Berhat and other [Arab] towns in Israel, civil initiatives began to operate to help evacuees from the surrounding area and the north. Amidst my despair, I cling to the glimmers of hope, in a civil society that helps everyone. In the willingness of my Bedouin friends to risk their lives to save lives on October 7, such as Amer Abu Sabila from Abu Talul, who was murdered while saving two girls in Sderot.

Friends, we have no choice. Two peoples will continue to live side by side, and therefore the forces of light must fight extremism, hatred, violence, and all the death-mongers. Only if we act together can we look into the eyes of our children and give hope for better days; this is the time to do everything for the common future of both nations. The moderate forces, who favor life, both in the Jewish public and in the Arab public, must say out loud the obvious—this is our country, and we must reach out for peace. The outstretched hand will meet many hands. We are the majority.

Eran Tzidkiyahu
Chapter 11: Comments on the Current Moment

October 18, 2023

> **Eran Tzidkiyahu**, PhD, is a postdoctoral fellow in the Department of Political Science at the Hebrew University of Jerusalem, and a research fellow at the Forum for Regional Thinking. He is also a geopolitical guide for Israel and Palestine, providing geopolitical consultancy and analysis, study-tours and lectures: www.erantzidkiyahu.com

Nothing will be as it was before the Black Saturday of October 7. From the present horror, one can move in two opposite directions: toward the abyss of hell or toward a political turning point, and ultimately—peace. Yes, peace. At a distance of a week and a bit from that Black Saturday, here are some initial thoughts from my home in Jerusalem.

I will start by stating the obvious that nevertheless needs to be said: Hamas is not legitimate. Its actions in the south are war crimes, atrocities against humanity, and massacres of civilian populations using Nazi- and ISIS-like methods. The horror cannot be overstated. Mass murder of women, the elderly, and children, obliteration of communities, kidnappings, torture, abuse, rape, and more. It is pure evil that must be condemned unequivocally. The Israeli occupation and the blockade on Gaza do not justify such evil. Anyone committing crimes against humanity forfeits the right to be called human and to belong to the family of nations—period.

This tragedy can strengthen the existing positions in Israel, both right and left. A person on the right will say: "We always knew they wanted to kill us—and here's the proof." Someone on the left will say: "We always said we must end the occupation and the blockade and seek a political solution. We always warned against the horror to come—and here's the proof." There may be truth in both arguments, but faced with such horror, every thinking person—especially those dealing with the Jewish–Arab conflict in this land—should introspect and reconsider their fundamental assumptions. The Israeli–Palestinian conflict has entered a new era, one we haven't fully grasped yet.

Only now, at a distance of more than a week from the events, I sit and write, trying to make sense of the chaos that has consumed my mind, body, and soul. Amidst the ongoing conflict, I feel the need to voice my criticism. Even if my words may sometimes sound harsh, rest assured that every word here is written with humility and uncertainty. Ultimately, every sentence poses more questions than answers. In the following lines, I will attempt to explain our reality, but explanation is not in any way a justification of the events in the south. Absolute terror must be condemned unequivocally and without hesitation.

The Hostages

Every effort should be made to bring back the Israeli hostages held in Gaza. As Yigal Karmon,[1] the President and Founder of MEMRI, and other security experts have made clear, Israel must take the initiative and inform the world and the public that it is ready to release all the Palestinian security prisoners held in Israeli prisons, in exchange for all the hostages. We need to do this for our sons and daughters, for our elderly and our youth, for the women and men who are currently in the hands of Hamas. We need to do it for their families and for ourselves as a nation. If Hamas refuses such an offer, the world will know, the families of the captives will know, and the Palestinian prisoners' families will know that Israel made a proposal, and Hamas rejected it. After such a move, Israel will have more freedom to act against Hamas.

It is possible that in the early days following the Black Sabbath, an opportunity might have been created to release the children, women, and elderly who were kidnapped. That moment likely passed with the start of the extensive Israeli bombings, and now, as long as it's still possible, more complex international mediation will be needed to reach a comprehensive agreement.

Alongside the public pressure to work for a hostage release agreement, it seems that the governmental tone regarding the fate of the captives is beginning to change [i.e. becoming more open to a prisoners' deal]. However, we must not forget the resolute and heartless pronouncements of Bezalel Smotrich[2] [finance minister] and Tzachi Hanegbi[3] [head of the National Security Council], who expressed complete disregard for the lives of the hostages.

"To Conquer Gaza and Topple Hamas"

It is imperative not to allow a ground incursion into Gaza without a clear purpose, without an exit strategy, and without considering what the Strip will look like the day after.

---

1 MEMRI (2023).
2 Haaretz Editorial (2023).
3 Haaretz Update (2023).

After the 9/11 attacks, the United States invaded Afghanistan and Iraq to fight terrorism and change the regime in the occupied countries. The operations turned out to be resounding failures: the Taliban now controls Afghanistan, Iraq has torn into factions, and the absence left by Al-Qaeda led to the rise of ISIS. I don't know of one example from the last two decades of an external occupying force taking control of a foreign and hostile territory and successfully and sustainably replacing its government with a better one. Such a move almost always leads to failure and spells huge humanitarian catastrophe for both the occupiers and the occupied.

Returning to our case, there are over two million people living in the Gaza Strip. Among them, Hamas has tens of thousands of trained fighters waiting for IDF forces in an underground fortified city. Even if the occupation of the Strip is militarily feasible, the cost of the invasion would be enormous, and its purpose unclear. It is reasonable to assume that a ground invasion into the Gaza Strip without a clear exit strategy and without considering "the day after" would lead to a protracted presence of IDF soldiers in Gaza. Such a move would play into Hamas's hands, and we must not repeat past mistakes.

Furthermore, there is no doubt that on the heels of the calls for action by some past military figures, such as Yaakov Amidror and Effi Eitam,[4] the likes of Bezalel Smotrich and Itamar Ben-Gvir are waiting with a complete plan[5] for renewed Jewish settlement in Gaza.

The Humanitarian Crisis in Gaza

Israel's "no-choice war" against Hamas will inevitably cause unavoidable harm to civilians, but it must not be our goal from the outset. In clear condemnation of Hamas's crimes, political sociologist Ameer Fakhoury writes in the present volume, "Human morality is indivisible. Opposition to the massacre that took place on that terrible Shabbat needs to be accompanied by no less determined opposition to crimes being planned and carried out in the Gaza Strip ... It's impossible to hold human morality in one hand and beat it with the other."[6]

According to the Ministry of Health in Gaza, as of October 15, and since the war began on October 7, approximately 2,670 people have been killed in the Gaza Strip, including many children. Among the approximately 9,600 wounded, the majority are innocent civilians. As I write these lines, there is no running

---

[4] Hidaboroot (2023).
[5] Segal (2023).
[6] Chapter 9 in this volume.

water in the Gaza Strip, and approximately one million people have been displaced from their homes by Israel.

The destruction of Gaza was born out of failure and is condemned to fail. It seems that in his conduct, Benjamin Netanyahu is attempting to cover up his horrific failure in rivers of blood. The purpose of complete destruction, it seems, is to shift the focus from the humiliation of October 7, to the number of casualties in Gaza, in a disingenuous presentation of a disproportional calculus, following the "logic" that "if they killed a thousand of us, we will kill three thousand or ten thousand of them." This is a fundamentally abhorrent idea. Wars should not be waged out of a desire for revenge. On the contrary, victorious wars are conducted with careful consideration and the setting of defined strategic goals, which also elaborate a plan for the day after.

Israel must now rally the moral justification and the international attention it receives due to the horrors it suffered at the hands of Hamas to establish a regional and international coalition involving Arab states and Western powers. Together, they can isolate Hamas. At the same time, an alternative to Hamas rule in Gaza must be built. There is no other solution. The indiscriminate destruction of Gaza is undermining the moral and international support that Israel currently "enjoys." The harsh images documented from the Gaza Strip in recent days are already changing the international tone, and it is possible that in the coming days the world will cease to support Israel.

The Middle East has always been a battleground for struggles among great powers. China, Russia, and even Iran are already in the "field." The United States has issued a clear and strong statement and even deployed in the region to deter Hezbollah. In this context, Israel must encourage Saudi Arabia (which has already frozen its contacts with Israel due to its bombardment of Gaza) along with Egypt and Jordan to participate in a regional initiative involving NATO (including Turkey) and the European Union.

The continuation of destruction in Gaza will undermine such a broad initiative, and likely ignite additional conflict zones on Israel's borders (including the Jordan border), in East Jerusalem, and within Israel itself, potentially even endangering the lives of the Jewish diaspora.

Israel is not the initiator here, but is rather reacting to its enemy's actions. Hamas dictates the moves and the pace of response by Israel. The organization's terrorists are waiting for IDF soldiers within the Gaza Strip, having prepared well for an invasion. To topple Hamas, it is better for Israel to halt, regroup, and regain its composure and initiative, especially against the backdrop of the misguided and hollow bluster currently overtaking Israel's politicians and spokespersons. Among the few who consistently warned in recent years about such a blunder, the figure of Major General (ret.) Yitzhak Barik stands out, as he clearly and consistently explained[7] why Israel should, at this stage, satisfy itself with surgical strikes and cease planning to occupy Gaza and annihilate Hamas. We can only hope that our decision-makers are aware of this.

Hamas

> And the height of absurdity: if we look back over the years, one of the key figures who contributed to the strengthening of Hamas was Bibi Netanyahu, starting from his first term as Prime Minister.
> (Former Shin Bet Chief Yuval Diskin in a 2013 interview)[8]

Hamas has engaged in ruthless and horrifying actions that have strategic implications. An improper response from Israel may grant Hamas a diplomatic victory in addition to its military achievement. Large segments of the Arab world and Muslim communities in the West are already taking to the streets to demonstrate solidarity with the Palestinian side. The continued blind pounding of Gaza might undermine Israel's regional relationships, both old and new. The Palestinians in Gaza refused to play the role of eternal regional underdog assigned to them by Netanyahu. Through its horrifying actions, Hamas has undermined the Israeli concept of "conflict management" and the possibility of bypassing the Palestinian issue on the way to integration in the region.

Hamas is not ISIS, and Gaza is not Mosul. In recent years, I've reviewed numerous studies and testimonies on this movement (in fact, more than half of my doctoral dissertation focuses on it), from which emerges a consensus that Hamas is not merely a structured organization with an internal hierarchy. It is the ideological flag-bearer of the religious-nationalist current of the Palestinian national movement.

Hamas emerged during the First Intifada from the "Muslim Brotherhood" movement that took root among Arabs in Mandatory Palestine in the 1930s and 1940s. Similar to other religious-nationalist movements, Hamas provides an infrastructure that envelops the individual, family, and community throughout all stages of life, from birth to death. This includes work through education, universities, mosques, and countless professional organizations, associations, and clubs.

In this century, Hamas has undergone a consistent process of politicization, aspiring to integrate into the existing regional order, and has even achieved partial success by combining violence and politics. Since its participation in the 2006 Pal-

---

7 Haaretz Podcast (2023).
8 More (2023).

estinian election and then with the publication of its 2017 document of principles, Hamas has aimed to institutionalize itself. The cancellation of the Palestinian election in 2021 was likely a turning point in the movement's strategy, leading to the war between Hamas and Israel, dubbed in Israel "Guardian of the Walls."

Now, after the Black Sabbath, Hamas's future is uncertain. On one hand, Hamas has proven that, contrary to Israel's intent, it will never become a "subcontractor of the occupation." It proudly waves a banner of resistance which has been long abandoned even by Fatah and the PLO. The Palestinian Authority's lack of legitimacy among Palestinians, combined with the deadly blow on Israel in the past week, may position Hamas as the leading body of the Palestinian national movement.

On the other hand, Hamas is responsible for war crimes, crimes against humanity, and atrocities committed against Israeli civilians in the Gaza Envelope. This is a moral stain that marks the movement and the Palestinian nationalist struggle as a whole. Hamas's horrific acts may lead to its isolation and rejection by the international community.

At this point, we must do everything in our power to actualize the second option and ensure that the moral stain clinging to Hamas does not adhere to us as well. We must fight Hamas while maintaining our moral high ground, and act according to the laws of war to avoid resembling our enemies. In parallel, we must extend a hand to the moderate Palestinian partners who are likely to govern Gaza after Hamas.

The Israeli Government

The current government does not have a mandate to lead Israel into a war. It is clear that we must continue the campaign against Hamas, keep Israel free from terrorists, and concentrate efforts on bringing back the hostages. However, the Israeli government includes individuals who are criminals, corrupt, religious fanatics, and extreme Kahanist nationalists who, over the past year, have torn the nation apart. The time will come to hold each member of the failed government accountable for the disaster and the most severe military failure in the country's history. The extent and magnitude of the failure is incomprehensible. As time passes, more evidence accumulates, revealing the political leadership's disregard for intelligence warnings from Egypt, ignoring countless warnings from domestic sources, weakening the military, diverting significant military forces to protect settlers in the West Bank, plus complete inaction by the state and military authorities in real time, and more.

The central blame, however, falls on Benjamin Netanyahu, who has been at the helm of the country for the past fifteen years (almost). Since 1996, Netanyahu has consistently worked to manipulate and split the groups that make up Israeli society. Since 2015, he has openly incited and waged an overt war against state bodies. He has acted tirelessly to weaken civil society and the state (including the judiciary) and to disintegrate social solidarity. In his actions, he has significantly eroded national resilience and prosperity, and the state's ability to protect its citizens. In an interview with Eyal Kitsis a few years ago, Netanyahu asked to be remembered as the "guardian of Israel's security." To his disgrace, he will be remembered as the one who entrusted Israel's security to bloodthirsty terrorists.

According to former prime minister Naftali Bennett,[9] Netanyahu talked a lot about the Iranian nuclear threat but did little in practice. During Netanyahu's years in power, Hezbollah's conventional existential threat of missile fire from the north was established along the borders. Under Netanyahu's rule, his natural allies from the religious Zionist camp, guided by their messianic blindness, deepened the Israeli occupation in the West Bank and East Jerusalem. Meanwhile, Netanyahu operated without restraint, fostering division and tension between communities within Israel—between Mizrahim and Ashkenazim, religious and secular, left and right, Jews and Arabs.

All these factors have resulted in Israel facing numerous threats, including Hamas in Gaza, Hezbollah in Lebanon, and a constant fear of a Palestinian uprising in the West Bank and East Jerusalem that could spill into violence among communities within Israel, sowing chaos across the country. In the face of this multifaceted threat, after years of incitement and division, Israeli and Jewish society lacks the resilience and solidarity necessary for recovery.

The ultimate stated goal of some current government members is to establish a totalitarian theocracy on the ruins of Israel and build a temple on the ruins of Al-Aqsa Mosque (I have dedicated another half of my doctoral dissertation to these people, so I know them well). In recent years, I have read everything written about them, spoken to them, and immersed myself in mountains of research and relevant testimonies. The implementation of their political program, deeply rooted in theology and a rigid ideology, requires ethnic cleansing of the Holy Land, which may also lead to genocide against the Palestinian population. This horrifying scenario may become a reality only under the umbrella of the organized chaos of multifront war, including a civil war. Hence, it is not surprising that this is precisely the direction in which Israel is currently heading.

---

9 Zaken (2021).

Ethnic Cleansing and Genocide

"Never again" is the dictum under which the State of Israel was established, to provide a safe haven for Jews fleeing persecution and crimes against humanity. Regrettably, it is precisely under the leadership of Netanyahu that Israel has failed in this mission. For the survival of the State of Israel, we must not be on the side that perpetrates such crimes.

We tell the story of the Admor of Klausenburg,[10] who lost eleven of his children during the Holocaust. When asked about the Holocaust, he stated that it could have been worse. His sons wondered how it could have been worse than the horrors of that dark period. His answer was especially poignant considering his moral strength: "It would have been worse if we were the murderers." Carrying out ethnic cleansing on a wide scale in Gaza and the West Bank is not possible. However, the mere attempt would spell the end of the State of Israel. Let's be clear: carrying out genocide in Gaza and/or the West Bank would be the death knell for the State of Israel.

At the same time, extreme nationalist settlers in the West Bank are promoting a genocidal discourse. By their doctrine, the Palestinians are Nazis, and they should be annihilated through a preemptive attack on their settlements in the West Bank. With the support they receive from the National Security Minister, Itamar Ben-Gvir, these extremists arm themselves and venture into the territories. In the week following the Black Sabbath, fifty-four Palestinians were killed in the West Bank, many by the settlers' gunfire. Now, as the olive harvest season begins, Kahanist networks are calling for the prevention of the Palestinian olive tree harvest.

Last week, a video was released by the human rights organization B'Tselem, in which a settler was documented entering the village of Susiya. The settler walked toward a Palestinian standing in front of him and shot him in the abdomen from a meter away—while an IDF soldier stood behind him, assisting. In a Palestinian village near Nablus, settlers invaded homes, beat residents, and abducted one of them to a settlement, where they held him captive for several hours. Palestinian social networks in East Jerusalem are flooded with videos showing Israeli police officers beating Palestinians violently in the streets (in recent days, I watched numerous such videos). Policemen are documented smashing cell phones and randomly deploying roadblocks around the neighborhoods. If this situation continues, the Palestinians will react. An uprising in Jerusalem and the West Bank in parallel to the war with Hamas might also push Hezbollah to attack Israel. Religious nationalists

---

10 Hitbonenut (2010).

on both sides are pushing for such an escalation and feeding off it. We, as people seeking to live in a normal, democratic, and prosperous state, must do everything we can to prevent this.

***

In the twilight of former prime minister Ehud Olmert's term, Israel came very close to reaching a peace agreement with the leader of the Palestinian Authority, Abu Mazen (Mahmoud Abbas). However, Olmert's corruption prevailed over him—and us. As soon as Netanyahu came to power, for the second time (the first time was following the assassination of Yitzhak Rabin), he dismantled the Oslo Accords and prevented any possibility of a political solution.

Throughout his long rule, my colleagues and I consistently called for a political solution. We warned that another intifada was inevitable and that those who live by the sword will die by it. Under Netanyahu's leadership, members of his party and his supporters silenced us, labeled us as traitors, and denigrated our professional and moral stances. Inevitably, the occupation and the oppression of Palestinians creeped into Israel in the form of a judicial overhaul—an attempt at regime change—that undermined the foundations of our society and the state, pushing us toward a fast track to becoming a failed state.

Gaza has been under Israeli siege for about eighteen years. Netanyahu did everything in his power to ignore this issue, and actively encouraged Palestinian division and the empowerment of Hamas. All this despite numerous possibilities and solutions at his disposal. Some pointed out his failures. Geologist Yossi Langotsky[11] has warned for fifteen years about the fragility of the Gaza barrier, and two years ago, Major General (res.) Amiram Levin[12] called for ending the siege, opening the Strip, and allowing hundreds of thousands of laborers to enter Israel, saying, "If we don't solve the Gaza issue, we'll go from one conflict to another." But Netanyahu's governments chose to ignore these warnings.

***

Although acts of horror have long accompanied human history, there cannot and should not be any justification for massacre, rape, abduction, and terrorism. Even today, horrors occur worldwide, in Yemen, Syria, Iraq, Myanmar, Ukraine, Nagorno-Karabakh, and other places. While each case has its political and social context,

---

11 Langutzki (2023).
12 Heller (2021).

that does not mean that killing and acts of terror are justified in any of them. Indeed, it means that if we had ended the occupation and striven resolutely toward a reality where all the people of this land share it with mutual respect and equal rights, thousands of our sons and daughters would still be alive today.

There is no solution to the Gaza problem other than a comprehensive political one. To achieve this, a moderate alliance should be formed that will combat all enemies of peace. Netanyahu, Smotrich, and Ben-Gvir are willing to abandon the state, the abducted, and the captives. The first is willing to do so for personal gain, while the latter are willing to do so, and to sacrifice all of us, for the sake of destroying Gaza, expanding settlements, and fulfilling their messianic vision.

Some years after World War II, the European Economic Community was established (in 1957). Less than a decade after the Holocaust, Israel established its relations with Germany. After the Yom Kippur War, Israelis and Arabs drew closer. Arabs lifted their heads a little, and Israelis slightly lowered their gaze, and their eyes met in the middle. Thus, despite the difficult situation, a political breakthrough occurred in Israel, and a peace agreement was signed with Egypt.

We should not rush to mourn the possibility of Israeli and Palestinian partnership in this land—even though the situation we find ourselves in now is horrendous and makes such a scenario seem imaginary. The main reason not to give up on the potential for peace and mutual respect between Israelis and Palestinians is that such a surrender means giving up on a future for Israel.

For our future, we must protect ourselves.

For our future, we must create an alternative: a life based on a political vision of partnership.

Orit Kamir
Chapter 12: Fighting on Two Fronts: Between Hamas's Atrocities and Israel's Extremist Government

November 28, 2023, and January 11, 2024

Orit Kamir, SJD, is a leading legal scholar and activist, feminist legal theorist, founder of the Israeli Center for Human Dignity, and author of several books, among them *Betraying Dignity: The Toxic Seduction of Social Media, Shaming, and Radicalization*; *Framed: Women in Law and Film*; and *Every Breath You Take: Stalking Narratives and the Law*.

I have been writing articles and op-eds for over thirty years; none of them was as challenging to write as this short piece regarding the Israel–Hamas war of October 7, 2023.

I consider myself a humanist—an avid believer in universal human dignity and rights, and a strong supporter of socialist liberal democracy. I remain as strongly committed to the two-state solution, Palestine and Israel, as ever; I have not lost faith in all Palestinians, nor do I seek revenge.

Yet, it was only on December 6th, three months into the war, that I participated for the first time in a demonstration calling onto the Israeli government to stop it. It was the first time that such a demonstration took place in Jerusalem, my home town. Minutes after it began, a large police force forcefully ended it (a few days later the Supreme Court issued a temporary injunction, prohibiting the minister of national security, the extreme right winger Itamar Ben Gvir, to interfere with the police handling of demonstrations). Previous attempts by smaller groups to protest the war were similarly quashed. But that is not the only reason I did not raise my voice against the war. From the first day of the Israeli invasion of Gaza, it broke my heart to see neighborhoods there turned into rubble, the long lines of dead bodies brought to communal burial, and above all else—helpless children who have lost everything. Hearing personal accounts of loss and grief devastated me. The images of Gazans fleeing, long lines of refugees holding on to their few remaining belongings, are unbearable. Why did I not immediately take a strong stand, demanding that Israel stop the war, as did many of my friends abroad?

I believe that humanists abroad have a moral right to pose this question; I feel obligated to offer an answer. To contextualize my answer, let me narrate the circumstances in which I encounter the war, and my state of mind since October 7. I imagine that the complexity of the situation is fully clear only to those closely familiar with the details of life in Israel; I will therefore expand the boundaries of the discussion to flesh out my experience.

During the first two months following Saturday, October 7, I was overwhelmed by deep grief and mourning. Like every other Israeli I know, Jewish and Palestinian alike, I found it hard to contain the magnitude of the brutal, savage, dehumanizing atrocities committed by Hamas. On what we refer to as the Black Sabbath, more than 1,200 human beings were tortured in the vilest of ways before they were slaughtered mercilessly. Parents were brutalized in front of their children and vice versa. Women and girls were gang-raped, assaulted both before and after being butchered. Men, as well as women, were sexually mutilated both before and after their execution. Children and babies were murdered as viciously as were their parents and grandparents. People were tied together in family groups and burned to dust, seated at their holiday tables. Some bodies were beheaded, and heads apparently taken as trophies. Arms, legs, and other body parts were similarly severed. The terrorists reveled in the destruction they committed and in the unimaginable suffering they perpetrated. Documenting their actions, they live-broadcasted them on social networks. They used their victims' phones to do so, targeting victims' families.

We have all heard of such barbarism committed in the distant past, in faraway places; nothing prepared us for the possibility that such atrocities could occur on this scale, here and now. The initial shock we experienced is rightly compared to that felt by Americans—particularly New Yorkers—during and after 9/11. But then the extent of the cruelty set in. Broad comparisons of Hamas to ISIS and to the Nazis may be inaccurate in many respects; they do seem accurate, however, regarding the absolute, deliberate, premeditated dehumanization of their victims. Dehumanization that evokes a loss of faith in humankind. Such blunt, outward rejection of human dignity—the inherent, immeasurable value of every human being—reduces people to worthless, disposable objects.

Hamas undoubtedly meant to cause horror, deep insecurity, and trauma. It may have succeeded beyond its expectations. It took weeks before I, like everyone around me, could sleep quietly, eat properly, breathe deeply, or smile. Three months later it is still difficult to concentrate, watch a movie, or talk about anything other than the horror and its consequences. I cry a lot, as do my friends. Encountering ruthless, radical evil scars the human soul.

It may be particularly traumatic for those who, like many Israelis, have already been scarred in a similar manner. Fifty years ago, at the age of thirteen, I went through the 1973 Yom Kippur War, which started on Saturday, October 6. The combined Egyptian and Syrian attack on Israel that day caught us woefully unprepared, and for several days Israel fought for its existence. The collective trauma is still deep. The Hamas attack on Saturday, October 7, exactly fifty years later, was clearly intended to evoke that past event. Furthermore, my mother and grandparents survived the Holocaust—five years of hell on earth in Poland. Like many Israelis, hearing stories from survivors of October 7 took me back to those that I grew up with and which have tormented my dreams ever since; back to the heart of darkness.

The Hamas attack on Israeli kibbutzim and towns and its intent to traumatize Israelis are in line with this terrorist organization's goals, ideology, and previous conduct. Hamas, the Islamic Resistance Movement, founded in 1987, took power over Gaza in 2007, savagely murdering members of Fatah, who ruled Gaza up to that time. Its rule over the Gazan population has been autocratic, oppressive, and brutal. According to its ideology, Hamas aims to establish a theocratic, Muslim Palestinian state, from the Mediterranean Sea to the Jordan River, hence eliminating the State of Israel and expelling its non-Muslim inhabitants (according to Hamas's understanding of Islam, only Muslims are allowed to live in Palestine).

Israel has been ruling the West Bank since 1967 in blunt disregard of international law. This long occupation is utterly unjustified and deeply immoral, and should have long been unequivocally condemned by the international community. Palestine, the West Bank and Gaza combined, must be free to rule itself, and Israel must be pressured to pull out of the West Bank. But Hamas is not a liberation organization; it is an oppressive autocratic regime, repressive for Palestinians and threatening for Israelis. Furthermore, no context can explain or justify barbaric crimes against humanity, unqualified renunciation of human dignity. Radical evil that materializes in cruel torture and murder is utterly reprehensible, both morally and legally. Amira Hass, an Israeli reporter for the *Haaretz* newspaper, stated that under oppression such as the Israeli occupation of the West Bank some people sometimes turn into monsters. Hamas actively encourages this transformation.

Israel was founded by refugees like both my maternal and paternal grandparents, who were victimized in their homelands and forced out of them. Israel must be made to end its cruel occupation of the West Bank, but is fully legitimate within its international borders. A terror organization attempting to demolish it by randomly torturing and murdering civilians must be disempowered.

All of this has brought me, together with the great majority of Israelis, to the understanding that Israel will not be safe as long as Hamas rules Gaza. There is no guarantee that Israel will be safe if Hamas doesn't rule Gaza; in fact, I fear that until Israel accepts the right of Palestinians to found an independent, liberal Palestinian state, it is not likely to be safe. But as long as Hamas is in power, it appears that Israelis run the risk of falling victim to inconceivable atrocities such as those committed on October 7.

As no international force is willing to end Hamas's rule, Israel must take it upon itself to do so. As Hamas members are merged within the civilian population of Gaza, the only way to fight Hamas is to conduct warfare within the cities. Such fighting is extremely difficult and dangerous both for the Gazan civilians and for Israeli soldiers: my neighbors, students, colleagues, friends, and acquaintances. There is nothing I want less. Yet what other option is there? This dilemma has been haunting and paralyzing me.

In the October 7 attack, Hamas kidnapped 240 people of all ages, imprisoning them in Gaza. The youngest of the hostages was nine-month-old when he was kidnapped, and the oldest are in their mid-eighties. As an Israeli citizen, I felt from the first day of the war that the most urgent task was releasing them. Initially, the Israeli government and its supporters were intent on combating Gaza and destroying Hamas; they preferred to minimize the issue of the hostages, in fear that negotiations with Hamas for their release might interfere with the warfare and hinder it. That it might force ceasefires that would allow Hamas to regroup after Israeli attacks.

On the third day of the war I joined the first protest, organized by the grassroots group Mothers Against Violence, demanding that the Israeli government negotiate with Hamas to return the hostages. Together with this group and others I stood almost daily in city squares, beside ministers' residences, in front of official buildings both in Jerusalem and in Tel Aviv. At first, we were as few as a dozen at a time. Even these small, quiet gatherings were treated as if they were sabotaging the government's war effort, and were rudely interrupted by the police. Passersbys cursed and threatened us. We persisted. At night we hung hostages' photos on billboards in our neighborhoods. They were repeatedly taken down by government supporters trying to silence the public discourse regarding the hostages. This started the battle that is now raging between Israelis bent on redeeming the national honor by destroying Gaza, and those of us who place human dignity and rights above all else; dignity and rights of the hostages and of Palestinians alike. I have spent the last 20 years warning against Israel's waning commitment to human dignity and its growing fascination with national honor. I now found myself fighting on what currently seems to be the losing side of this internal battle.

A week into the war, hostages' families began to lead the protests, calling on the public to join. After several weeks, when thousands were on the streets demanding negotiations, the media finally gave voice to the hostages' families, and the IDF's chief of staff announced that returning the hostages was a primary goal. The government was pressured to embark on serious negotiations to release the hostages.

From this point on, the IDF and the government have been claiming, time and again, that fierce war in Gaza is the only way to force Hamas to negotiate the hostage release. Hamas's need for a ceasefire, they argue, would cause it to offer the return of hostages. In other words, if Israel stops fighting, Hamas is not likely to release the hostages any time soon. Did I believe this claim? My faith in the Israeli government is minuscule. So too is my faith in every other institution. Yet I knew of no counterargument. In fact, after six weeks of fierce fighting, Hamas, needing a ceasefire, indeed offered to return some of the hostages. Soon after, more than a hundred children, mothers, and elderly women were released from captivity in return for Palestinian women and children held in Israeli prisons and several days of ceasefire. Hamas abruptly stopped the release of hostages and has since not agreed to resume it. All IDF attempts to find the hostages and release them forcefully have failed. The Israeli government continues to claim that only fierce fighting will coerce Hamas to release the remaining hostages. I no longer believe it.

My lack of faith in the Israeli government is not unrelated to the war. The October 7 fiasco brought about a widespread loss of faith in the state and its institutions, the government in particular. Israelis felt betrayed and abandoned; their state left them to fend for themselves and die alone at the hands of gleeful terrorists. Their communities were devastated and their homes were burned to the ground. The army, Israel's most trusted and cherished institution, let them—and all of us—down; it failed to fulfill its fundamental role of guarding the border and defending Israel. During the long, horrible hours of October 7, it was mostly absent from the scene. Furthermore, the authorities have been completely ineffective in responding to the dire consequences of the attack. Civil society quickly organized to take their place and fulfill necessary tasks, including driving reserve soldiers to the front and providing them with warm clothes and other necessary supplies. The disillusionment with the state is crippling, and many Israelis continue to feel lost and terrified. Many purchase weapons for self-protection (encouraged by the far-right minister of national security).

Yet my mistrust of the Israeli government did not start with the war. October 7 came on the heels of a deep political crisis, in which general elections were held five times in three and a half years. At the heart of the crisis was Benjamin Netanyahu's unwavering insistence on remaining at the head of his party, Likud, and serving as prime minister of Israel despite very serious criminal charges of corruption brought against him by the attorney general and the ministry of justice.

Netanyahu, a populist politician who has served as prime minister for more than 16 years, built a loyal base of supporters by inciting them against Israel's "old elites," and by manipulating and enhancing the historical animosity felt by Israeli Jews who immigrated to Israel from Arab countries (Mizrahim) toward European Israeli Jews (Ashkenazim), who had originally founded the state in 1948 (my paternal grandparents included). Presenting himself as the Mizrahim's representative and savior, who is persecuted on their behalf and victimized by the old Ashkenazi elites, Netanyahu, himself an Ashkenazi and a very wealthy member of Israel's elite, managed to secure enough power to prevent anyone else from establishing a sustainable government.

In November 2022, after the fifth round of elections, Netanyahu managed to obtain enough votes to build a stable coalition. His coalition consisted of Likud (by this time a populist, extreme right-wing party), Jewish ultra-Orthodox parties, and parties representing extreme right-wing, fundamentalist settlers. Living in the West Bank, these settlers believe that the biblical God promised them the whole territory from the river to the sea. They view any acknowledgment of Palestinians' rights to self-rule and governance as sacrilege. A like-minded Israeli, Yigal Amir, had in 1995 assassinated Prime Minister Itzhak Rabin, who attempted to advance a peace accord between Israel and the Palestinians. Netanyahu incited the protest against Rabin, and was elected as prime minister after the assassination.

Netanyahu's new 2022 government declared its intent to cripple Israel's already unstable liberal democracy, seeking absolute power. This would enable Netanyahu to terminate the criminal cases against him, and allow the fundamentalist settlers, together with the other extreme right-wingers, to turn Israel into a theocracy, annex the West Bank and cleanse it of its Palestinian inhabitants. The government's planned first step, following the Hungarian and Polish models, was to weaken the judiciary, nominate new judges, and legislate provisions affording the government absolute power.

In January 2023, in reaction to the government's announced plan, Israeli civil society responded promptly. Hundreds of organizations were immediately set up all over the country, and we took to the streets. Hundreds of thousands of us demonstrated from January until September, every Saturday night, and often several more times each week. Like many others, during these months I did very little other than protest in every possible way. During the second half of September and the beginning of October demonstrations were fewer and smaller, due to the Jewish high holidays. On October 8 we were to resume the intense resistance.

We, therefore, reached October 7 after nine months of continuous internal struggle; of economic decline caused by the government's irresponsible policies; of the government depleting the state and the civil service; of a deep split between rivaling sectors of Israeli society. We found ourselves facing an unprecedented traumatic moment when we were on the brink of a civil war, with an extreme right-wing, populist, fundamentalist government whom many of us do not trust.

There is more. As a part of his strategy, Netanyahu tolerated and even supported Hamas's rule in Gaza, believing that this would weaken the Palestinian Authority and the PLO who rule the West Bank, prevent the unification of Gaza and the West Bank, and thwart the establishment of a Palestinian state. Also as a part of this strategy, IDF troops were moved from Israel's border with Gaza to the West

Bank to protect fundamentalist settlers, including Knesset members, as they harassed Palestinians in the West Bank and robbed them of their land. Citizens in the kibbutzim near the Gazan border (many of them Ashkenazi left-wingers, not Netanyahu supporters) were abandoned to fend for themselves.

Even now, Netanyahu attempts to shift responsibility for the disaster from himself to the army and the opposition protestors, suggesting that Hamas's attack was somehow enabled by them as an attempt to undermine him. Members of his government are eager to occupy Gaza, force the Palestinian population out and settle it with Jews. They continue in their attempt to weaken the civil service, the media, and every other public institution. They use the war to restrict civil rights, including free speech and the right to demonstrate. The general outrage is immense. And yet Netanyahu's government refuses to resign. There is no political procedure that can bring it down.

I have no faith in my government. In fact, I believe that it threatens Israeli democracy and even Israel's mere existence. I protest against many of its policies. I do not trust it to conduct the war in Gaza. I condemn its abandonment of the hostages, and abhor its dismissal of the horrendous devastation the war has caused Gazans. But in order for me to demand an end to the war, I felt that I had to suggest an alternative course of action. To this day, I have no such suggestion. I felt paralyzed by a cruel Sophie's choice: abandon the dignity and safety of Gazans, or that of my fellow Israeli citizens. A binary division; a zero-sum game.

Concurrently, I am disheartened and horrified by the overwhelming wave of anti-Semitism in the Western world. I am shocked by the enthusiastic support for Hamas. I am disgusted by the denial and refusal to acknowledge the atrocities committed by the organization. I have lost faith in the judgment of international organizations and the international community. This deepens my paralysis.

Three months into the war, I can't help but acknowledge that Israel is starving the civilian population of Gaza, demolishing its hospitals, schools and courts, and systematically flattening its residential areas. Voices openly calling for brutal revenge and the annihilation of Gaza have become legitimate. Hamas has not been defeated; the hostages are still in captivity, and I am no wiser regarding peaceful courses of action. But I know that the assault on Gazans must stop; the dismissal of their human dignity cannot continue. I now demonstrate for ceasefire, even though I know not what to do next.

I implore anyone wishing to assist both Gazans and Israelis to pressure their governments to bring Israel and the Palestinian Authority to negotiate a peaceful, diplomatic resolution to the conflict. Otherwise this futile, bloody feud will consume us all.

Orly Noy
Chapter 13: Listen to Israeli Survivors: They Don't Want Revenge

October 25, 2023

> **Orly Noy** is an editor at Local Call news website, a political activist, and a translator of Farsi poetry and prose. She is the chair of B'Tselem's executive board and an activist with the Balad political party. Her writing deals with the lines that intersect and define her identity as Mizrahi, a female leftist, a woman, a temporary migrant living inside a perpetual immigrant, and the constant dialogue between them.

Against the prevailing public mood, many survivors of the October 7 massacres and relatives of those killed or kidnapped are opposing retribution on Gaza.

"Everyone is talking about unity. Guys, unity is terribly beautiful, but in the field, there is revenge, and there is cruelty … We will have our whole lives to grieve, and we will grieve. But now, there is only one goal: to take revenge and to be cruel."[1] These were the words of Israeli reserve soldier Guy Hochman—usually an entertainer and online influencer—in an interview on Channel 12 in the first days of Israel's assault on the Gaza Strip following the October 7 massacres by Hamas militants. In just a few words, Hochman captured the sentiment that appears to have taken hold in Israel, from the far right all the way to many who self-identify as leftists: justification of the catastrophe that Israel is currently wreaking on more than 2 million Palestinians in Gaza.

Some are explaining their justification in terms of "defeating Hamas." Others, like Hochman, are putting sweeping revenge above all else. It is thus all the more remarkable that, in the face of the prevailing political mood, more and more of those Israelis who survived the massacres, or whose loved ones were killed or kidnapped to Gaza, are expressing unequivocal opposition to the killing of innocent Palestinians, and saying no to revenge.

In a eulogy for her brother Hayim, an anti-occupation activist who was murdered in Kibbutz Holit, Noi Katsman called on her country "not to use our deaths and our pain to cause the death and pain of other people or other families. I demand that we stop the cycle of pain, and understand that the only way [forward] is freedom and equal rights. Peace, brotherhood, and security for all human beings."[2]

---
1 Hochman (2023).
2 Mechazkim (2023).

Ziv Stahl, executive director of the human rights organization Yesh Din, and a survivor of the hellfire in Kfar Aza, also came out strongly against Israel's assault on Gaza in an article in *Haaretz*. "I have no need for revenge, nothing will return those who are gone," she wrote. "Indiscriminate bombing in Gaza and the killing of civilians uninvolved with these horrible crimes are no solution."[3]

Yotam Kipnis, whose father was murdered in the Hamas attack, said in his eulogy: "Do not write my father's name on a [military] shell. He wouldn't have wanted that. Don't say, 'God will avenge his blood.' Say, 'May his memory be for a blessing.'"[4]

Michal Halev, the mother of Laor Abramov, who was murdered by Hamas, cried out in a video posted to Facebook: "I am begging the world: stop all the wars, stop killing people, stop killing babies. War is not the answer. War is not how you fix things. This country, Israel, is going through horror … And I know the mothers in Gaza are going through horror … In my name, I want no vengeance."[5]

Maoz Inon, whose parents were murdered on October 7, wrote on Al Jazeera: "My parents were people of peace … Revenge is not going to bring my parents back to life. It is not going to bring back other Israelis and Palestinians killed either. It is going to do the opposite … We must break the cycle."[6]

When Yonatan Ziegen, the son of Vivian Silver, was asked by a journalist what his mother—who is thought to have been kidnapped—would think about what Israel is doing in Gaza now, he replied: "She would be mortified. Because you can't cure dead babies with more dead babies. We need peace. That's what she was working for all her life … Pain is pain."[7]

And, in a video that has since gone viral, a nineteen-year-old survivor of the massacre at Kibbutz Be'eri offered a soul-stirring monologue about the government's abandonment of the residents of the south, in which she pleaded for: "Returning the hostages. Peace. Decency and fairness … Maybe some of you will find it hard to hear these words. It's hard for me to speak. But with what I went through in Be'eri, you owe it to me."[8]

We owe it to them. I listen to them and read their words, and I bow my head before their courage. And I think about the strange insistence by so many in this moment, including so-called leftists, on measuring our degree of solidarity, pain, or

---

3 Stal (2023).
4 https://twitter.com/democrat_tv/status/1716052156258676784.
5 Haleve (2023).
6 Inon (2023).
7 Channel 4 (2023).
8 Reuveni (2023).

rage in accordance with our willingness to support the fire that our army is raining down on Gaza.

What will you say to this bereaved father? To that survivor of the massacre? Do they also lack solidarity? How do you have the audacity to determine what is going on inside each one of our broken hearts and minds?

I see the accusations against those who beg for an end to this futile carnage, this terrible and menacing war crime in Gaza, and I think of the sentence uttered by Ben Kfir, a member of the Bereaved Families Forum, that was engraved in my head years ago when he spoke of the futility of revenge: "I lost my daughter, not my mind."[9]

This man, who lost the person most dear to him of all, and many others who have now joined the circle of bereavement, understand what so many are today still refusing to understand: that the path we are being offered, of more blood and more "deterrence," is exactly the path we have been offered so many times before, and that led us to the horrors we are seeing today.

Beyond the immorality of justifying the atrocities Israel is committing in Gaza, the expectation that this time the mass slaughter will lead to a different result than all the previous military campaigns—which achieved nothing but deepening the despair, suffering, and hatred on the Palestinian side—is a terrible self-deception, the price of which will be paid again by the residents of the south.

Don't say that Israel is doing it for them. Israel abandoned the south in a colossal crime, and cannot redeem itself with the blood of innocents in Gaza. Instead of indulging in this lust for revenge, let's listen to the families of the victims.

---

9 Moshe (2023).

Noam Shuster-Eliassi
Chapter 14: Picking Up the Pieces of Our Grief

October 20, 2023

> **Noam Shuster-Eliassi** is a comedian, performer, peacebuilder, and activist. A graduate of Brandeis University, she grew up in Neve Shalom Wahat Al Salam ("Oasis of Peace"), the only community in Israel where Jews and Palestinians live together by choice, and she performs in three languages—Hebrew, Arabic, and English. In 2018, she was named the "New Jewish Comedian of the Year" in London. That same year, she was also the first Jewish performer at the Palestine Comedy Festival and her content went viral in the Arab media. Shuster-Eliassi has been a fellow at Harvard Divinity School's Religion, Conflict, and Peace Initiative, where she developed her one-woman show in Hebrew, English, and Arabic.

There is an awful silence, so loud that it is numbing. It is the silence of frightened people trying to mourn while the war maniacs blast their bombs so they don't have to hear us, or provide any answers for their failures. Behind the horrible screens of social media, I see friends abroad being so loud while friends locally sit in silent grief. My soul aches for us, for the silence imposed on us, for the fear of saying very basic human things—as basic as "Have mercy on the children of Gaza."

Government ministers have lined up every day for the past two weeks to declare, even to the families of the kidnapped: now is not the time to place blame or to investigate. "Be quiet. We're at war." I keep getting messages from friends all around the globe: "How are you? We know this is an especially heavy moment for you, we're sending you our love." What can I answer? We are broken. There is so much grief. Unfolding, ongoing, ancient, personal, political, violent, endless grief.

I think I am writing this for those who have the capacity to mourn for two peoples. I know I am. And it is a heavy weight. When news of the Hamas attack started spreading on the morning of October 7, we experienced many hours and even days of uncertainty, but we knew something out of the ordinary was happening. We just did not understand how horrific the scale of it was.

The first news I received was about my friend Osnat Trabelsi, an outstanding filmmaker among whose amazing films is *Arna's Children*—a powerful documentary about the Jenin Freedom Theater and a generation of Palestinian children born into the violence of the occupation. Her nephew was at the music festival in Re'im and was murdered. The next news was about Vivian Silver, a peace activist and a friend of my mother: she had been kidnapped. Right after that we got word that Hayim Katsman, another peace activist, had been killed as well; he was protecting his neighbor, saving her life as he was murdered guarding the door. The nightmare kept on going. My friend Moria, a comedy writer, was searching for her cousin who went missing at the festival; after a few hours, she received the devastating news that he, too, had been murdered. The parents of my friend Maoz Inon, an incredible entrepreneur and peace activist, had also been killed in a kibbutz.

More and more names and faces we knew. So many that we stopped counting. It was overwhelming. And on top of that, many of them were people who always stood beside us in the peace and justice community, firmly against aggression and war, actively resisting the occupation.

As I write this, a hospital in Gaza has been bombed. Maoz is grieving on the phone and telling me we must do something to stop this madness, that the deaths of his parents cannot be used to justify more blood. Our grief has been turned into a senseless revenge campaign in a split second. A cyberwar of narratives plays out over our heads: who bombed the hospital? But the children are already dead, watching us go on stupid Twitter to find out how they died. Miserable. Your war machines killed them, you useless militants, whoever you are.

Can Anyone Hear Us?

I am so proud of my friends who, despite losing family members in the Hamas attack, did not lose their moral compass, immediately using their platform to say clearly: do not use this pain for revenge, or to inflict more pain—that is not the solution. But can anyone hear us?

During her nephew's shiva (Jewish mourning ritual), Osnat was crying. "It's like I have two rooms in my heart now," she said. "One for my personal grief, and one for everyone's grief. And I don't want my pain to be used to cause more people grief." I've heard that even the families of the kidnapped are hesitant to criticize the government, out of fear that it will disturb the efforts to bring their loved ones back. It is heartbreaking to see videos of heartless people attacking those families at their demonstrations, thinking that their protests will stop the Israeli army from pummeling Gaza. These families received more attention, answers, and warmth from President Biden than from their own leader, our failed leader.

Admitting how deep our pain is—the lonely people who have space to mourn and care for two peoples—is too heavy to bear. It is easier to simply stare at my phone and hope my brain will shut down. But actually, my phone is my nightmare; God, Instagram is my nightmare. Who are all these Americans posting from their comfortable homes? Let go of your phones immediately. Except Bassem Youssef, he can stay; his interview on Piers Morgan's show was genius. He is trolling the anchor and telling him: "My wife is using my kids as a human shield, Palestinians do that even in my home, it's crazy!" What a way to deal with dehumanization. Comedians are always so needed during times like these.

Another iconic figure who emerged from the October 7 atrocities is Rachel Edry from Ofakim, who saved her and her husband's lives through the power of hospitality. A Persian Jew married to a Moroccan, she described in the funniest, most heartbreaking way how for fifteen hours she used her expert guest-hosting skills to feed and entertain the Hamas militants who entered her home with song, until the police arrived and freed them.

I am also a comedian, but I am struggling to find anything funny to say. Should I write a joke about the right-wing bigots who always shout, "Leftist traitors to Gaza!" and say, "Here, you got what you wanted"? No, it's too soon for that. But Jewish comics have done well with their trauma in the past, so I am sure I will catch up soon—stay tuned.

Filling the Vacuum

Ministers from our fascist government who try to visit the Israeli survivors are being yelled at and chased away. People are blaming them for what happened. But it is like we do not have a voice, because there is no challenge to the government response. People are too busy with survival.

There is a huge civil force filling the vacuum of the government's inability to answer the needs of the citizens, including those who were evacuated from the south. I hope they can translate this movement into political power, so we can know exactly who all these amazing people are that sprang into action, and vote for them.

And even though the government is nowhere to be found when we need it, somehow, miraculously, it still has time to arrest hundreds of Palestinian citizens of Israel for sharing or liking a post on social media that expresses sympathy with the people of Gaza. And when two activists in Jerusalem from the Standing Together movement hung posters saying "Jews and Arabs will overcome this together" in Hebrew and Arabic, they were detained, their posters confiscated by police. The state can, it seems, function when it wants to. In leftist social media groups, friends are warning each other that right-wing bigots are doxxing leftists and inciting violence against them—as we saw with prominent left-wing journalist Israel Frey, who is now in hiding due to threats against him and his family. The fear is numbing.

Can I ask you for something? Can you check on your friends who live in Israel-Palestine before posting on social media? Because we are not OK. We are broken. Why do I say "we"? Because I do not want to feel alone. Yes, I knew some of the people murdered, and I know some of the people kidnapped. But I, compared to others, am relatively OK. No, I am lying to myself. What is OK? No one is OK. I am trying to put the pain down on paper. I am not doing it very well, because every few moments I get another message about another person we knew who is gone. And the sad truth is that in the name of this pain, our government is carrying out atrocities on people who had nothing to do with it.

Alone in Our Grief

When people experience a great deal of grief, they usually also feel shame and anger that they need to channel somewhere. People's capacity to see beyond their wounds and pain is limited. We need recognition, compassion, solidarity, and a voice. By having a voice, you feel like you have agency. By having agency, you are able to imagine taking action. And when that action is tangible, you get the sense that you might actually be able to influence the situation and help your loved ones.

Wow, I'm so happy I wrote that. But the truth is that the amount of grief here from what happened that day is so huge that I'm not sure I or people like me have a voice anymore. I feel so numb and scared I can hear the silence in my friends' voices without even speaking to them. Both peoples are retreating inward right now, and it is extremely difficult for those of us who are trying to hold the pain of everybody grieving. Our mental, emotional, and political space is shrinking all at once. I am torn in pieces. I am sure many of you are too.

There is a lot of death, displacement, and horror unfolding in this moment, and not much hope to offer. But I will say this: it is OK to acknowledge that we felt abandoned for a moment, alone in our grief. The scale of the violence that hit us was nothing like anything we had experienced before. It is OK to sit with your grief and not have answers or be active all the time. I wish I had told that to myself straight away, but instead I was immediately a participant in the cyber-war madness. What a mistake for my mental health and my close relationships. I'm so sorry.

Jessica Ausinheiler
Chapter 15: Child Loss: A Mother's Reflection

December 12, 2023

> **Jessica Ausinheiler** is an Israeli American community organizer and consultant focused on capacity building and conservation in East Panama. She is a 2023–24 IIE Centennial Fellow and a 2020 Fulbright Scholar. She holds a master's in public administration from the Harvard Kennedy School and a BA in Near Eastern studies from Princeton University. She lives in Panama with her husband and two living daughters, twenty feet from where her son is buried.

A smile forms around the edges of my mouth as I hear her suckle, sense the warmth of her breath, feel her chest expand into mine as I nurse-nap her in our family bed. My older daughter chitter-chatters about Lego in the other room. I close my eyes, and my mind wanders …

***

A loud boom resounds inside my head, sends chills down my spine. I smell cement crumble. I feel the earth shift the bed beneath me and I hold my baby tighter. A bomb? This is how her dad will find us, then, tethered to each other in our safe space beneath the rubble …

No… We are safe…

But my six-year-old is in the other room. Kidnapped? How she would fare in those dark tunnels under the earth with strangers and only the trauma of separation replaying in her mind to soothe her …

No… She is safe…

***

But my son did really die, right? I remember running toward his little body, peeling him from the mud-smeared rocks and into my arms after the car accident. I remember how quickly the skin turns cold, the cold looks blue, on a little boy.

Since my son Zev's accident in April 2021, my flesh and my bones know what it feels like to hold a dead baby. This has made the daymares involving his living sisters since October 7 so real. I feel his death every time I see or hear another child has died. To stay sane, I must be careful what I allow into my ears and eyes.

But when I feel strong, I seek out images of suffering there. I break open afresh to the pain.

After Zev died, I began a Tonglen meditation practice. I continue that practice now, filling my chest with the suffocating thick red goop of the pain of children and their mothers and fathers and aunts and uncles and grandparents in Nachal Oz in Israel, in Jabaliya camp and Shujaiyah in Gaza, in Deir Yassin in Palestine, in Warsaw in Poland, in Odessa in Ukraine, inhaling so deeply I could explode. On the exhale, I transform the goop into a blue lagoon where all of us are laughing and reunited with our loved dead ones, and I wish healing upon all of us.

***

I am a US-born daughter of settlers—my father and mother Peruvian nationals of Ashkenazi, Sephardic, and Incan descent, respectively. My parents made aliyah to Israel in the late 1980s to start a new life and found themselves in Ariel, one of the largest settlements in the West Bank. Blissfully ignorant of the history and context they emigrated into, they were immediately brought into the right by the need for protection in a remote settlement nestled deep in Occupied Palestinian Territories.

My childhood was spent in snug separation from my Palestinian neighbors. Young male Palestinians often joined us as manual laborers. My father, a furniture salesman, would take little me with him to Nablus and Jenin to meet his Palestinian business partners and their families. That kind of interaction was certainly not the norm, especially after the First Intifada, but I still knew them as Other. Their houses were often unfinished. Their smell was different. Their language was foreign. It was understood that we belonged apart.

I remember the First Intifada. One particular memory stands out, when we had spent hours getting dressed as jovial clowns for Purim and arrived at school to the news of suicide bombings on buses and dismembered costumed bodies on the sidewalks of Tel Aviv. I wrote poems to soldiers and gifted them at IDF checkpoints.

My parents took us back to the US before we were of military age. But when I was in college something drew me back, not to my home but to the other side. Perhaps it was a love interest with a Muslim classmate, or simply that I was at the age of peak neophilia. I heard Arabic spoken while walking an Arab neighborhood in the course of a study-abroad program in France, and strangely, it struck me as familiar and mellifluous ... far from the Adhan I recalled blaring over loudspeakers in my childhood.

I became obsessed with better understanding the context in which I was raised. I majored in Near Eastern Studies at Princeton. I learned Arabic. I lived with a Palestinian family fifteen minutes from where I grew up, but on the other side of the Wall, and documented the efforts of activists working with youth on the ground. I stayed at home with the women making food during the

Friday afternoon protests. I tightened in bed when I heard shots fired by the IDF in our neighborhood during night raids. I joined my host mother in mourning the arrest and two-year detention of her sixteen-year-old son, Mohammad, without trial.

My work in Palestine ended when a Palestinian mentor warned it wasn't safe for me, an Israeli American, to be there anymore. And I had student loans to pay. So I got a job working for a consulting firm that focused on the Middle East North African region, and on the philanthropic organizations that influence its politics. Through marriage I ended up working with grassroots leaders in Central America.

But I still have Israeli citizenship. I have friends in Israel. In the Occupied West Bank. In Gaza. And my heart is breaking open for all of them.

***

A fellow loss mom once shared that losing a child is like having a chronic illness that won't kill you, but often feels like it could. With over 6,000 children injured, dead, and kidnapped, and missiles still raining down, roofs falling in, bullets piercing through, I imagine the whole place sick with loss and trauma.

As I watch our cousins in Gaza, hear parents screaming to Allah with pain that should break open the sky, my mind goes back to the day I found Zev. I too screamed louder than I had ever screamed. I screamed for an eternity. I screamed until I realized my daughter, who was still in the car, was listening. For weeks and months later I screamed when I was alone, pressing my head into the mud-smeared rocks or raising my arms to the sky. I wonder how it is possible to not hear their screaming.

And then I remember. When I was a girl, surrounded by a sea of Palestinian villages in a mountainous settlement, how the reverberating call to prayer seemed like a threat. It wasn't until I fell in love with Arabic and lived amongst those who speak it that I came to see and appreciate the beauty on the other side. Could it be that the cries to Allah have the same impact as the call to prayer did for me, when spoken in a language that one considers foreign, that has been depicted as the sound and color of danger for so long?

I feel the crushing weight of so many dead children, and look up to find the world around me humming along unperturbed, and I feel deeply alone. I feel alone in feeling so much.

I can understand why we as humans so often tend toward only feeling the pain of our side and not the other's. The pain of one child is enough. The pain of one family is enough. Adding the pain of the Other is too much. Human empathy was baked in the warm hearth of Us. I didn't choose to feel the loss of both sides; life just brought me to a point where I do, and it aches.

***

Friends who support the invasion by Israel have asked if I would have supported the World War II bombings in the German cities of Cologne, Hamburg and Dresden. My response is that no one can justify to me the death of anyone's child. I cannot imagine any military strategy for ensuring the safety of Israelis and Jews worldwide that involves the murder of thousand children and civilians who are prisoners in their own land. I cannot imagine carpet bombs killing a movement or an ideology. I cannot imagine so much trauma and pain resulting in anything other than more trauma, and more pain ... Similar to the way in which the killing of our ancestors in the Holocaust has led to the current apartheid reality, and to the war atrocities we see in Israel and in Palestine today.

So for now, I post. And I write. I light Shabbat candles while wearing a keffiyeh and pray that the Divine in us leads us to ceasefire. Now. To dress the wounds of October 7 and address the sickness of the occupation, on us all.

Meirav Jones
Chapter 16: From the River to the Sea

December 14, 2023

> **Meirav Jones** is Assistant Professor of Religious Studies at McMaster University and a fellow of the Kogod Research Center at the Shalom Hartman Institute of North America. Her research, which has been published in such outlets as *Journal of the History of Ideas*, *Review of International Studies*, and *Political Studies*, focuses on the intersection between Jewish sources and Western political thought, on political understandings of Judaism and the Jews, and on sovereignty and Jewish sovereignty.

With pro-Palestinian protests around the world, the question of whether the now-popular chant "From the river to the sea, Palestine will be free" is or should be threatening to the Jews has become hotly contested. Some have argued that freeing Palestine clearly involves the dismantling of the State of Israel and the exile, killing, or subjection of its Jewish population. Others have said that the chant calls only for equal rights and freedoms for Palestinians, as equals in a single state, or free of domination in their own.

At the height of this controversy, a few weeks into the war in Gaza, a video was sent out in an Israeli WhatsApp group I follow, in which Palestinians were interviewed in Israel and the Occupied Territories, and asked the following question: When people chant "From the river to the sea, Palestine will be free," what do they mean? The video was filmed three years ago by Jewish Canadian Corey Gil-Shuster, whose YouTube channel "The Ask Project"[1] claims to offer viewers insight into "what Israelis and Palestinians really think" by asking questions generated by viewers to random people on the street in Israel and Palestine. The video was shared in the group to show that, indeed, "from the river to the sea" means that Palestine will be free from Jews or at least from the State of Israel. The video was presented as evidence that the phrase supports genocide.

But the video actually offered a far more complex picture of Palestinians' understanding of "from the river to the sea," and it is one with which Jews around the world and Israelis should be sympathetic. First, when asked what people mean when they chant "from the river to the sea, Palestine will be free," most of those asked placed some distance between themselves and the chant. They themselves were not protesting with these words, and some were visibly uncomfortable being asked about it, perhaps feeling unsafe (one person said this explicitly). Those interviewed generally agreed that the phrase means that Palestine will

---

[1] Gil-Shuster (2019).

https://doi.org/10.1515/9783111435046-017

be free in the sense that there would ultimately be no state of Israel in "Palestine," from the river to the sea, and that Jews would either leave Palestine or stay on as guests or as a minority in a state where Palestinians have full rights and self-determination. But the idea of a free Palestine from the river to the sea was also clearly remote, for all those asked. Some who were hopeful that this would be reality described it as destined to take place "not very soon," or alluding to a "miracle" or "the last day." This is a far more important part of the video than most viewers appreciate. I will return to this after considering an example of a similar phrase, chanted by Jews, that if asked about would generate a similar response.

In the "Amidah" prayer, said three times a day, Jews around the world recite the following words: "May it be your will, Lord our God, that the Temple [Beit Hamikdash] may be built speedily in our times." The temple being referred to is to be located on the Temple Mount in Jerusalem, the site of the Al-Aqsa Mosque. If "The Ask Project" were to ask Jews on the streets in Israel what people mean when they pray for the temple to be built speedily in our time, many people would distance themselves; if they are secular then they themselves do not recite these words, or if they are religious, most would prefer not to think about the real-world implications. Pushed for an answer about the meaning of the prayer, Jews would likely share that the prayer means that "not very soon," with a "miracle" there will be a third temple built on the site where the first and second temples stood. If the interviewer were then to ask what would happen to the Al-Aqsa Mosque, the answer would be that the prayer alludes to messianic times, and that while many Jews believe in this, they don't work to bring it about and it is imagined as a peaceful time. Yet there are some zealous Jews who believe in working toward that messianic time, disregarding the status quo and the rights of Muslims, and pushing—even violently—for a third temple in Jerusalem in our times. These extremists are in positions of power in Israel today and have used violence, both state-sponsored and not, to harm Palestinians and Muslims and advance their messianic agenda.

If we return now to "from the river to the sea," we can appreciate the extent to which those interviewed were confronted with what was, on their understanding, a messianic moment; something that they believe would happen in a remote future, imagined as a time of peace. Further, even those who spoke of injustices in Israel and of their hope for a just future did not express the belief that "from the river to the sea" was a vision that justified bloodshed. Yet there are zealous extremists who believe in working toward this messianic time, and freeing Palestine of Jews now, in our time. Such extremists have shown incredible cruelty and caused unbearable terror and bloodshed in recent weeks. These were not the Palestinians interviewed in the streets, who confirmed that "from the river to the sea" means—to them—a peaceful future without domination, imagined as a distant time.

Taking only the responses of the Palestinians I have cited from the video into account, and disregarding what Americans, English, Canadians, and Australians believe they are calling for when they chant "from the river to the sea, Palestine will be free," it is worth considering the significance and the divisive effects of bolstering messianic agendas in pro-Palestinian protests. If at a parallel rally in support of the Jewish cause, people were to chant "may the temple be built in our time," would this be considered supportive of a peaceful vision, even if Jews imagine this as a peaceful moment in messianic times? The idea of such a chant, or of backing Jewish messianic agendas in support of Israel at this time, is not so far-fetched. At the rally supporting Israel and the Jewish people that took place in Washington in November, John Hagee spoke, saying that "there is only one nation whose flag will fly over the ancient walls of the sacred city of Jerusalem. That nation is Israel, now and forever." One of the Palestinians interviewed pushed for the recognition that there are some Jews—even Jews in power in Israel—who call for a Jewish state from the river to the sea. Hagee would certainly stand with them.

There is some temptation to describe the conflict in Israel-Palestine as irresolvable, as zealots on both sides are those promoting the image of a zero-sum game, with "us" or "them" on the land or flying a flag over Jerusalem as part of their respective visions. Zealotry and messianic agendas are not new on the world's political stage nor is the agenda that advances war as endless in this world. At the dawn of modernity, with Europe's often ruthless wars of religion that followed the Protestant reformation, modern political thought sought to end bloodshed and protect life by suspending messianic time. Thomas Hobbes, who claimed in his journal to have written *Leviathan* because he "could not tolerate so many atrocious crimes being attributed to the commands of God," set up the sovereign as a "mortal God"—a political entity that would protect life until the Second Coming. There was nothing to be done politically to bring about messianic times, and the best that could be achieved was human rule that would protect life, and cultivate religion that would support the protection of life, for the time being. Modern politics, at its inaugural moment, was critically aware of the extent to which it was holding back messianic agendas that if allowed to enter politics, would cause endless violence and bloodshed.

There are different models for how Palestinian and Israeli life could be protected and how these peoples might even flourish, suspending messianic time. One of the Palestinians interviewed said that establishing two states, a Jewish state alongside a Palestinian state, is the only way to avoid "from the river to the sea" discourse, which he understood as problematic whichever side it was coming from. While the majority of those interviewed would not accept partition, they were prepared to talk more openly about their lack of freedom in the present —whether their freedom of movement, freedom of religion, or freedom of assembly—than they were of their ultimate visions. Advancing messianic agendas in pro-Palestinian protests is hardly conducive to peace and promotes the zero-sum nature of the conflict as portrayed by zealots. Addressing subjection, domination, and oppression in the present and consolidating politics for the time being—a temporary solution to protect both peoples until messianic times—may in fact be the only way to counter zealotry that is tearing both peoples, their allies, and the region apart.

Tal Correm
Chapter 17: The Imperative of Thinking in Dark Times

December 16, 2023

> **Tal Correm**, PhD, is Clinical Assistant Professor in Liberal Studies at New York University. Her research focuses on the intersection of ethics and political theory, specifically with relation to political violence, transitional justice, and democratic theory. Her research has appeared in edited volumes and journals including *Arendt Studies*, *Theoria: A Journal of Social and Political Theory*, and *Listening: Journal of Communication Ethics, Religion, and Culture*. She holds a PhD in philosophy from Temple University and a BA and an MA in philosophy from Tel Aviv University.

Arendt used the often misunderstood phrase "the banality of evil" in her writings about the trial of Adolf Eichmann in Jerusalem, to describe the evil that ordinary people perpetrate rather than monstrous inhumane radical evil. Evil is not radical in the sense of the depth of its roots (the etymological source of radicality); rather it is shallow. Evil is the result of thoughtlessness. What Arendt identified in Eichmann was his shallowness or inability to think. How can thinking save us from committing evil? In what sense is thinking itself moral? Thinking is the silent dialogue we carry within ourselves. Arendt's model is Socrates, whose integrity led him to declare in Plato's dialogue *Gorgias* that he prefers to suffer injustice than live with the one who perpetrates it, namely, himself. The moral and political implications of thinking come to the fore in times of emergencies when things fall apart.

> At these moments, thinking ceases to be a marginal affair in political matters. When everybody is swept away unthinkingly by what everybody else does and believes in, those who think are drawn out of hiding because their refusal to join is conspicuous and thereby becomes a kind of action.[1]

Arendt was probably more circumspect with regard to the ability of thinking to prevent evil in these moments of crisis. Nevertheless, in a Kantian twist, her legacy as I see it is the imperative to think in dark times.

The shattering events of October 7 and their lingering, devastating aftermath in the war in Gaza form our current dark time. The shock and the grieving are disorienting, draining, and traumatizing. They seem to defy any attempt to make sense of them. What could have been a moment of reckoning with Israelis' false

---

[1] Arendt (1971), p. 36.

https://doi.org/10.1515/9783111435046-018

sense of security and indifference to the fate of the conflict, and perhaps a turning point to send an urgent plea to the world for its resolution, was quickly swept away by military action, international response, and a wave of protests, solidarity statements, opinion columns, and social media wars that forced many, whether they have direct stakes in the crisis or not, to take sides.

One recurring theme in the campus protests in North America and their coverage was decolonization. Images of breaking through fences with bulldozers, Israeli tanks in flames, and paragliders piercing the sky were quickly captured in a banner as acts of liberation, while students' and other academic statements construed these acts as resistance to what they deem a settler-colonial project. The violence executed and documented by Hamas on the same day became counter-violence against the brutality of the colonial state, and some explicitly blamed the escalating violence exclusively on Israel, exonerating Hamas from responsibility, if not excusing their acts.

When more and more evidence accumulated on the atrocities, their scale, and nature—including an unprecedented number of civilian hostages, including Israeli women, young children, and the elderly, and Thai and Nepalese citizens; massive air strikes on Gaza while rockets are still fired to Israel; and an impending land invasion—the initial response of solidarity with the Palestinian cause did not acknowledge the horrific crimes committed in its name. Protestors ripped down photos of Israeli hostages, which they considered to be Israeli propaganda. Casting all Israelis as settlers might explain the lack of empathy, the indifference, and in some instances the denial of the atrocities of that day.

The claim that Israel is a settler-colonial state is not new. It is sufficient to say that it is a growing paradigm in settler-colonial studies and it fits well with longstanding Palestinian claims. Indeed, as the recent protests showed, it does not remain an academic debate and gets traction as a framework to explain the over one-hundred-year-old conflict. While it is important to understand this framework if we want to understand what decolonization will look like in Israel/Palestine, I want to point to its limitations.

The settler-colonial framework does not capture the complex situation of the Israeli-Palestinian reality, and it makes impossible avenues for resolution of the conflict and the realization of the right of both societies to live in peace and dignity. Let me explain these shortcomings.

First, this framework fails to capture the reality of inexplicable suffering and the sheer horror of two traumatized societies. Settler-colonialism emphasizes structures rather than events. While the history of the conflict does not begin on October 7, events, and especially traumatic events, have the power to shake and transform our understanding of reality and our sense of ourselves. Neither Israeli nor Palestinian societies will be the same after October 7. Hannah Arendt writes that human action has the capacity to bring to life what was before unprecedented. The unpredictability and irreversibility of action are what makes it both miraculous and pernicious.[2] In order to continue from here, we have to acknowledge the reality of the violence perpetrated on October 7 and the violence that continues in its aftermath.

Second, we cannot ignore how the current events echo past traumas in the histories of both peoples. The burning of whole families in their homes, mass killings, and displacement bring painful memories of pogroms, the Holocaust, and the Nakba. Trauma means living past horrors as if they are part of the present. The settler-colonial framework casts clear moral boundaries between the just, dispossessed indigenous population and the invading settlers who are there to eliminate the natives from their land together with their culture, ways of life, and language. The histories of the Jewish people and the Palestinian people defy these clear boundaries. Understanding the reality of the conflict through the settler-colonial lens perpetuates a Manichean framework that decolonization aims to overthrow.

This brings me to the next point: settler-colonialism is a theoretical framework and as such its power and limitations lie in the interpretive lens it offers to the present and the past. However, this is not the only available framework, and the case of Israel and Palestine challenges a neat application. The history of Israel and Palestine is understood also through the lens of national liberation and self-determination. Zion (Heb. צִיּוֹן) is the old Hebrew name for Jerusalem that became a metonym for the land of Israel in the exilic prayers and lamentations. It is the word from which Zionism received its name. The Zionist movement was a national movement to establish a homeland for the Jewish people. The Palestinian struggle for liberation and the establishment of a Palestinian state are legitimate national aspirations. The constitution of national identity in both groups in many ways was shaped in relation to each other.

Another related framework involves the plight of refugees. The State of Israel was established three years after the end of World War II with the promise of a safe haven for Jewish refugees and stateless people. It became one for refugees and Holocaust survivors from Europe, but also for Jewish refugees from majority-Muslim states in the Middle East. At the same time, the establishment of the nation-state of Israel created another refugee crisis, a wave of dispossession, and a call for the return of the Palestinian refugees.

To think through the complexity of the lived reality of Israelis and Palestinians is to resist an all-encompassing totalizing explanation and consider the multiple frameworks through which we make sense of that reality. But we need to think

---

2 Arendt (2013 [1958]), p. 191.

beyond these frameworks and confront the reality of dark times. What does that entail? Acknowledging our affiliations, sympathies, and complicities, and trying to see clearly. I am not saying that it is easy. Both societies will go through a process of reckoning to come to terms with their own failures, acts of violence, and responsibilities, even if it will take time. Even when it is hard to imagine such reckoning while the war is still ongoing.

This requires confronting reality pragmatically. The generations who were born and live in this country cannot be removed; they have no other home. At the same time, the continuation of the occupation is untenable. It perpetuates war and the threat of war, suffering, and injustice.

We need to take our cue from civil society organizations that live this complexity, such as the Parents Circle—Families Forum, an organization of bereaved families on both sides of the conflict. The members of the Parents Circle, more than 600 families who lost their loved ones, organize public meetings, share personal narratives, and promote their vision for reconciliation as a prerequisite for lasting peace through education, direct action, exhibitions, and the media. These families who build connections do not only envision a different reality, but transform reality through their actions.

Anwar Mhajne
Chapter 18: Silencing Dissent: Suppression Tactics in Israel Since October 7

November 15, 2023

Anwar Mhajne, PhD, a Palestinian citizen of Israel, is Assistant Professor of Political Science at Stonehill College. She specializes in international relations and comparative politics. Her research focuses on gender, religion, cybersecurity, digital politics, disinformation, and Middle Eastern politics. She is the co-editor of *Critical Perspectives on Cybersecurity*, which will be published with Oxford University Press in the spring of 2024. Her writing has been featured in the *Journal of Women, Politics & Policy*, *The International Feminist Journal of Politics*, *Political Research Quarterly*, *Religion and Politics*, *Culturico*, *The Carnegie Council for Ethics in International Affairs*, *Foreign Policy*, *The Conversation*, *The Times of Israel*, *Haaretz*, *Middle East Eye*, *+972 Magazine*, *Quartz*, *The Defense Post*, *The Jerusalem Post*, *Carnegie Endowment for International Peace*, *Al Bawaba*, *The New Arab*, and *The National*, among others.

Introduction

Since October 7, scholars,[1] President Biden,[2] and Israeli officials[3] have likened the recent terrorist attack to a heightened version of "Israel's 9/11." While this comparison faces scrutiny,[4] it provides a starting point to understand and contrast the experiences of the Arab-Palestinian community in Israel. Drawing parallels with the aftermath of 9/11 in the United States, where a significant expansion of mass surveillance occurred to address perceived security lapses, sheds light on the current situation in Israel. Six weeks after the 9/11 attacks, the USA PATRIOT Act was enacted, initiating changes to surveillance laws and enabling increased government monitoring of citizens. This legislation granted authorities expanded surveillance powers over phone and email communications, access to bank and credit reporting records, and the monitoring of online activities of American citizens.[5] Similarly, in Israel, the government, leveraging the state of shock and crisis, has altered the political landscape for Palestinians/Arabs, introducing bills and legislative amend-

---

1 Kupchan (2023).
2 White House (2023a).
3 Wall Street Journal (2023).
4 Cohen, R. (2023).
5 ACLU (2011).

https://doi.org/10.1515/9783111435046-019

ments that foster an environment conducive to political censorship and increased incitement against Palestinian citizens.[6]

On November 8, 2023, the Knesset [Israeli parliament] approved the Counter-Terrorism Law,[7] targeting the systematic and continued consumption of material from terrorist organizations like Hamas and ISIS. Offenses include direct calls to commit acts of terror or expressions of sympathy for terrorism under circumstances indicating identification with a terrorist organization, punishable by up to one year's imprisonment. Although valid for two years, this law faces opposition from civil society organizations in Israel.[8] Critics argue that it disproportionately impacts Palestinian citizens, potentially leading to the criminalization of innocent individuals based on their consumption of information. Uniquely, the law is more stringent than similar legislation invalidated in France, and Great Britain's law only criminalizes the consumption of publications in the context of preparing for a terrorist act. Concerns include that the law penalizes thoughts and feelings, its ambiguity in defining prohibited consumption, potential criminalization of consuming news documentation, violations of freedom of expression, and the public's right to access information.

Moreover, privacy concerns arise due to increased surveillance of citizens' digital activities, especially during national emergencies, posing risks of unfair penalization for those seeking information during chaotic times, such as the conflict with Gaza. This law exemplifies the broader trend of backlash, censorship, and silencing of Arabs/Palestinians within Israel, mainly through intensified surveillance of social media posts.

In the censorship of Arabs/Palestinians in Israel, we see how state and non-state actors and institutions such as colleagues, employers, and universities have become essential elements in surveilling what Arab-Palestinian colleagues, students, and professors are posting online. This phenomenon illustrates the convergence of state and societal surveillance, creating a complex web of monitoring and control that impacts individuals on both personal and professional fronts. Surveillance, censorship, and resistance will undoubtedly shape public discourse and individual freedoms in an interconnected world as digital technologies evolve.

---

6 Mada al-Carmel (2023).
7 Amendment No. 9 and temporary order Consumption of terrorist publications (2023).
8 Adalah (2023b) and Baker (2023).

Post October 7

Since October 7, the Israeli government has implemented various measures to address dissent and maintain order within the Palestinian community in Israel, amidst the ongoing conflict with the Gaza Strip. These measures aim to manage opposing perspectives on the war and responses to the violence in Gaza. The Israeli government's framing of the war as an existential and domestic challenge, combined with the broader security and political crisis since October 7, creates an environment where controlling dissenting voices against the war, killings, and destruction is a priority. The government led by Benjamin Netanyahu is currently implementing a crackdown in the aftermath of the recent attack, granting expanded powers to the police to identify what qualifies as support for terrorism without the involvement of state prosecutors. This shift removes a critical level of legal protection for individual free speech. The consequences of this move are observable not only in the suppression of criticism but also in the stifling of expressions of compassion.

Demonstrations expressing solidarity with Gaza have faced forceful dispersal, and Yaakov Shabtai, Israel's chief of police, publicly expressed openness to facilitate deportation to Gaza of individuals identifying with the suffering of the people of Gaza. Additionally, we saw a wave of arrests based on social media posts. Following the recent attack by Hamas, Israeli police have apprehended more than a hundred individuals due to their social media engagement. In Jerusalem alone, there have been sixty-three detentions and interrogations.[9] Yaakov Shabtai has warned against incitement, vowing a firm response. He stated, "Anyone inciting against the State of Israel, its government symbols, elected officials, military personnel and police, should be aware that the Israel Police will respond firmly and without leniency".[10]

Furthermore, workplaces, academic institutions, cultural entities, and social media platforms have become arenas where individuals expressing solidarity with the people of Gaza may face consequences. Social media, in particular, is being utilized by Israel and some Israelis to monitor and regulate expressions of critical perspectives on the war by Arab-Palestinian citizens and leftists. This use of social media aligns with broader discussions on surveillance practices and managing dissenting voices, as previously explored in the literature.[11] The current situation highlights the complex ways in which surveillance, both institutional

---

[9] Monetta (2023).
[10] Monetta (2023).
[11] e.g., Andrejevic (2005), Gandy (1993), Lyon (2003, 2017).

and social, is being applied to manage freedom of expression and political dissent within the Palestinian community in Israel.

Targeting Influencers

The arrests have mainly targeted Arab-Palestinian citizens who have a large following on social media. For instance, the influencer Muhannad Taha was detained for disseminating content related to Gaza. The Haifa Magistrate's Court ruled to keep him in detention from October 12 to October 13. This decision was based on a post where he expressed solidarity with the children of Gaza, stating, "My heart is with the children of Gaza"—he was charged with "engaging in behavior that may compromise public safety."[12] This relates to a post visible for only an hour on the same day as his arrest. Although the prosecution sought a six-day extension for his detention, the court first agreed to extend it until the following day, providing the prosecution with time to substantiate the impact of Taha's posts on "compromising public safety and state security".[13] The prosecution argued that Taha's influential posts about Gaza posed a threat to public safety, given his approximately million followers. Eventually, he was released on the 13th and placed under house arrest for five days, with a bail of 8,000 shekels.[14] Additionally, he was prohibited from using social media platforms during this period.

As another instance, in the Bedouin city of Rahat, authorities detained Dr. Amer al-Huzail, a former mayoral candidate, for a four-day period starting October 14. This action was taken after he shared on social media a map of the Gaza Strip along with an analysis of potential outcomes for an anticipated ground operation by Israeli forces.[15] The Israeli police allege that al-Huzail collaborated with Palestinian factions through a post on social media.[16] He was eventually released without any restrictive conditions.[17] In another case, Palestinian singer Dalal Abu Amneh was released on bail on October 22 after a two-day detention for a social media post deemed as "promoting hate speech and incitement" by Israeli authorities.[18] She posted a Palestinian flag emoji with the words "There is no victor but

---

12 Arab48 (2023).
13 Arab48 (2023).
14 Arab48 (2023).
15 Bwaret (2023).
16 Bokra (2023).
17 Bokra (2023).
18 Tusing (2023).

God" on Instagram to her 340,000 followers, resulting in her arrest.[19] Placed under house arrest, she faces a forty-five-day ban on discussing the war, and the possibility of charges is uncertain. Lastly, Maisa Abdel Hadi, a prominent Arab-Israeli actor, is facing charges, including "incitement to terrorism." She was briefly arrested after sharing a picture of an elderly Israeli woman supposedly being abducted to Gaza by Hamas, accompanied by a caption suggesting amusement. In subsequent posts, Abdel Hadi shared images of the attack with the comment "Let's go Berlin-style".[20] With 27,000 followers on Instagram, her posts were deemed to express sympathy, encouragement, and support for acts of terror, leading to charges of "identifying with a terror group".[21] These charges are part of a broader trend, highlighting the sensitivity of such expressions, especially considering Israel's diverse population, which includes Israeli Arabs.

Silencing influencers holds immense significance on domestic and international fronts, wielding power over public opinion and mobilization efforts. Domestically, influencers with large followings can shape narratives and garner support, making their suppression a strategic move to control dissenting voices and maintain a preferred narrative, particularly in times of conflict. It sets a model for others, instigating self-censorship and discouraging the use of influential platforms for expression. On the international stage, influencers can impact global perceptions and draw attention to human rights issues, conflict, or government repression. Silencing them aims to manage local and international narratives, avoiding negative scrutiny and potential diplomatic consequences.

Additionally, it serves as a model for other repressive regimes, inspiring similar measures globally. This strategy creates an environment of fear and self-censorship, regulates online behavior, and undermines advocacy efforts, limiting the potential for coordinated movements and solidarity networks. Overall, suppressing influencers is a nuanced tactic with far-reaching consequences, affecting the dynamics of local and global conversations.

Higher Education

Israel's attorney general's office has directed universities and colleges to report instances of students posting "words of praise for terrorism" to the police.[22] Minister

---

[19] Tusing (2023).
[20] Hashmonai (2023).
[21] Hashmonai (2023).
[22] Borger (2023).

of Education Yoav Kish has publicly endorsed disciplinary measures, advocating for the immediate suspension or expulsion of any student or employee supporting terrorist acts in Israel. The Chairperson of the National Union of Israeli Students has also voiced backing for the removal of students expressing strong support for terrorism.[23] Several Israeli academic institutions have officially declared "zero tolerance" for "supporting terrorism," resulting in the suspension or expulsion of students, with a notable focus on Palestinians expressing their identity or solidarity with the Palestinian people in Gaza.[24] This directive has triggered a purge in Israeli universities, with numerous Palestinian students facing disciplinary actions and some being suspended from their studies. What makes this case unique is the prominence of universities in surveillance and censorship, marking a distinct shift in their role in the ongoing situation. Intimidation, both online and offline, targeting individuals with dissenting views, whether Jewish or Arab Israelis, is also on the rise, often orchestrated by anonymous entities and groups.

Since October 7, 2023, Israeli universities and colleges have taken disciplinary actions against Palestinian students, resulting in suspensions and, in some cases, expulsions based solely on their personal social media posts. The institutions claim that these posts violate disciplinary regulations, either by "supporting terrorism" or "sympathizing with terror organizations".[25] As of November 14, Adalah, a legal center for Arab minority rights, is monitoring 110 cases and directly representing ninety-one Palestinian students across thirty-two Israeli academic institutions in disciplinary procedures. Among these cases, fifty-two students faced suspension before a hearing, eight were expelled without a hearing, and three were removed from dormitories without prior notice or a hearing.[26] Adalah has been involved in forty-seven disciplinary hearings, with thirty-two cases seeing decisions delivered. Eleven resulted in acquittals or dismissals due to reasonable doubt; three led to up to one-semester suspensions, two resulted in longer suspensions, and seven ended in expulsions.

Additionally, academic institutions imposed "educational punishments" in seven cases, including reprimands, mandatory apologies, educational courses, and volunteer work. Many of these cases involve students expressing solidarity with the Palestinian people in Gaza, posting content unrelated to the war or Hamas, providing context to the October 7 attack, quoting verses from the Quran, or engaging in actions well within the bounds of freedom of expression

---

23 Adalah (2023c).
24 Adalah (2023c).
25 Adalah (2023c).
26 Adalah (2023c).

and religion.[27] These disciplinary actions stemmed from complaints by political far-right student groups targeting Palestinian students and monitoring their social media accounts. Reports of disciplinary actions against students and incendiary publications highlight a concerning trend, with collaboration between universities, colleges, and student unions escalating to a dangerous attack on students. In this context, surveillance, censorship, and policing are conducted by higher education institutions that are supposed to provide a space for critical reflection and diverse informed perspectives. Suppressing academic freedom could result in a deficit in more varied perspectives, limiting the effectiveness of responses to crises. Furthermore, a society that restricts academic freedom risks sliding into authoritarianism. Academic institutions that are free to challenge authorities, question leadership, and develop new ideas play a crucial role in keeping checks and balances on power, contributing to a healthy democracy.

Workplace

Adalah reports a higher number of detentions following October 7, raising concerns that the police are adopting a broader definition of incitement and what is considered support for terrorism under the new amendment to the Counter-Terrorism Law discussed above. Adalah's lawyers reveal that as of November 14, there have been over ninety cases of Arab workers being suspended or fired.[28] One example is the cardiac intensive care unit director at a Petah Tikva hospital, Abed Samara, who was arrested last week after fifteen years of service. His suspension was prompted by his social media profile picture, which featured a dove carrying an olive twig and a green flag with the shahada, the Muslim declaration of faith. Although Samara had adopted this picture before the recent Hamas attack, it was interpreted as expressing support for the incident.

Additionally, he posted a quote attributed to the Prophet Muhammad, emphasizing Muslims being held accountable for their actions on the day of judgment. Samara clarified that this was directed at Muslim leaders and clerics whom he believed were not doing enough to prevent bloodshed. Despite his explanation, hospital authorities considered his actions to be supportive of the enemy.

Similarly, Samah Abou Shhadeh, who was an economist at a prestigious Israeli financial services company in Tel Aviv, was fired from her job for posting a clip on her personal Instagram account from the 2022 Israeli documentary *Tantura*, shed-

---
27 Adalah (2023c).
28 Adalah (2023c).

ding light on a tragic massacre in a Palestinian village in 1948.[29] She shared the clip without personal commentary.[30] Samah Abou Shhadeh faced the professional consequences of expressing historical perspectives that some found discomforting within the corporate setting.

This strategy of utilizing social media for censorship is particularly effective because it goes beyond direct state surveillance. The broadening definition of incitement and support for terrorism, as outlined in the amended Counter-Terrorism Law, allows authorities to interpret a wide range of expressions as potential threats. The cases of individuals like Abed Samara and Samah Abou Shhadeh highlight how seemingly innocuous content, such as a social media profile picture or a historical documentary clip, can be misconstrued and result in severe consequences. This indirect form of surveillance, driven by employers and institutions, creates an atmosphere of self-censorship, where individuals fear expressing dissenting views or sharing content that may be deemed critical by those in positions of power. Unlike direct state surveillance, this approach relies on societal and professional repercussions, contributing to a chilling effect that stifles open discourse and historical perspectives within various spheres.

Conclusion

The situation in Israel since October 7 reflects a concerning trend of suppressing dissenting voices across various sectors of society. The Israeli government's measures, from crackdowns on social media to the targeting of influencers, demonstrate a concerted effort to control the narrative surrounding the conflict with Gaza. The broadening definition of incitement and support for terrorism, as seen in amendments to the Counter-Terrorism Law, enables authorities to interpret a wide range of expressions as potential threats, leading to arrests and disciplinary actions.

The impact of this suppression extends to influencers, higher education, and workplaces. Influencers, particularly those with large followings, are being targeted for expressing solidarity with Gaza, highlighting the strategic importance of silencing voices that can shape public opinion both domestically and internationally. In higher education, Israeli universities and colleges are taking disciplinary actions against Palestinian students based on their social media posts, raising concerns about the erosion of academic freedom and the stifling of diverse perspectives.

---

[29] Diaz and Frayer (2023).
[30] Diaz and Frayer (2023).

Workplaces have become arenas for censorship, with individuals facing professional consequences for seemingly innocuous expressions on social media, creating a pervasive atmosphere of self-censorship.

The use of social media for surveillance and censorship, coupled with the collaboration between state institutions, employers, and educational institutions, underscores the multifaceted nature of the efforts to control dissent. This approach, relying on societal and professional repercussions, goes beyond direct state surveillance, contributing to a chilling effect that stifles open discourse and historical perspectives. Ultimately, the suppression of voices in Israel reflects a tactic with far-reaching consequences, impacting the dynamics of local and global conversations and raising questions about the health of democracy and the protection of fundamental freedoms.

IV. Going Forward: Questions of Morality and Hope

David Kretzmer
Chapter 19: Reflections on International Law

December 11, 2023

> **David Kretzmer**, Dr.Jur., is Professor Emeritus at the Hebrew University. Kretzmer's areas of expertise include public international law, administrative law, and constitutional law. He is the author of many books and articles on such subjects as the Supreme Court's protection of human rights, judicial review over actions in the occupied territories, the legal status of Arab citizens of Israel, freedom of expression and racist statements, the right of protest, the concept of human dignity in human rights discourse, and the applicability of the Geneva Convention in the occupied territories. Kretzmer is a former chairperson of the boards of B'Tselem and the Association for Civil Rights in Israel and from 1995 to 2002 served as a member of the Human Rights Committee that monitors compliance with the International Covenant on Civil and Political Rights.

Introduction

The murderous attack on October 7 by Hamas on Israel, its residents, and communities, and the subsequent hostilities between the IDF and Hamas in Gaza, have sparked petitions, statements, blog posts, and newspaper articles on the issues of international law involved. In reading these one cannot fail to be struck by the widely differing perceptions of the relevant norms of international law and their proper interpretation in the present context, especially in relation to the armed force being used by Israel in its attempt to eliminate Hamas military and governmental capacity in Gaza. At one end of the spectrum are spokespersons for the IDF and many Israeli and foreign lawyers, who claim that we are dealing with an armed conflict in which the IDF is by and large conducting its operations in compliance with the applicable laws of armed conflict. At the other end are some foreign lawyers and international organizations who deny that Israel has the right to use armed force to defend itself, or who claim that Israel is committing war crimes, crimes against humanity, and even genocide against the Palestinian people. In the middle are some experts in international law who try to distinguish between various practices of the IDF and show why specific practices are either compatible or incompatible with international norms.

Even if one's own perception of the situation is not entirely determined by one's affiliations and political outlook, it is certainly going to be influenced by them. It is unlikely that an Israeli lawyer who was devastated by the horrors and atrocities of Hamas's attack, the ongoing shelling of Israeli towns and villages, the abduction of people and holding them in Gaza as hostages, and the huge number of internally displaced persons from communities that were ravaged by Hamas is going to castigate the whole IDF action in Gaza as unlawful. It is equally unlikely that a Palestinian lawyer in Gaza, whose family or that of their friends has been killed and whose houses have been destroyed by Israeli bombings, will concede that Israel's offensive meets the requirements of international law.

What can I, an Israeli academic lawyer, add to this discussion? The truth is, very little. It is doubtful if anyone will be able to raise arguments that convince one side or the other that their perception of the law and its implementation in the present situation is misguided. Hence, I do not purport to add anything new to the legal arguments that have already been raised. Rather what I intend to do is to present the different views in a critical framework, and to conclude with some personal conclusions on the limitations of law in assessing the rights and wrongs of the situation.

I shall begin with a number of assumptions that I do not believe are, or certainly should not be, controversial.

Assumptions

1. Hamas's attack

Nobody who faces the facts that have been revealed could make a serious argument that Hamas's murderous acts had even a colour of legality, let alone morality. Many of the critics of Israel's actions following the October 7 attack condemn Hamas's murderous attack in no uncertain terms. Those who defend or even praise Hamas's attack do so simply by denying the nature of the horrific acts Hamas committed, or by claiming that in resisting occupation and colonialism all means are legitimate.

The latter claim is incompatible with a basic legal principle that should be beyond dispute: even people who believe that they are fighting for a just cause, such as resisting occupation or oppression, are bound to comply with the most fundamental rule in armed conflict that applies to all. To cite Judge Higgins's opinion in the Advisory Opinion of the International Court of Justice on the legality of constructing the separation barrier in the West Bank:

> I think the Court should also have taken the opportunity to say, in the clearest terms, what regrettably today needs constant reaffirmation even among international lawyers, namely that the protection of civilians remains an intransgressible obligation of humanitarian law

not only for the occupier but equally for those seeking to liberate themselves from occupation.[1]

There is ample evidence that the crimes against civilians committed by Hamas were part of a widespread, planned, and systematic attack on the civilian population. Hence the acts of murder, extermination, rape and other forms of sexual violence, and the enforced disappearances of the persons abducted amounted not only to war crimes, but to crimes against humanity. There are also strong grounds for asserting that since the murders of Israelis were committed with the intent to destroy a national, ethnic, or religious group, wholly or in part, they constituted the crime of genocide, the most serious crime known to the international community.

Abduction of civilians is a war crime, and when part of a widespread attack on a civilian population it is also a crime against humanity. Those who continue to hold the abductees are committing the crime of taking hostages, and by failing to provide any information as to their condition or whereabouts they are also committing the international crime of enforced disappearance of persons. Their act intentionally causes severe suffering not only to the abductees themselves, but to their family members too, thus constituting the international crime of torture toward them.

Most critics of Israel's conduct have stated quite clearly that all hostages should be released immediately and unconditionally. This demand must be repeated until all the hostages have been released.

2. Israel's response

In its response to Hamas's attack, which included firing hundreds of rockets into Israel, Israel has bombed huge areas in Gaza; thousands of Palestinians have been killed, many of them children; whole families have been wiped out; there has been massive destruction of buildings of all sorts, and huge displacement of civilians, many of whom were warned that they should leave their homes in order to avoid being killed or wounded by IDF attacks. At first Gaza was placed under siege, and even after Israel agreed that humanitarian aid could enter from Egypt, the UN reports that the humanitarian situation in Gaza remains catastrophic, with families lacking adequate food, water, and medical attention, and with growing chances of an epidemic breaking out. According to UN sources, there

---

1 https://www.un.org/unispal/document/auto-insert-208728/.

are still huge problems in the access of aid to Palestinians. The UN Food and Agricultural Organization has expressed deep alarm over growing hunger in the area and the risk of famine. Medical services have all but broken down and the hospitals that are still functioning suffer from severe lack of medicine and essential equipment. Large parts of Gaza have been rendered uninhabitable, so that when the fighting ends hundreds of thousands of people will not have homes to which they can return. The situation of the huge civilian population in Gaza is catastrophic.

3. Statements by Israeli political and military leaders

At the beginning of and during the campaign, Israeli political and military leaders made statements that conveyed that the use of force by Israel was not aimed solely at neutralizing the threat posed by armed Hamas groups, but was also a form of revenge against Gaza (" revenge"[2]; "remember what Amalek did to you";[3] "while balancing accuracy with the scope of damage, right now we're focused on what causes maximum damage";[4] "all the Palestinian civilians in Gaza are responsible for the Hamas actions, since they did not rise up against the Hamas regime";[5] "Gaza won't return to what it was before. Hamas will no longer exist. We will eliminate everything";[6] "there will be a siege on Gaza—no electricity, no food, no water, no fuel—we are fighting human animals and we will act accordingly";[7] "you wanted hell, you will get it"[8]). One can understand why, when combined with the massive loss of life and damage caused by the Israeli use of force, these statements led many outside observers to conclude that the military action involves collective punishment of the Palestinians or even that Israel is committing the crime of genocide towards the Palestinians.

---

[2] Aichner (2023).
[3] Netanyahu (2023).
[4] McKernan and Kierszenbaum (2023).
[5] Blumenthal (2023).
[6] Bloomberg (2023).
[7] Galant (2023).
[8] Pacchiani (2023).

4. The Palestinians are civilians

The vast majority of Palestinians in Gaza are civilians, who are not legitimate targets in war. The fact that some residents of Gaza support Hamas does not deprive them of their civilian status. Unless they are active members of one of the armed groups, principally Hamas or Islamic Jihad, they lose their protection as civilians only if and for such time as they take a direct part in hostilities.

Hamas operates from within or under civilian houses and buildings. When they do so they may be responsible for using civilians as human shields, or for failing to avoid locating military objectives within or near densely populated areas, in clear violation of international law. This violation by Hamas does not absolve Israel from its legal obligations toward civilians. It does, however, present it with huge problems of how to meet these obligations.

5. The failure of Israeli authorities to prevent Hamas's attack

Both the political and military leaders of Israel failed miserably in the first and primary duty of any government and any army: protecting the citizens of their country from attack. Rather than trying to reach a political agreement with the PLO, which Israel recognized as the legitimate representative of the Palestinians, the government supported the Gaza Hamas regime, mainly by allowing Qatar to send large sums of money into the territory. The prime minister was warned that his divisive plan to undermine Israel's democratic institutions [with his "judicial overhaul"] was having a disastrous effect on the security of the state, and was also warned that the enemies of the state might well attack it. He remained oblivious to these warnings. When his minister of defense warned of the threats to security by the so-called "legal reform" his response was to fire the minister, rather than to deal with the threats.

The military and secret service were apparently locked into a rigid paradigm, assuming that previous rounds of force against Hamas in Gaza had deterred it from attacking Israel. They refused to reconsider this paradigm even when provided with intelligence information that Hamas was preparing an attack.

One cannot exclude the possibility that the shame of the government and military over their abysmal failure to prevent the October 7 attack has contributed to the nature of their response in Gaza, which is causing far more loss of life and damage than previous rounds of hostilities there.[9]

---

9 See report here: Abraham (2023).

The Legality of Israel's Response

The horrific nature of Hamas's attack, the international crimes that were planned and committed in that attack, and the trauma caused to the Israeli people by that attack cannot, and do not, per se, mean that Israel's response is lawful.

In judging the legality of the response, three questions arise: 1. Was it lawful for Israel to use armed force in Gaza in response to Hamas's attack? 2. If Israel was legally entitled to use force against Hamas in Gaza, what limits are there on this use of force? 3. Are the means and methods of force being used compatible with the laws of armed conflict?

1. Laws of armed conflict

Israeli decision-makers place the emphasis on the last question, namely the laws of armed conflict. The Israel Ministry of Foreign Affairs has published lengthy statements[10] setting out the reasons[11] why Israel claims that it is complying with these laws.

I do not make the claim that the IDF is consistently complying with all the rules relating to conduct of hostilities in an armed conflict. On the contrary, the original refusal of the IDF to allow entry of needed humanitarian aid for the civilian population is not compatible with these rules; nor are the difficulties it allegedly poses in allowing access of humanitarian aid. There is also growing evidence that many of the rules have been ignored or given a wide interpretation, so as to allow, for example, massive bombing of what are called "power targets", attacks that will cause excessive "collateral damage", use of indiscriminate weapons or indiscriminate bombing, and destruction of property that was not demanded by military necessity.[12] Despite this evidence, in order to make a responsible assessment of *wide-scale* compliance or noncompliance with these rules, one has to have more detailed information than is available at present.

This may seem surprising to the lay reader, who may well assume that the vast loss of life and damage caused proves that Israel has been violating the laws of armed conflict. This assumption ignores the fact that the rules relating to conduct of hostilities in armed conflict are some of the more problematic norms of international law. They do not attempt to prevent use of force, nor even to hamper a party

---

10 Israel Ministry of Foreign Affairs (2023a).
11 Israel Ministry of Foreign Affairs (2023b).
12 Abraham (2023).

in an armed conflict from pursuing its legitimate war aims. On the contrary, they accept that the parties involved in an armed conflict may conduct hostilities whose aim is to kill members of the enemy force and to destroy its military objects. While it is forbidden to make civilians and civilian installations the object of an attack, it is not forbidden to attack a legitimate military target because civilians will be killed or civilian buildings destroyed. Hence, the fact that many civilians have been killed and civilian objects destroyed or damaged does not per se mean that the laws of war have been violated. It is for this very reason that I have always objected to the current practice of referring to the laws of war as international humanitarian law (IHL). There are certainly humanitarian norms that apply in times of conflict, but they do not capture the real nature of the rules that apply in conduct of hostilities. The better term is the law of armed conflict (LOAC), or the laws and customs of war. At the same time, whatever the terminology, we must be aware of the potential resort to law as a legitimizing factor for acts and policies that result in massive loss of human life and vast destruction of property.

Assuming that the laws of armed conflict apply in the present conflict, let us see how they may provide the basis for the argument that the IDF is acting lawfully in its attack on Gaza.

The law of armed conflict rests on an attempt to create a balance between military necessity and humanitarian considerations. In conduct of hostilities three main principles apply:

a. **Distinction:** The parties must distinguish between combatants and civilians, and between military objects and civilian objects. Attacks must be directed only against combatants and military objects. It is totally forbidden to direct attacks at civilians and at civilian objects. Indiscriminate attacks that do not distinguish between military targets and civilians or civilian objects are prohibited. In case of doubt whether a person is a civilian, that person shall be considered a civilian.

Members of Hamas or Islamic Jihad armed forces are fighters who may be targeted. Civilian objects may become military targets if by their nature, location, purpose, or use they meet two conditions: 1. they make an effective contribution to military action; and 2. their total or partial destruction offers a definite military advantage. Thus a house, school, or mosque may become a legitimate military target if weapons are stored in it, or if Hamas fighters fire rockets from it. A hospital also loses its immunity if it is used to commit, outside its humanitarian duties, acts that are harmful to the enemy, although in this case adequate warning must be given before action is taken against the hospital. At the same time the house of a Hamas fighter is not a legitimate military target unless it is making an effective contribution to military action and its destruction will offer the IDF a definite military advantage.

Civilian buildings of the Hamas regime in Gaza are also not legitimate targets unless they fulfill both of the above conditions. Hence, it would seem that in the absence of clear evidence that the Gaza parliament, courthouse, and other government buildings and the Islamic University were making an effective contribution to military action and that bombing them would offer a definite *military* advantage, they were not legitimate military targets.

b. **Precautions:** Parties must take precautions so as spare the civilian population and civilian objects. Thus, for example, if civilians are likely to be harmed by an attack on a military object, advance warning should be given, unless circumstances do not permit it. In choosing the means and methods of attack, feasible precautions should be taken with a view to avoiding or at least minimizing loss of civilian life, injury to civilians, and damage to civilian objects.

c. **Proportionality:** When the target of an attack is a legitimate military target, the fact that civilians or civilian objects might be harmed by the attack does not make that attack unlawful, unless the expected damage to civilians or civilian objects is "excessive" in relation to the anticipated direct and concrete military advantage. Note that the question relates to the expected damage and anticipated military advantage, and not to the damage actually caused or to the military advantage obtained.

There is no objective standard for assessing what will be "excessive." Hence there is probably going to be a huge difference between the assessments made in advance by military commanders and those made after the fact by human rights NGOs. It is far from clear to the outside observer what criteria are being used in deciding how many civilian deaths will be regarded as excessive in targeting Hamas leaders or other military targets. The large number of civilians who have been killed in attacks on civilian buildings, or on Hamas fighters, raises serious concerns regarding the permissiveness of these criteria.[13] It would also seem that if a civilian building is being used by Hamas fighters, the IDF does not regard the damage to the civilian use of the building as collateral damage that must be considered in the proportionality assessment.

From this short description of the main rules in hostilities it should be clear that even if they are strictly applied (and that is probably not a realistic expectation in any prolonged armed conflict), there may be huge loss of civilian life and extensive damage to property. This is certainly likely to be the situation when the armed forces of the enemy are embedded in the civilian population and seem indifferent

---

13 Lattimer (2023).

to the harm caused by the hostilities to that population. One can therefore understand why attempts may be made not only to challenge whether the IDF is complying with the rules, but also to deny that these rules apply in the present situation. In relation to the latter claim it should be pointed out that the international commissions of inquiry established by the UN after previous rounds of fighting between Hamas and Israel have all judged the legality of the IDF actions under this set of rules. The prosecutor of the International Criminal Court has also intimated that the criminal aspects of noncompliance with these rules will be the subject of his investigation into alleged crimes committed in the present conflict.

2. The legality of using force in response to Hamas's attack

The reader may find the first question—whether Israel had the right to use force in Gaza after Hamas's attack—rather puzzling. Could it possibly be that Israel was attacked by an armed force from Gaza, that hundreds of rockets were being fired into its territory from Gaza, that Hamas was holding over 200 hostages in Gaza, and yet Israel did not have the right to use armed force in response? Yet, surprising as it may seem, a number of international lawyers have questioned the very right of Israel to use armed force against Hamas in Gaza. One argument is that since all Israel's actions in Gaza since 1967 have been unlawful, Palestinians in Gaza had the right to use force to resist Israeli forms of control there, and after repelling Hamas's attack on Israeli territory, Israel did not have the right to use force in Gaza. The second argument is that since Gaza is still occupied territory, Israel did not have the right to use force in self-defense in that territory.

I do not think that either of these arguments has any merit. Firstly, both arguments ignore the fact that Hamas's attack included massive firing of rockets at civilian centers in Israel, some of which resulted in Israelis being killed. These attacks continued even after the IDF managed to repel the ground attack. The idea that Israel had to sit idly by while rockets were fired into its territory cannot be taken seriously. Secondly, Hamas's attack was not an isolated "incident"; it was part of the declared strategy of Hamas to wipe out the State of Israel, an aim expressly mentioned in Hamas's Charter. Spokespersons for Hamas stated quite clearly after October 7 that they intend to carry out further attacks in the future. In such a situation, after Hamas launched its murderous attack, Israel must surely have had the right to act in self-defense against Hamas.

Whether Gaza remained occupied territory after Israel withdrew its forces and settlements from the area in 2005 under the "Disengagement Plan" is controversial. The widely accepted view in the international community seems to be that since Israel has retained forms of control over life in Gaza from outside, and has not allowed the inhabitants of Gaza to act as if they were in a free state, the territory is still occupied territory. The weakness of this view, pointed out by leading experts in international law, is that the very essence of occupation is effective control over the territory by the hostile army. The effective control must be such that the occupying power can fulfill the first and major obligation of an occupying power: maintaining public order and civil life in the territory.

It is quite clear that since the withdrawal of Israel from Gaza, and especially since Hamas took control of the territory in 2007, Israel does not have the effective control over the territory that would enable it to fulfill the obligation of an occupying power to maintain public order and civil life. In fact, the present war is the ultimate proof that Israel does not have effective control over the area: if a massive military campaign is required in order to gain control over the main cities in the area, in what sense can it be said that Israel had effective control before that campaign?

To be quite honest, it is not at all clear which conclusions those who rely on the status of Israel as an occupying power in Gaza wish to draw. One possibility is that Israel cannot resort to the rules of armed conflict in its attempt to destroy Hamas, but is confined to a policing model of law under which the use of lethal force is highly restricted, and the principle of proportionality does not apply.

The notion that Israel could have dealt with the rockets that Hamas was firing from Gaza into Israel, and the preparations of Hamas for another ground attack in Israel, by employing a policing model of law ignores both the real situation in Gaza and the nature of Hamas as the de facto government of the territory, commanding a highly organized and large armed force. What policing methods could have been used to neutralize this force that posed a huge security risk to Israel and its residents? Furthermore, when wide-scale organized hostilities take place in occupied territory, the law on conduct of hostilities will apply, just as it does when such hostilities take place in the sovereign territory of a state.

Much of the legal discussion on the right of Israel to use force in self-defense has revolved around the question of whether this right of a state as recognized in the UN Charter is restricted to inter-state relations. I do not intend on joining this discussion. Given the fact that Israel does not have effective control over Gaza, and that Hamas is the de facto government of this territory and has a highly organized armed force, it seems to me that after it was under attack Israel was in principle entitled to use force in self-defense against Hamas armed force, whether this is grounded in the UN Charter or in customary international law. At the same time, this use of force was, and continues to be, subject to serious legal constraints. These constraints are of two kinds. Firstly, all use of force in self-defense must meet the demands of necessity and proportionality. Secondly, the use of force must comply with the laws that relate to conduct of hostilities in armed conflict.

I mentioned the problematic nature of these laws above, and explained why it is difficult at this stage to judge the extent to which they have been respected. I turn now to discussion of the constraints on use of force in self-defense.

3. Constraints on use of force in self-defense: necessity and proportionality

Since the second half of the nineteenth century it has been a fundamental principle (admittedly often violated) that the only legitimate aim of using force in an armed conflict is to weaken the military forces of the enemy. This idea was strengthened in the post-World War II era, in which a state may only use force beyond its borders when it has to defend itself against an armed attack. As the right to use armed force is limited to the right of self-defense in the face of an armed attack, the object of military action against the enemy must be to weaken or destroy its military capacity to continue the attack. Revenge and general deterrence are not legitimate war aims. As mentioned above, irresponsible statements from political and military leaders of Israel since October 7 and the massive destruction in Gaza have provided critics of Israel with strong grounds for arguing that the aims of Israel's actions have not been solely to destroy the military capacity of Hamas. To the extent that places were bombed or property destroyed as a form of revenge, it was clearly unlawful.

It is hard to believe that the initial attacks on Gaza were not in any way influenced by the statements of the prime minister and minister of defense, the latter of whom declared that he had removed all the brakes on the military. Nevertheless, failing evidence that the IDF actions were indeed influenced by these statements, one cannot conclude that these actions were necessarily unlawful. The legal questions that must be addressed are the issues of necessity and proportionality.

Necessity means that the legitimate war aim—weakening the military capacity of Hamas—could not be achieved without using armed force, and that the armed force that was used was necessary to achieve this aim. In this regard the first question that arises is whether all possible political avenues were explored to address the serious threat that the Hamas regime in Gaza does indeed pose, as so horrifyingly revealed by the October 7 massacre, the abduction and subsequent holding of 240 hostages, the firing of rockets into Israel, and the declarations by Hamas leaders that there would be further attacks, the aim of which is to destroy Israel.

Hamas is reviled by many of the Arab regimes, and has been designated as a terrorist organization by many states. The horrific nature of the October 7 attack might have opened the opportunity to enlist support from the surrounding countries and other countries to eliminate that threat and to force Hamas to release all the hostages. Should Israel have tried to neutralize the Hamas threat and secure release of the hostages through political means before resorting to the massive use of force that inevitably resulted in the large number of Palestinians killed and wounded, and the vast level of destruction in Gaza? From the point of view of domestic politics, it might have been difficult for the Government of Israel to seek a political solution to the Hamas threat, and in practice it might have proved impossible to enlist the international support needed for effective intervention to disarm Hamas and force it to release the hostages. It could be argued, however, that since it was quite clear that use of force against Hamas would result in massive loss of life of civilians and vast destruction, unless every attempt had been made to try this path before resorting to massive use of force, the use of such force was not necessary.

In addressing the issue of proportionality, it is important to distinguish between the meaning of this requirement in relation to the use of force, and its meaning in relation to specific attacks on legitimate military targets. In the first context the term refers to the overall proportionality of the force used, whether or not it was in all cases compatible with the laws on conduct of hostilities. In the second context the term refers to the proportionality of the collateral damage expected to be caused by a specific attack on a military target. I addressed the second context above. I turn now to the first context.

It is accepted that a state that uses force in self-defense must comply with the demands of necessity and proportionality. There is, however, little agreement on the meaning of the latter term in this context. One can in fact discern two lines of thought.

The first is that the armed force used in response to an armed attack must be proportionate to the need to achieve the legitimate goal of self-defense. If the force used is necessary to achieve this goal, it cannot be disproportionate, no matter what damage is caused in pursuing that goal. Assuming that totally destroying the military capacity of Hamas is a legitimate war goal (an assumption that is challenged by many scholars), unless Hamas surrenders Israel may continue to use the force necessary to achieve this goal, no matter the cost in terms of human life and suffering of Palestinians and Israelis. The only constraints will be the rules relating to conduct of hostilities that were discussed above. From what one can discern, this is the official approach of Israel.

According to the second line of thought, in assessing proportionality in use of force one has to examine not only whether the force used is necessary to achieve the legitimate war aim, but also the loss of life and damage that will be caused by the force used. This is not a one-time assessment to be carried out when the initial decision to resort to force is made, but an assessment that must be made again and again while the use of force continues. Even if the use of force was originally justified, at some stage the damage might be so great that further use of force will be disproportionate, since the damage that it will cause will outweigh the benefit of furthering the legitimate war aim.

Like all assessments of proportionality, there is no objective standard for making this assessment. Each side will place much greater value on protection of its own people than that of civilians on the other side. The side causing the damage will have to consider not only what damage will be caused by continuing to use force, but what damage it is likely to suffer if it abandons use of force while leaving the enemy capable of continuing or resuming its attack. In the present context Israel must also consider whether the internally displaced persons from communities in the south will be able to return to their towns and villages if the military capacity of Hamas remains more or less intact.

However difficult it is to make this assessment, in the present context proportionality in this sense might mean that given the damage that would inevitably be caused by using vast military force against Hamas, Israel should have refrained from use of force altogether; should not have defined an overambitious war aim, the achievement of which would necessarily lead to massive loss of life and damage to property; or that even if at first it could have used force, it may at some stage have had to refrain from further military action due to the damage it was causing.

In the discussions of Israel's use of force, both lines of thought have been advanced. Some, including former US military lawyers, have argued that as long as the aim is to eliminate the continued threat of Hamas, the extent of loss of life and damage do not make the use of force disproportionate. Others have argued that the massive loss of life and damage to property of Palestinians have rendered the use of force to destroy Hamas disproportionate.

Although I am on record as having advanced the second strand of thought, and still hold by this view, it does not seem fruitful for me to try to decide which of the two views reflects prevailing standards of international law. There is no agreement, and there are no clear decisions from international decision-making bodies on the meaning of the term in this context.

Moral and Political Issues

From the above discussion it should be apparent that the law regarding the horrific crimes of Hamas and its duty to release the hostages is clear. But when it comes to the war in Gaza itself, the law is going to give us limited guidance as to the rights and wrongs of the present round in the Israel–Palestine conflict. Each side will inevitably cite law as a legitimizing factor for its position. Israel will cite the rules on conduct of hostilities that apply in armed conflict and claim to be abiding by them. Under this view, the massive loss of life and destruction of property may place the burden on Israel to show that it acted in accordance with the rules on conduct of hostilities, but they do not necessarily prove that Israel violated these rules. Critics will either deny that Israel had the right to use armed force in Gaza, or claim that even if it did, the force has been or has become disproportionate, and in all events that Israel is violating the laws of armed conflict. Even if there were a clear answer to all the difficult legal questions that arise in regard to the present conflict, and even if we were to assume for the sake of argument that everything that Israel has done is "lawful," we would still have to address the more important moral and political questions.

The Secretary-General of the UN condemned Hamas's attack in no uncertain terms and stressed quite correctly that "the grievances of the Palestinian people cannot justify the appalling attack by Hamas." He later stated, however, that it should also be recognized that the attack did not take place in a vacuum. Making this statement may have been insensitive, since Israelis could interpret it as lessening the horrific and unlawful nature of the attack. Nevertheless, it seems to me that what the SG said is quite true. Hamas's attack, murderous, horrific, and pernicious as it was, was an especially vile use of violence in the context of the Israel–Palestine conflict. The background of the Israeli occupation of Gaza, its treatment of the population there since the Disengagement, and the continuing uncontained settler violence toward Palestinians in the West Bank cannot and do not in any way justify Hamas's massacre. They are, however, highly relevant in gauging the implications of Israel's reaction to that massacre.

On the moral level one must ask whether Israel's security interest in destroying the military capacity of Hamas can justify causing the death of such a large number of civilians, including thousands of children and whole families, and huge damage to the homes of hundreds of thousands of people. All readers should ask themselves this question. In contending with it I suggest that *some* of the many pertinent questions are these: Assuming for the moment that unless Hamas is totally crushed, Israelis will not be able to live securely in towns and communities close to the border with Gaza, and that the chances of another war with Hamas in the fairly near future are high: 1. What price in terms of the lives of Palestinians in Gaza may be demanded in order to achieve this goal? Has Israel not exceeded the acceptable price? 2. Is it quite clear that the declared aim of crushing Hamas is achievable by use of more and more force? And if not (as many experts claim, and as now seems increasingly apparent), how can one justify the killing of many civilians by force that will not achieve its intended goal? Under traditional Just War theory, a war for what appears to be a justified aim will not be just if that aim is not achievable. 3. Is it absolutely clear that this legitimate aim could not have been achieved without the use of the massive force that has been used, with its dire consequences for the civilians in Gaza? 4. To what extent, if any, can Israel's moral responsibility for the massive loss of life and damage to property be diminished, due to the Hamas tactics and their declared and actual lack of care for the safety of the civilian population?

As to the political questions—the vast majority of Palestinians in Gaza are civilians, who are not responsible for the horrific crimes of Hamas and Islamic Jihad. Most of them are refugees or the descendants of refugees from the 1948 war—victims of the Israel–Palestine conflict who have been forced to live their whole lives in intolerable conditions. Israel was not solely responsible for their plight, but it certainly is not devoid of responsibility for it. Israel was an occupying power in Gaza from 1967 until 2005 and did little to improve the conditions of the Palestinians during that time. And since it withdrew the IDF and Israeli settlements from the area, Israel has still maintained forms of control that had an enormous effect on the daily lives of the people there. Gaza was described even by a former senior Israeli security official as a large prison. The civilians there were treated as pawns whose interests were always subject to the overriding security interests of Israelis. Israel adopted severe measures against the population in Gaza after Hamas wrenched control in 2007, and despite having recognized Gaza and the West Bank as one territorial unit, it cut off Gaza from the West Bank. Since Netanyahu became prime minister in 2009 the government has made no attempt to reach an agreement with the Palestinians. It has continued with its settlement policy in the West Bank and has refrained from enforcing the law against settlers who use force against Palestinians or their property. Netanyahu is on record stating that those who oppose creation of a Palestinian state should support allowing Qatar to provide financial aid to Gaza. The minister of finance stated in the past that "Hamas is an asset."

Israel entered this war with no clear strategic plan as to the future of Gaza and its residents. The government did not consider the implications of the vast loss of life and destruction of homes in the context of the conflict with the Palestinians. But if we do not want to face more and more wars and continuation of the conflict as a zero-sum game that will only end when one side destroys the other, it is essential to ask questions that relate not only to Hamas, but also to the Palestinians in Gaza and the West Bank. What does the enormous price being exacted from Palestinians in Gaza mean for the future relations between Israelis and Palestinians in this troubled land? Does it not destroy any hope for a political settlement of the conflict between the two peoples? Will the bitterness caused to Palestinians who have lost their families and homes not be the breeding ground for more extreme Palestinian organizations, as more and more Palestinians seek revenge or become convinced that Israel's existence is a threat to their continued existence? If these are the results of the present conflict, Hamas will have won, even if its military capacity is destroyed.

Israel is not an island unto itself. It cannot continue to exist and thrive without political support from other countries. The loss of life and damage to the Palestinians in Gaza in the present war have increased hostility toward Israel and its people in many parts of the world. Will this growing hostility lead to delegitimization of the State of Israel, thereby posing a threat to its very existence?

Omer Bartov
Chapter 20: What I Believe as a Historian of Genocide

November 10, 2023

> **Omer Bartov**, PhD, is the Samuel Pisar Professor of Holocaust and Genocide Studies at Brown University. He is the author of numerous books, including most recently, *Erased: Vanishing Traces of Jewish Galicia in Present-Day Ukraine* (2007); *Anatomy of a Genocide: The Life and Death of a Town Called Buczacz* (2018), which received the National Jewish Book Award and the Yad Vashem International Book Prize for Holocaust Research, among others, and has been translated into several languages; *Tales from the Borderlands: Making and Unmaking the Galician Past* (2022); *Israel-Palestine: Lands and Peoples* (2021); *The Butterfly and the Axe* (2023); and *Genocide, the Holocaust and Israel-Palestine: First-Person History in Times of Crisis* (2023).

Israeli military operations have created an untenable humanitarian crisis, which will only worsen over time. But are Israel's actions—as the nation's opponents argue—verging on ethnic cleansing or, most explosively, genocide?

As a historian of genocide, I believe that there is no proof that genocide is currently taking place in Gaza, although it is very likely that war crimes, and even crimes against humanity, are happening. That means two important things: first, we need to define what it is that we are seeing, and second, we have the chance to stop the situation before it gets worse. We know from history that it is crucial to warn of the potential for genocide before it occurs, rather than belatedly condemn it after it has taken place. I think we still have that time.

It is clear that the daily violence being unleashed on Gaza is both unbearable and untenable. Since the October 7 massacre by Hamas—itself a war crime and a crime against humanity—Israel's military air and ground assault on Gaza has killed more than 10,500 Palestinians, according to the Gaza Health Ministry, a number that includes thousands of children. That's well over five times the number of the more than 1,200 people in Israel murdered by Hamas. In justifying the assault, Israeli leaders and generals have made terrifying pronouncements that indicate a genocidal intent.

Still, the collective horror of what we are watching does not mean that a genocide, according to the international legal definition of the term, is already underway. Because genocide, sometimes called "the crime of all crimes," is perceived by many to be the most extreme of all crimes, there is often an impulse to describe any instance of mass murder and massacre as genocide. But this urge to label all atrocious events as genocide tends to obfuscate reality rather than explain it.

International humanitarian law identifies several grave crimes in armed conflict. War crimes are defined in the 1949 Geneva Conventions and subsequent protocols as serious violations of the laws and customs of war in international armed conflict against both combatants and civilians. The Rome Statute, which established the International Criminal Court, defines crimes against humanity as extermination of, or other mass crimes against, any civilian population. The crime of genocide was defined in 1948 by the United Nations as "the intent to destroy, in whole or in part, a national, ethnical, racial or religious group, as such."[1]

So in order to prove that genocide is taking place, we need to show both that there is the intent to destroy and that destructive action is taking place against a particular group. Genocide as a legal concept differs from ethnic cleansing in that the latter, which has not been recognized as its own crime under international law, aims to remove a population from a territory, often violently, whereas genocide aims at destroying that population wherever it is. In reality, ethnic cleansing may escalate into genocide, as happened in the Holocaust, which began with an intention to remove the Jews from German-controlled territories and transformed into the intention of their physical extermination.

My greatest concern watching the Israel–Gaza war unfold is that there is genocidal intent, which can easily tip into genocidal action. On October 7, Prime Minister Benjamin Netanyahu said that Gazans would pay a "huge price" for the actions of Hamas and that the Israel Defense Forces, or IDF, would turn parts of Gaza's densely populated urban centers "into rubble."[2] On October 28, he added, citing Deuteronomy, "You must remember what Amalek did to you."[3] As many Israelis know, in revenge for the attack by Amalek, the Bible calls to "kill alike men and women, infants and sucklings."

The deeply alarming language does not end there. On October 9, Israel's defense minister, Yoav Gallant, said, "We are fighting human animals and we are acting accordingly,"[4] a statement indicating dehumanization, which has genocidal echoes. The next day, the head of the Israeli Army's coordinator of government activities in the territories, Major General Ghassan Alian, addressed the population of Gaza in Arabic: "Human animals must be treated as such," he said, adding: "There will be no electricity and no water. There will only be destruction. You wanted hell, you will get hell."[5]

---

[1] https://www.un.org/en/genocideprevention/genocide.shtml.
[2] Lis (2023).
[3] NPR (2023).
[4] Fabian (2023).
[5] Pacchiani (2023).

The same day, retired Major General Giora Eiland wrote in the daily newspaper *Yedioth Ahronoth*, "The State of Israel has no choice but to turn Gaza into a place that is temporarily or permanently impossible to live in." He added, "Creating a severe humanitarian crisis in Gaza is a necessary means to achieving the goal."[6] In another article, he wrote that "Gaza will become a place where no human being can exist."[7] Apparently, no army representative or politician denounced this statement. I could quote many more.

Taken together, these statements could easily be construed as indicating a genocidal intent. But is genocide actually occurring? Israeli military commanders insist that they are trying to limit civilian casualties, and they attribute the large numbers of dead and wounded Palestinians to Hamas tactics of using civilians as human shields and placing their command centers under humanitarian structures like hospitals.

But on October 13, the Israeli Ministry of Intelligence reportedly issued a proposal to move the entire population of the Gaza Strip to the Egyptian-ruled Sinai Peninsula (Netanyahu's office said it was a "concept paper").[8] Extreme right-wing elements in the government—also represented in the IDF—celebrate the war as an opportunity to be rid of Palestinians altogether. This month, a videotape emerged on social media of Captain Amichai Friedman, a rabbi in the Nahal Brigade, saying to a group of soldiers that it was now clear that "this land is ours, the whole land, including Gaza, including Lebanon." The troops cheered enthusiastically; the military said that his conduct "does not align" with its values and directives.[9]

And so, while we cannot say that the military is explicitly targeting Palestinian civilians, functionally and rhetorically we may be watching an ethnic cleansing operation that could quickly devolve into genocide, as has happened more than once in the past.

None of this happened in a vacuum. Over the past several months I have agonized greatly over the unfolding of events in Israel. On August 4, several colleagues and I circulated a petition warning that the attempted judicial coup by the Netanyahu government was intended to perpetuate the Israeli occupation of Palestinian land. It was signed by close to 2,500 scholars, clergy members, and public figures who were disgusted with the racist rhetoric of members of the government, its antidemocratic efforts, and the growing violence by settlers, seemingly supported by the IDF, against Palestinians in the occupied West Bank.

---

6 Eiland (2023b)
7 Eiland (2023a).
8 Teibel (2023).
9 Kaplan Sommer (2023).

What we had warned about—that it would be impossible to ignore the occupation and oppression of millions for fifty-six years, and the siege of Gaza for sixteen years, without consequences—exploded in our faces on October 7. Following Hamas's massacre of innocent Jewish civilians, our same group issued a second petition denouncing the crimes committed by Hamas and calling upon the Israeli government to desist from perpetrating mass violence and killings upon innocent Palestinian civilians in Gaza in response to the crisis. We wrote that the only way to put an end to these cycles of violence is to seek a political compromise with the Palestinians and end the occupation.

It is time for leaders and senior scholars of institutions dedicated to researching and commemorating the Holocaust to publicly warn against the rage- and vengeance-filled rhetoric that dehumanizes the population of Gaza and calls for its extinction. It is time to speak out against the escalating violence on the West Bank, perpetrated by Israeli settlers and IDF troops, which now appears to also be sliding toward ethnic cleansing under the cover of war in Gaza; several Palestinian villages have reportedly self-evacuated under threats from settlers.

I urge such venerable institutions as the United States Holocaust Memorial Museum in Washington, DC and Yad Vashem in Jerusalem to step in now and stand at the forefront of those warning against war crimes, crimes against humanity, ethnic cleansing, and the crime of all crimes, genocide.

If we truly believe that the Holocaust taught us a lesson about the need—or really, the duty—to preserve our own humanity and dignity by protecting that of others, this is the time to stand up and raise our voices, before Israel's leadership plunges it and its neighbors into the abyss.

There is still time to stop Israel from letting its actions become a genocide. We cannot wait a moment longer.

Rawia Aburabia
Chapter 21: On the Need for Moral Clarity and Political Complexity

December 21, 2023

> **Rawia Aburabia**, PhD, is an associate professor at Sapir College School of Law. She earned her PhD from the Faculty of Law at the Hebrew University of Jerusalem in an interdisciplinary doctoral program, "Human Rights Under Pressure—Ethics, Law, and Politics," which was jointly held by the Hebrew University and the Freie Universität Berlin. Aburabia received her LLM in International Human Rights Law from the American University Washington College of Law, Washington, DC. Aburabia teaches and researches in the fields of family law, international human rights law, feminist jurisprudence, and minority rights. She has received several awards for her academic and feminist work. She was awarded the Ma'of Scholarship of the Council of Higher Education for Outstanding Arab Scholars (2020), and the Polonsky Postdoctoral Fellowship (2019). Aburabia was selected as one of *Globes Magazine*'s "40 Under 40" most promising young leaders in Israel (2018), and as *+972 Magazine*'s "Person of the Year: Woman Activists of the Arab World" (2011). Aburabia practiced as a human rights attorney for the Association for Civil Rights in Israel and has been at the forefront of several civil rights initiatives, concerning the unrecognized Bedouin villages and Bedouin women's rights in Israel.

More than two months have passed since that cursed Saturday on which Hamas slaughtered innocent Israeli citizens, most of them residents of the area around the Gaza Strip, in a horrific and inconceivable massacre. Entire villages were uprooted, thousands of residents were forced to leave their homes, others are missing, and over a hundred hostages remain in Hamas captivity. The stories of the horrors and terror will not leave me; the images of dead or kidnapped children, women, and the elderly make it impossible to sleep. I am a lecturer at Sapir College in southern Israel, a mere 6 km from Gaza. And I cannot stop thinking about the people we have lost, the students and staff members uprooted from their homes, and their terrible pain. I think about my peace activist friend Vivian Silver from Kibbutz Be'eri, murdered in her home, and I lament this tremendous loss. I think about Tal Haimi from Kibbutz Nir Yitzhak, the nephew of my good friend Haia Noach, who was killed on October 7. The pain and loss are unbearable. We are not the same people we were before the events of October 7, and it is difficult to find words to express what we are feeling.

The despicable acts committed by Hamas are war crimes; there can be no possible justification for them. Following the events of the appalling massacre, a war broke out between Israel and Hamas, the declared aim of which is to destroy Hamas's military capabilities and bring about its collapse. However, the people bearing most of the heavy burden of this war are not members of Hamas but rather the innocent citizens of Gaza, entire families killed by Israeli bombs or uprooted from their homes to an unknown fate of loss and life as refugees. At the time of writing, there are reports of around 20,000 killed in Gaza, most of them citizens and innocent children who had no connection with Hamas.

It is difficult to be a Palestinian citizen of Israel today. Our hearts suffer doubly. We feel the pain of the Israeli families who lost their loved ones in the horrific events of that Black Saturday, follow with worry the fate of the hostages—those who were released and those who remain in captivity. However, our hearts also bleed for the deaths and flight of Palestinians from Gaza, our brothers and sisters driven to Gaza by the events of the Nakba in 1948 and now forced to flee again: they are paying the highest price in this cursed war. While Hamas's rockets do not distinguish between Jews and Arabs and are fired indiscriminately at targets all over Israel, Israeli policymakers discriminate between Jews and Arabs when they treat unrecognized Bedouin villages in the Negev as open spaces—not only do these villages lack any kind of bomb shelters, but Israel's Iron Dome missile defense system does not shoot down rockets set to fall in their lands. This has led to the deaths of residents of these villages, among them children.

The atmosphere of war creates a dichotomy of good versus bad, barbarism versus a moral army, victory versus defeat. Leftists are rethinking their stances in the face of those who say "We told you so," silencing any attempt to question or criticize the Israeli government headed by Benjamin Netanyahu, and its continued failures, which led to the horrific catastrophe of October 7. A government that was occupied with judicial overhaul and destroying the Israeli democratic space. While most of the Israeli public is exposed mainly to the terrible pictures and stories of the horrors committed on October 7, as published by the Israeli media, the world also sees the appalling pictures from Gaza that show death, destruction, flight, and deep despair. Pictures of thousands of dead children, buried under the ruins caused by Israeli bombings, pictures of refugee camps flooded with water, and an emerging humanitarian crisis.

This binary plays several roles. One is psychological: relieving the massive collective pain and calming fears by providing a concrete response in the form of a simple, easily absorbed message. Likewise, it silences the criticism of governmental failures. Moreover, it justifies the war and the collective punishment of the Palestinian population by dehumanizing the residents of Gaza and constructing them as an enemy in a way that warrants their systematic killing. The binary and superficial nature of the discourse leaves no room for complex thinking amidst the political context in which the events unfold—silencing any attempt to go beyond the victim–perpetrator dichotomy, or to offer a framework in which it is possible to subscribe to several truths.

Are we allowed to maintain moral clarity and cling to complex political perspectives? Can we at the same time take a stand against the crimes of Hamas and also recognize the suffering of the Palestinian people, protest against the killing of innocent citizens in Gaza who have no connection to Hamas? Can we both oppose Hamas and present a diplomatic solution alongside the military response for the day after the war, one that will lead to the end of the Israeli–Palestinian conflict and stop the cycle of violence and bloodshed? Are we allowed to feel pain and hope, without hope being a radical concept?

In Israel, many conceptions have collapsed since October 7, the arrogant and irresponsible conceptions of a reckless and incompetent leadership. Conceptions that strengthened Hamas in order to weaken the Palestinian Authority and to prevent the establishment of a Palestinian state alongside the State of Israel. Conceptions of economic peace at the expense of a political solution, and more. Did the critical thought propounded by some liberal intellectuals in Israel also collapse? Or did it never exist in the first place?

The horrors of October 7 shook the foundations of critical intellectual thought in Israel. Those who were previously critical began to question the paradigms to which they had clung, in particular the settler–colonial paradigm that analyzes power relations and control in the space between Israel and Palestine, and the question of decolonizing that space. Intellectuals who defined themselves as liberals began to reframe their stances, adopting more conservative approaches appropriate to the time. Some even joined the witch hunt against Arab staff and students in Israeli institutions of higher education, investigating their activities on social media and whether they had signed petitions against the war in Gaza. An entire public that demonstrated every Saturday in Kaplan Square, Tel Aviv, against the judicial overhaul in Israel changed its tune, proving that the battle for Israel's democratic space was and remains a matter of perpetuating the ethno-national privileges of the Jews. They did so despite all the stories of the heroism displayed by Arab residents of the Negev, who helped save their Jewish neighbors from the terrible slaughter at the party in Re'im and the villages surrounding Gaza. Despite the heavy price paid by residents of unrecognized and undefended villages in the Negev, to whom the rockets of Hamas show no mercy. Despite the Arabs killed and kidnapped on that awful Saturday. All these did not change perceptions of the Arab population in Israel or the need to redefine the Israeli citizenship of Arabs so that it will be based on egalitarian principles. Various calls to change the Israeli law on nationality have not found a sympathetic ear among the Israeli public, even when these calls originated among the leadership of the Arab Druze community, whose soldiers have been killed in Gaza during the war. Such events highlighted even further that it is easier to promote critical or liberal discourse in times of peace—or, in the Israeli case, between wars—and to depict oneself as an enlightened liberal intellectual when talking about regime change. In times of war, the challenge is far greater.

Our challenge today, as Israeli Palestinians, those who have both Israeli citizenship and a Palestinian national identity, is even more complicated. Our complex identity is similar to that of African-Americans. We are Israeli citizens, part of the State of Israel; our fate is tied up with that of the country. Yet we are also part of the Palestinian people—we have a national and collective history, language, culture, and narrative. And we have relatives in Gaza, in the West Bank, and in the Arab world. Some of them refugees of 1948, uprooted from their homes during the Nakba. The expectation that we will hide our national identity is not realistic and embodies the logic of colonial elimination.

Despite this challenge, we must demonstrate at once moral clarity and political complexity. We must unequivocally and clearly oppose the criminal slaughter and terror attack carried out by Hamas against innocent citizens, children, the elderly, women, and men. The cruel slaughter was inhuman and totally unacceptable. At the same time, we must oppose the Israeli occupation and see the residents of Gaza as double victims—of Hamas, which terrorizes them, and of Israeli policy, which imposes a lengthy siege on Gaza with no sign of hope on the horizon.

We seek to end the Israeli occupation of the West Bank and Gaza, and we support the right of the Palestinian people to a sovereign state alongside Israel. Our support of the right of the Palestinian people to self-determination does not mean that we support Hamas, or any other terror organization responsible for crimes against humanity. As Arab citizens of Israel it is our right to express our opinions freely and without fear, without being marked as traitors. Our citizenship is not conditional. Only recognition of our complex position and unconditional acceptance will provide an opportunity for a new period in relations between Jews and Arabs in Israel.

While the political situation is complex, the moral stance must be clear. Whether I am Jewish or Arab, I must cling to both possibilities at once. Moral clarity together with political complexity will allow us to extricate ourselves from the binary situation and propose possibilities for a different, shared existence. In the absence of a moral stance and recognition of the political complexity, each side will become entrenched in its own position and pain without the possibility of recovery or resolution. We must level our gaze at the future to extricate ourselves from the current situation.

Only if we succeed in humanizing the story and viewing each other as equals, only if we understand the pain of Jewish mothers and Palestinian mothers (and fathers) alike, only then will we be able to release ourselves from the dichotomy of good versus bad and create the hope that is so desperately needed today. The radical hope of a shared Jewish–Arab future.

Hannah Safran
Chapter 22: If Not Now, When? Time for a Feminist Peace Vision

December 3, 2023

> **Hannah Safran**, PhD, is a lesbian, peace, and feminist activist. She turned to the study of feminist history and activism after years of working at Isha L'Isha, the Haifa Feminist Center. Her research on the Jewish suffrage movement in 1920 and the feminist movement in Israel in the 1970s was published in 2006. She has taught gender and women's studies at different academic institutions and is now dedicating her time to promoting research at the Haifa Feminist Institute, including a feminist library and archives. She has been active in the anti-occupation women's movement, demonstrating every Friday since 1988 with Women in Black, and was a founding member of the Women's Coalition for Peace. Her writings include articles on lesbian activism since the 1980s, the history of gender studies in the academy, the history of the women's peace movement, and more.

Following the development of the Israel–Hamas war in the fall of 2023, is it possible to imagine a future for people in Palestine and Israel when one is moving between anger, frustration, despair, and hopelessness? I turn to a feminist vision to find a different perspective and imagine other possibilities for people to exist and share their lives. To look for a worldview that is in absolute negation to the reality currently unfolding.

The basic idea of feminism, that man and woman are equal and deserve equality, is so simple and yet impossible to achieve. Thousands of years of society's structures are standing in the way. The struggle between Israeli Jews and the Palestinians is similar. Around 140 years of Zionist settlement makes it difficult to look at Palestinians and Jews as equals. But the only way for us all to survive is to practice equality. It has to be possible.

The war caught me in New York City, which makes going to demonstrate so much more difficult, worrying as I do about getting arrested in a foreign country and standing in the bitter cold weather. Although it is so important, I have decided not to join the demonstration demanding a ceasefire and a return of the hostages. It is a strange feeling. I have been attending demonstrations in Haifa (Israel/Palestine), where I usually live, for the last thirty-five years. Demonstrating endlessly against the occupation, for social justice, for women's rights and for LGBTQ rights.

We hear the news of the approaching ceasefire and the promised return of those kidnapped to Gaza. Is going to a demonstration important at all? Demonstrating might not change reality but it does help us, ordinary people, to keep going. I do need to keep going. It took the Israeli government forty-nine days to start returning

https://doi.org/10.1515/9783111435046-023

the hostages, and this move was due largely to the mounting pressure of the demonstrations by the hostages' families. The pressure was not loud enough or strong enough for this to happen on the first day of the war. Yet demonstrations are our way to be in community with each other, to feel the power of a group, the anger and frustration of the group, and to communicate with the people around us.

Feminist, antiwar (and antiviolence) women, and the men who join us, are capable of creating a new vision for humanity. This is particularly important in the present crisis, as the right wing has a messianic vision for a Greater Jewish Israel based on biblical law. Hundreds of thousands of Israelis went out to the streets around the country in an attempt to stop the usurpation of power promoted by the government in the last ten months leading to the current crisis. What is at stake now has a direct relationship to women's status in our society. Jewish supremacy and patriarchal theocracy are the goals of the current right-wing government in Israel.

Thus, we have no choice. This is exactly the time for a feminist vision. Having a vision for peace in a time of war, fear, anxiety, and anger is bordering on a sense of "hutzpah." A rare form of daring in spite of it all. In this war, there are people—Israeli and Palestinian women, men, and children—who are struggling to stay alive. Feminism requires me to see people behind the groups to which they belong, and to insist that we have enough in common. People might not listen, people might disagree, and some might use an extreme form of violence to make you (me) shut up.

Now, "DAVKA" now, especially, I will persist. I will insist. I am not willing to give up my hope and dream for a different and better world. If we can offer a vision for a better world, it will allow us fresh air to breathe. It is so difficult to breathe in times of war.

There are many things unknown and unexplained in the present war unleashed by Hamas and continued by Israel. One thing is known for sure. The road taken this time, while I write these thoughts, has been tried before and has failed terribly. No clear-thinking policy should pursue war if it has failed repeatedly to achieve peace.

Why was Gaza important in the pursuit of peace with the Palestinians? As the Gaza Strip became isolated under Israeli rule, the normal state of affairs became unbearable. Normal life in Gaza was not possible anymore. To what end are the lives of over 2 million people devastated? What political horizon remains open after such a devastation? What can the fear and anxiety suffered by Israeli Jews bring about?

All through the last decade I kept the news from Gaza and its surrounding area close to my heart. I traveled the length of Israel, joining demonstrations demanding a peaceful solution to the conflict. To no avail. Then that horrific Saturday arrived, and its aftermath. This has been a disaster for everyone in the region. I, like many others, continue to feel shock, anger, and frustration. These feelings have led Israelis to call for revenge and for the total destruction of Palestinian lives in Gaza. This is not only immoral; it is a road that leads to devastation for both sides. We desperately need a different solution.

In 2018, we at the Haifa Feminist Center, Isha L'Isha, came together with Physicians for Human Rights to help Palestinian women diagnosed with cancer. As there is no adequate treatment available for these women in the Gaza Strip, they needed to get permission to cross to East Jerusalem. We had to organize meetings to raise public awareness of the plight of these women and help reach the people with the power to issue permits. As a result, 90% of women were allowed to enter Jerusalem and receive the necessary treatment. However, this achievement did not improve the overall health disparities in Gaza. The fact that over 2 million people are not able to access basic medical services was obvious.

Since the First Intifada in 1988, the women's peace movement in Israel has been demanding an end to the occupation and a political solution to the conflict. Women have organized in many and differing ways to oppose war as the only way to resolve conflict in the narrow strip of land between the river and the sea. From Women in Black and the Coalition of Women for Peace, who started in 1988, to the current Women Waging Peace of today, which started in 2014 soon after one of the many wars against Gaza, women have been demanding peace to enable life.

We must insist that negotiations can lead us down a different path than violent engagement. Feminist ideas on war have been discussed in the past hundred years by many thinkers. Virginia Woolf laid out her feminist approach to war in the book *Three Guineas* (1938) when she postulated that "We will be able to prevent war in the best way not by repeating your words and your methods but by finding new words and new methods ... Our common target is to ensure the right of everyone, men and women, to respect the ideals of justice, equality and freedom."[1] In Israel, the writer Orna Coussin published an essay called "More Than Three Guineas or: Feminism Will Prevent the (Next) War," calling for inclusion of women in the day-to-day management of the current situation. The special point of view that women can add to the running of the country is necessary in order to achieve peace.

Following these and many other feminist peace theorists, what can a feminist vision offer and why is it so important? If we are to remain alive, between the River Jordan and the Mediterranean Sea, we have to guarantee equal rights to all those living here. I know that basic human rights, a given to anyone living in

---

[1] Woolf (1938), p. 131.

the West and supporting Israel, is not a given when it comes to the lives of Palestinians and Israelis. Extreme groups on both sides wish for the entire country to belong to them. This will not work. For the rest of us, the only way to survive is to think of ways to share this land with equality, generosity, and humility.

Three weeks ago, in a Zoom meeting held by the High Commission of the Palestinians within Israel, 400 people, Jewish and Palestinians, committed themselves (ourselves) to working together for a sustainable society based on equality and freedom. The struggle today is not between Jews and Palestinians; it is the struggle between those who hold a vision of religious domination and those who share humane compassion and love.

We need more leaders whose ideals are not a result of a holy book, of power and control, but the lived reality of experience: women who will not give up the desire for life and compassion. Men who are ready to forgo macho manhood for ideals of caring and loving. For that, I am ready to start demonstrating again. If what we are seeing now in Gaza and the West Bank is not aimed at genocide against the Palestinians, or as pure aimless revenge, then the only way out of the current horror is to envisage a shared future for both peoples. Sharing the land between the river and the sea in equality, dignity, and mutual respect. [Update: Hannah returned to Haifa and continues to oppose the war and to demand the return of the hostages.]

Tanya Zion-Waldoks and Galit Cohen-Kedem
Chapter 23: On Hope I: In Search of Generational Hope

November 2023

> **Tanya Zion-Waldoks**, PhD, is an associate professor in the Seymour Fox School of Education at the Hebrew University of Jerusalem. Her areas of research and teaching are religion, gender and education, feminist and anti-racist activism, and qualitative methodologies. She completed her doctorate at Bar-Ilan University, and postdoctoral studies at Ben-Gurion University of the Negev and at Princeton University, supported by the Rothschild (YadhaNadiv) Fellowship and ISF (Israel Science Foundation). She is co-author of the book *Holy Rebellion: Religious Feminism and the Transformation of Judaism and Women's Rights in Israel* (Brandeis University Press, 2024). Tanya is a feminist activist and lives in the Negev with her husband and four children.
> Rabbi **Galit Cohen-Kedem** holds a BA in Hebrew Language and Literature from the Hebrew University of Jerusalem and an MA from Bar-Ilan University's Gender Studies Program. Ordained as a rabbi at HUC Jerusalem in November 2014, she founded and currently leads Congregation Kodesh V'Chol in Holon, established in October 2010. Dedicated to her roles as a rabbi, wife, and mother of three, Rabbi Galit brings a wealth of knowledge and passion to her community, fostering innovative cultural and educational municipal projects that connect spirituality and contemporary Israeli life.

Speaking of Hope

Tanya's story:

When first asked to write an essay about hope, I refused. I have no words, I explained. I still don't. How to reach for hope when there is so much raw pain and so little air? In the relentless grip of daily trauma, compounded with each passing hour, hope seemed to have gotten buried under the debris of lost lives, fractured by shattered hearts and broken limbs. Amid such brutality and terror, hope was rapidly seeping away like blood from an untreated wound, leaving us weaker and emptier, so that even our yearnings for better days lacked a life force. Yet aren't these precisely the moments when nurturing hope is most essential?

A deep ache in my womb has reawakened, reminding me that I have encountered such questions before. I was grieving the sudden death of my adopted-mother and mentor when I birthed my first child, I nearly died while birthing my fourth. I have learned that life and death—the wild existential powers that symbolize infinite hope and excruciating loss, the greatest joys and greatest dangers—are intertwined, intermingled, overwhelming us in their painful embrace of one another.

Committed to finding words that might rekindle the scarce resource of hope, I invited my beloved and wise friend Galit to a shared, tentative exploration. We debated, developed, and wrote the whole text collaboratively, yet chose to maintain a first-person perspective in parts of the essay, to honor the intimacy of the personal experiences that drive our narrative.

As we were completing this essay, we experienced a rare pause in the fighting that allowed some—though not enough—abducted children, women, mothers and grandmothers, to finally return home to their families. Despite a dreadful sense that the light in the world was being forcefully diminished by hate, violence, and hubris, a glimmer of hope had emerged.

Cradling Capsules of Hope

> With each birth, a new beginning is born into the world, a new world has potentially come into being.
> (Hannah Arendt, 1973.
> *The Origins of Totalitarianism*)[1]

Galit's story:

On October 7, a new soul entered the world, just as outside a war raged. The new mother, having eagerly anticipated the birth of her first child, now spends her days breastfeeding while watching the news. "I nurse and cry," she tells me, "my tears wetting my daughter's face." She fears for her brother, with whom she shared a womb, now a reservist fighting in Gaza. Cradling new life amidst the looming menace of death, she struggles to grant herself permission to embrace the vulnerable joy this moment holds. "Everyone is broken, grieving, displaced, shocked. Sometimes it feels wrong for me to rejoice in this small miracle when everything around us is so dark. What country did I bring her into? What world?" She lets out a sigh, and I join her.

Traditionally recited after one survives a dangerous experience, the Jewish blessing of recompense (*hagomel*) is often recited by mothers after giving birth: "Blessed is the one who rewards the undeserving with goodness, who has reward-

---

[1] Arendt (1973), p. 465.

ed me with all this goodness." The assembled community responds: "Amen, may the one who rewarded you with goodness, recompense you with every good thing, forever." This blessing promises that order can be restored after trauma, that we can be healed through a communal embrace that affirms that all is well, and that we live in a world that eventually rewards good deeds. But this young mother questions such closure—she is still in the thick of danger, she feels undeserving of celebration. She is stranded in limbo, caught between life and death, far from a safe shore. In the midst of a national and regional rift, she lashes out against "the one who rewards," asking: Why do I deserve all this goodness if you won't reward the others? What have they done to deserve their fates? How can I assure my daughter the world welcoming her is good? Her questions reverberate in the air.

In Greek tradition, the womb (*hystera*) is the source of unfounded and unruly anxiety—hysteria. The Jewish narrative, however, imagines the womb (*rekhem*) as the wellspring of mercy (*rakhamim*). The corporeal womb harbors the latent ability to bring forth new life. The metaphorical womb urges us to grow, to transcend our confines and reach toward another creature with compassion. It bids us to envelop others' sorrows, carry their humanity within us, and nurture their needs. The regenerating lining of the womb symbolizes a renewable source of optimism, a cycle that unfurls afresh. Seemingly indifferent to external circumstances, new layers of tissue are created monthly, a testament to the ceaseless possibility of vitality. Rarely, the womb absorbs a kernel around which it will extend and expand, enfolding a nascent cell in a protective cocoon. It will offer the delicate new life an embrace that shields and nurtures it even as it divides and develops in preparation to depart and face the world. Much more often, menstruation comes, and the uterus contracts to usher forth a tide of blood, allowing its passage and release. The tally of a woman's pregnancies fades in comparison with the frequent rhythms of her menstrual cycles. Despite this apparent futility, the body persists in its unwavering belief in potentiality, cultivating in humanity a consciousness of creativity, continuity, and compassion. The womb generates hope by consistently practicing the ebb and flow of care for a mysterious future, encapsulating yet-to-be-imagined prospects. Fertility, at its core, like education, is rooted in hope, in the relentless pursuit of actualizing a reality that reaches beyond one's self and beyond the here and now.

But this is not merely a romanticized story about female anatomy. Like Noah's ark, swaying amidst the flood's watery extinction; like Moses' basket, shielding an infant from the terror of a tyrant's annihilation, or the spacecraft that delivers Superman to Earth: we surround ourselves with cultural narratives about a life-saving womb dispatched to cradle us in a turbulent world. Retelling these narratives helps us oscillate between hope and despair. They are a cushioned capsule of hope to hold onto as we cry and nurse.

"I have set before you life and death, the blessings and the curses; therefore choose life, that you and your descendants may live" (Deut. 30:19)

Tanya's story:

November 16, 2023. As the tears of anger, grief, and despair threaten to spill forth, and I feel my throat tighten once again, I remind myself of how yesterday's tears tasted slightly different, lightly spiced with pride and hope. I had just learned that my eleven-year-old son, Netta, posted a letter in the "compassion corner" at his Jewish-Arab school in Beer Sheva, just 40 km from the Gaza border. He had drawn a dove with an olive branch in its beak, and its outstretched wings boasted Israeli and Palestinian flags. The picture seemed so out of place in the current political circumstances that it only stirred in me a sense of sadness and futility. However, above it, he scrawled a note which felt like a fragile and powerful offering of hope. Addressing his letter to "all the innocent children," Netta wrote: "You really need help and we are trying to help. If we could help, we would. We care and we want to help. But, for now, you need to survive! So don't stop believing. You will succeed." Netta was refusing to do what adults do almost every day: shield ourselves by ignoring others' pain, especially when we can't, or don't know how to, alleviate their suffering or fear. Instead, he engaged with the sense of helplessness. Writing from one innocent child to another, with wisdom beyond his years, Netta acknowledged there may be traumatic times when all you can do is survive, when merely hanging on consumes all your energy—at such times success means you have not yet stopped believing.

It is tempting to end this story here, with a letter both heartbreaking and heartwarming. But a few nights later, I awoke to find Netta shaken by my bedside. "I had a nightmare," he tearfully recounted, "there was someone outside our house. I opened the window and asked if I could help him. He turned, trained a gun on me, and shot me." Is this where the story ends? With the shattered innocence and breakdown of trust? Is it merely innocent and naive to suggest, especially at times like this, that mutual destruction is not the only conceivable conclusion to our lives here in this bloody, shared, and contested land? In a reality where fear of being killed in your own home becomes standard, where hate is a pedagogical preference, and violence or revenge are celebrated as a legitimate way of life, practicing compassion and enabling Jewish and Arab schoolchildren to share everyday lives becomes a radical act of hope.

When the Bible urges us to "choose life," it promotes a belief in the value of life and in cultivating lives worth living. Therefore, hope is an imperative—neither a choice nor a luxury. Hope is an existential need, a vital—life-giving and life-preserving—force. Hope is a theological stance, a subversive act that requires moral commitment. In his reflections on how to heal a fractured world, Rabbi Lord Jonathan Sacks argued: "Optimism and hope are not the same. Optimism is the belief that the world is changing for the better; hope is the belief that, together, we can make the world better. Optimism is a passive virtue, hope an active one. It needs no courage to be an optimist, but it takes a great deal of courage to hope."[2] Hope is the opposite of innocent naivete. It requires courage, because nurturing it can be quite a painful and painstaking undertaking.

Yellow Balloons

Tanya's story:

It is mid-November 2023; over five weeks have passed since everything changed. It feels like forever ago, and like one endless day. My day began when I dropped my eight-year-old son off at a local bomb shelter, where he was to finally meet his teacher and friends for a few rare hours of so-called school after several weeks of staying home. Our home, where our bodies and minds are caught in an unsustainable state of constant alert. We warily listen for sirens warning us of rockets aimed at our homes; and hear with mixed emotions the near-constant droning of military planes flying overhead, heading to drop bombs on our Gazan neighbors, 40 km away.

As I prepared to leave the parking lot, the radio blared to life and I learned that Itay Hadar (twenty-seven), whom I remembered for his warm smile and eternal guitar, had been murdered weeks ago with his girlfriend at a rave that took place on October 7. His body had only recently been identified. Time folded in on itself. Itay was a well-known local activist, promoting food security and social justice. His nickname was "Houston," as in "Houston, we have a problem!" because he joked he was in fact a compulsive problem-solver.

By noon, I had moved on to the funeral of feminist peace activist Vivian Silver, who had been assumed kidnapped for over a month, though it was later discov-

---

2 Sacks (2007), p. 166.

ered she had been viciously murdered in her home in Kibbutz Be'eri on October 7. Looking around the hundreds of gathered mourners, I marveled at the diversity of faiths and nationalities in the crowd, at the hijabs, the kippot, and the white shirts and blue scarves that serve as the "uniform" of "Women Wage Peace." Look, a friend said to me, we came to mark her brutal death but are celebrating her life.

Her son's eulogy eloquently merged this sense of hope and grief: "Not only have I become orphaned," he said, "this land is orphaned, the movement for peace has become orphaned. But don't worry, [Mother,] we—the living—will rise from our mourning and will work even harder to bring the tomorrow you spoke of. With your passing I have fallen in love again with the words 'peace, gender equality, and solidarity'."

An hour later, exhausted, Galit and I sat down at a café on a busy city street in the center of the country to try and string words together toward this essay. Unexpectedly, within a few minutes, the mood on the street shifted. Hundreds of strangers wrapped in Israeli flags and holding yellow balloons began streaming in, lining the streets in solidarity. They quietly awaited the arrival of a procession of hundreds of citizens whose family members were taken hostage by Hamas. Down the street we began hearing the swell of call and response: "Bring them home—NOW! Every last one—NOW!" Families of those abducted were commanding, begging, leaders they no longer trusted to do the right thing: to care. They were marching together, carrying photos of their loved ones to Jerusalem, to remind the government of its moral priority and its duties. This street, this town, was merely a tragic detour. They had come to pay their respects at the home of the Marciano family whose kidnapped daughter, Noa (nineteen), had just been pronounced dead. As we stood, tears in our eyes, we wondered how to make sense of this uniquely intimate public gathering. This was not quite a funeral, not quite a political protest, not quite a memorial, not quite a public prayer service. It felt like a spontaneous ritual that was creating a community of those who came to share their respect for the value of human life. A gathering for those who were lost, and for those who are lost beyond the borders, and for the sake of what must never be lost. They were taking a stand by standing shoulder to shoulder—for others, for themselves, for the hope that hope itself might be recovered.

It was yet another example of the incredible solidarity that Israeli citizens—both Jews and Arabs—have shown one another since the beginning of the war. Driven by sheer willpower and incredible tenacity, citizens have been organizing at every level to support and enable the maintenance of civil society. These efforts are a source of pride and outrage, since they highlight the staggering absence, ineffectiveness, and blatant disregard of the government, and the near-total collapse of the public sector and Israel's social welfare network.

In fact, the sense of collapse was emotional, structural, moral, and cognitive. In the fallout from October 7, everyone seemed to agree that most—if not all—preconceptions had crumbled, even if there was some disagreement about what these misconceptions were. That everything must be reimagined or rebuilt might sound like a revolutionary's utopia. However, for most regular people, invested in our everyday lives and relationships, a total collapse of preconceptions is a terrifying trauma that undermines anything but fight, flight, or freeze. Still, could the shaking up of conceptions generate opportunities? We have long been lulled into thinking that the status quo is all that is possible: that conflict is eternal, pain is inevitable, and the best—and only—thing we can do is manage them. But that no longer seems possible. Perhaps it is that very impossibility that might breed a different, radical, kind of hope for change?

***

We call on hope when the social order as we know it seems desperately incapable of reordering itself. Hope encapsulates a belief, a trust, a faith, in some force that is beyond current reality, that holds the potential for the impossible to breach what is possible. Such a concept of hope is predicated on acknowledging the limits of human agency, and on embracing the chaotic, unpredictable existence of the unforeseeable. Yet it is also a belief that something else, beneficial and positive, lies hidden at the edge of our current understandings and capacities. Such hope is a seemingly unwarranted but necessary investment in the unimaginable, a fervent insistence that such a future is, despite everything we now know and experience, inevitable. It is in essence a collaborative, shared, communal, and contagious endeavor. It draws its power from transcending any one individual desire, yet drawing together people's utmost and most deeply held human desires. Hope itself, when translated into human action and solidarity, generates more hope.

Despair is often considered an absence of hope. Hope and despair seem to have divergent energies and directions—where one lifts us up, another crushes us; where one draws us together, the other curls us inwards, distancing and detaching us from the world; where one mobilizes action, the other empties us of motivation and stills movement. Yet perhaps these are not quite opposites. For just as disappointment reveals the existence of unmet expectations, despair—in contrast with apathy—carries evidence of a lingering echo of hope. Despair is linked to hope like a shadow that trails alongside a flickering candle. It might feel like a gaping abyss, threatening to swallow us whole, yet it secretly urges us not to release our precarious grasp on hope and to take just one more tiny step forward.

Fig. 3: A yellow balloon at the march for the return of the hostages, Modi'in, November 16th, 2023. Photo credit: Tanya Zion-Waldoks.

Fig. 4: March for the return of the hostages, Modi'in, November 16th, 2023. Photo credit: Tanya Zion-Waldoks.

David Grossman, Israeli author and peace activist, who lost his youngest son Uri on the last day of the 2006 war between Israel and Hezbollah in Lebanon, said recently: "One could look at hope as a sort of 'anchor,' cast from a stifled, desperate existence, toward a better, freer future. Toward a reality that does not yet exist, which is made up mostly of wishes. Of imagination. When the anchor is cast, it takes hold of the future, and human beings—sometimes an entire society— begin to pull themselves toward it."[3]

Grossman imagines hope as an anchor. Perhaps sometimes it is a yellow balloon suspended in the air, being pulled in opposite directions by powerful forces; yet connected by a fragile string grasped by a collective of strangers who spend their days helping one another cope with disrupted lives, attending funerals of lost believers, and demanding freedom for the hostages: NOW.

---

[3] Grossman (2023).

Wrestlers: Israelis with Blessings and Scars

Galit's story:

As a community rabbi, I have the honor of guiding young boys and girls through the Jewish coming-of-age ceremony. I engage in studying the weekly parsha—the biblical verses read traditionally in the week of their birth according to the Hebrew calendar—with teenage boys, girls, and their parents. My rabbinical challenge lies in weaving meaningful connections between the ancient text and the immediate interests and realities of Israeli teenagers' lives today. This week, the eighth week of the war, I was privileged to mark a significant milestone for an insightful boy born in Holon to parents who immigrated from the former Soviet Union in the 1990s. Despite the absence of a structured Jewish education, the boy's parents have discovered a unique interest in learning.

This week's Torah portion recounts the story of how Jacob's name was changed to Israel. Jacob (*Yaakov*), so named for grabbing his twin brother's heel (*akev*) in a recurring bid to become the firstborn and secure a blessing and a birthright, embodies a tale of struggle, transformation, and resilience. In one poignant incident, Jacob wrestles with a mysterious counterpart until dawn, sustaining an injury which will forever leave him limping, but also emerging victorious with a blessing and a new name. This transformative encounter takes place in the in-between space of a riverbank, in the shadowlands of the terror-filled dark of night, symbolizing a link between the physical and transcendent reality. Jacob's past, present, and future journeys, and all his earthly struggles over recognition, love, belonging, and power get played out, as a rite of passage, with the divine. The story serves as a reminder that the Jewish narrative is one of a people continually rising and falling, embodying hope in the face of adversity.

One evening, during our joint study sessions, the Bar Mitzvah boy's father posed a profound question: "Do you think it is our destiny to fight? And will this limp never be forgotten?" In essence, he asked: Is there hope?

Indeed, regrettably, some have interpreted this story as evidence that Israel's destiny is an eternal fight. I reject this interpretation as dangerous. Portraying Israel as always on the verge of extinction, as a permanent survivor or victim, as a reluctant fighter, perpetuates militaristic and sacrificial traits that make me concerned for our ability to build a viable future. It hinders us from recognizing how some of our actions are those of an aggressor, and assumes one can either be conqueror or victim, even as it blurs the lines between defense and aggression. Such interpretations lend themselves to zealotry and righteous certainty which— too often coupled with violence—do not allow us to recognize others' humanity, or our own.

I, however, read this story through a Hasidic lens, interpreting it as an opportunity for self-reflection on how, in our darkest hours, we might come to see both our shadows and the others whom we encounter in a new light. This narrative tells of a struggle in which we tumble over and into one another—wrestling and embracing until dawn, since neither partner could vanquish and overpower the other. We then emerge with a blessing, a new name, and a lifelong limp. The story reflects on the blessed power of our scars: how we pass on both generational trauma, the emotional and physical burden of our fears, pains and losses; and generational hope, the practice of striving for resilience, for actions that rebuild trust, human capacities, and faith. "Your name will no longer be Jacob, but Israel, because you have struggled with God and with humans and have overcome" (Genesis 32:28). The "other" has not been vanquished. What has been overcome is despair.

The Israeli response of *"yihiyeh beseder"*—it will be fine—is a frustrating colloquialism that belittles and dismisses calls for accountability or for a strategic course of action. Perhaps, however, a more generous interpretation would see this mindset as a belief that even the most intractable problems will work out, somehow. Perhaps it is Jacob's legacy, an ingrained hope that even in darkness and difficulty, Israel will cope, wrestle, and become a blessing to itself and unto others. The symbolic lameness, akin to the "Achilles' heel," serves as a reminder of our vulnerabilities, and injects complexity into the masculinist national ethos. Being inherently, generationally, blessedly disabled fosters a cultural commitment to building unforeseen alternative pathways. The name Israel is an eternal reminder that in our struggles we must seek to recognize that when facing the other, "to see your face is like seeing the face of God" (Genesis 33:10).

***

Israelis know about intergenerational trauma, about being the children and grandchildren of hardened and hurting survivors. Perhaps we are also now learning something about intergenerational hope, about being the harbingers of a fragile, vulnerable, generative hope. What would tomorrow—or today—look like if we practiced regenerating compassion and expanding our wombs, even as we struggle? What if we rebuild ourselves and our collectives by taking on the most intimate and political of practices: laboring to nurture images, words, and actions of hope in our everyday lives? By facing this crisis while also facing one another, with all our vulnerabilities, cares, and strengths, we might begin to generate some freshly imagined futures.

Fig. 5: Protest for the return of the hostages, Beer Sheva, Jan 4th, 2024. Photo credit: Tanya Zion-Waldoks.

Avi Shilon
Chapter 24: On Hope II: Hope in Days of Despair

November 30, 2023

> **Avi Shilon**, PhD, is a historian who specializes in the field of Israel studies. He is the author of *Menachem Begin: A Life* (Yale University Press, 2013), *Ben-Gurion: His Later Years in the Political Wilderness* (Rowman & Littlefield, 2016), and *The Decline of the Left Wing in Israel: Yossi Beilin and the Politics of the Peace Process* (I.B. Tauris, 2020). Shilon has taught courses at NYU, Columbia, Rutgers and the Hebrew University and is currently a senior lecturer at the Tel-Hai Academic College in Israel, and the editor of the non-fiction department at Am-Oved Publishing House. He also writes op-ed columns for *Yedioth Ahronoth* newspaper.

Few have given deep thought to the significance of the Hamas massacre occurring on one of the most "Jewish" days in our calendar—Simchat Torah. In contrast to other holidays, like Hanukkah or Lag BaOmer, which were adopted by Zionism and even underwent changes to suit the modern national era in Jewish history, Simchat Torah is a holiday devoid of national orientation. It is primarily about rejoicing in the completion of the Torah readings throughout the passing year and the excitement of starting the cycle anew. You can read the Torah anywhere—not just in the Land of Israel. In fact, Simchat Torah is the religious holiday most celebrated by secular Israelis, who for most of the year do not engage in Torah study—but on that day, at least some of them join the local joyous processions held throughout the country with Torah scrolls.

It's likely that Hamas was less concerned about the significance of Simchat Torah. Its leaders chose to attack at this time due to the proximity of the date to the fiftieth anniversary of the Yom Kippur War, where Egyptian and Syrian armies surprised Israel on Friday, October 6, 1973. However, what Hamas managed to do, beyond the horrific massacre and kidnappings, was to restore Israelis to being Jews. There was a distinctly Jewish feeling in Israel during the days following the attack. This feeling primarily stemmed from the failure of the IDF to protect the residents of southern Israel bordering Gaza. If Zionism was intended to change the passive status of Jews in the diaspora and ensure their security in their homeland, on October 7 it seemed that the Zionist state was powerless to do so. I do not recall any time in the past when the association with the days of the Holocaust, or at least the era of pogroms—like the one that occurred in Kishinev precisely 120 years ago[1]—was so present and natural in Israel.

The very Jewish feeling in Israel intensified when it seemed that a second front might develop: a war with Hezbollah, Iran's proxy in Lebanon. The founding father of the state, David Ben-Gurion, said in his final speech in the Knesset that one of Zionism's achievements lies in the development of our ability to rely on our strength.[2] Yet in the first week after the Hamas attack, all eyes were turned specifically toward the White House, hoping to gain the support of Uncle Sam. The fact that the American superpower came to our aid and provided military backing alongside President Biden's visit to the country was touching. But simultaneously, it raised further reflections on Zionist weakness.

The very Jewish feeling in Israel intensified even more in light of reports of anti-Semitism around the world and on campuses in the United States—where it was not difficult to notice that the protests were also a kind of celebration, whether conscious or not, against Israel. Otherwise, it's difficult to understand why precisely at a time when one could expect at least some empathy with Israel and its pain, hatred and disgust were expressed toward it.

Two days after the attack, I wandered around central Tel Aviv. Few people were on the streets, and those that were seemed weary. Against the backdrop of sirens warning of rockets from Gaza and a Tel Aviv already scarred due to construction of the subway, a profound sense of national defeat was prevalent. I recalled a famous sentence that opens the book *Refuge* by the Jewish-Iraqi author Sami Michael: "If Israel is destroyed, what will future generations remember from it?"

What, indeed? That is a good question to reflect upon.

***

But Israel has not been destroyed, nor will it be destroyed so quickly. (Even though the country is in its seventy-fifth year, and we should remember that the ancient kingdoms of Israel in the past did not survive more than eighty years.) October 7 reaffirmed, as mentioned, the Jewish identity of many Israelis; and the return to Judaism is also an opportunity for a deep and new debate on questions that Zionism has neglected. That is the great hope I hold onto, even though for almost two months now, we've been living in constant dread, with reports of abducted infants

---

[1] Zipperstein (2018).
[2] Ben-Gurion (1971).

and vanished families, alongside an unprecedented number of casualties in Gaza as a result of Israel's response.

The hope I have stems from an expectation of a soul-searching process that will awaken Israel. Hamas's attack should not only be analyzed through military perspectives, or solely through the history of the conflict. The massacre must primarily be understood against the backdrop of a moral breakdown that has occurred in Israel in recent years. The neoliberal logic that infiltrated all spheres of life led us to prefer comfortable lives, to rely on technology as a means of defense, even as there was a clear moral and ethical decline in the political sphere and throughout society. In recent years, we thought we could go through five election cycles within just four years(!) over a personal question—whether you are for or against Bibi—without understanding that if we don't address the right questions, even if we get rid of the most narcissistic prime minister Israel has ever had, we will remain in the same stagnant place.

But now we can no longer avoid providing answers to the questions reality has imposed on Israelis of all backgrounds. Right-wing individuals cannot help but wonder why, precisely when Israel has its most radical right-wing government, it has been plunged into its greatest weakness. Conversely, what can left-wing Zionism offer to us, given that after Israel dismantled the settlements around the Gaza Strip as part of its disengagement in 2005, Hamas targeted kibbutzim and settlements inside the Green Line?

These questions also touch on Israel's military policy: while these lines are being written, the war is in its seventh week; at least the northern part of the Gaza Strip has been heavily bombarded by the IDF, and thousands have been killed. Raef Zreik, an Arab-Israeli philosopher and a friend, wrote to me in sorrow to say that what Hamas did is horrifying, and he does not intend to discuss the proportionality in Israel's response; but, he added, Israel is currently immersed in blood, and with no glimpse of hope for the future, it will be impossible to maintain proper relationships between Arabs and Jews. I thought a lot about his words and did not know how to answer.

***

I believe that Israel needs to continue fighting until Hamas's ability to rule is eliminated. At the same time, I know that more deaths in Gaza are not the solution, neither morally nor politically. Ethical issues should be reconsidered: is it possible to strive for the elimination of Hamas and ignore the price of the lives that will be taken from innocent civilians in Gaza? Therefore, is the moral obligation to stop the war? Or, on the contrary, is the moral duty and challenge now is to acknowledge that there's no good without evil and that Israel must increase its attacks? In other words, what is more ethical: to take a clear side, contrary to our intellectual tendency, as otherwise no deep change can be instigated? Or is it precisely the time to delve deeper into a more complex perspective? And overall, why isn't Hamas considered a common enemy for Palestinians and Israelis seeking peace alike?

Some optimism can be drawn from a close examination of the relations between Jews and Arabs within Israel since Hamas's attack. A surprising calm prevails in the mixed cities and throughout the country since the massacre. Many Arab Israelis are volunteering and expressing support for the release of the hostages. I think it reflects authentic revulsion at Hamas's cruelty among Palestinian citizens of Israel. Perhaps the Palestinian people are now divided about their path in a way they have never been before, and this too could have implications for the future of coexistence.

***

I conclude this writing as the first groups of hostages begin to return to Israel amid the ceasefire. Similarly to other parents of young children, we didn't tell our children what was really happening on October 7. We just talked about the rockets. When the streets were filled with images of the hostages, my five-year-old son, Roee, asked who they were. Initially, I told him they were heroes living near Gaza. After some time, he directly asked me if I knew that Hamas kidnaps children.

The trauma will remain—but as the images of the captives and their families tear our hearts, they also present us with a human splendor reminiscent of the pioneers of Zionist activity. The calm, the restraint, and the dignity of the returnees from captivity—one of the hostages, Adina Moshe, seventy-two, even demanded that they first release a woman older than her—offer a moving human vision.

Populist and pseudo-intellectual discourse has spread in Israel in recent years, particularly regarding the struggle of "First Israel against Second Israel"—meaning the struggle of Mizrahim, Jews from Muslim countries, lacking privileges, against Ashkenazim, Jews of European descent, who hold these privileges. Although there is indeed a need for a mending of relations within Jewish-Israeli society, the proponents of the "First Israel against Second Israel" thesis did not seek to advance equality. Instead, they served a government that worked to secure its continued political might by creating social rifts and fissures.

Therefore, much of what we have heard and read in recent years about the kibbutzim members and the residents of development towns like Ofakim, who were affected together in Hamas's attack, touched on confrontations and accusations of discrimination and condescension. The contribution of the kibbutzim to the establishment of the state was almost forgotten, and the domestic debate in Israel focused mainly on their privileges.

Ofir Toubul, editor of Avishay Ben Haim's book, who was among those who promoted the "First Israel against Second Israel" thesis, has already expressed regret. "I feel that identity politics," he said, "contributed to the very vulnerable place that invited the external attack." It's likely that Hamas's attack would have occurred anyway. However, Toubul is correct in pointing out that we weakened ourselves through domestic conflicts. The image of emotional residents of Ofakim who went out to welcome the kibbutz children and women returning from captivity is so far the first victory in the war—a victory over the unnecessary factionalism and hatred that has developed in Israel. It's time to eliminate it fully.

No, it can't be that the emotional turmoil we're experiencing won't affect us. Israel will change! I believe that, in the spirit of Hannah Arendt's call after World War II to engage in practical public activity and not just theoretical philosophy, good people from all streams will join a journey of domestic soul-searching—a journey that will eventually lead to positive developments between Israelis and Palestinians.

Hagar Kotef and Merav Amir

Chapter 25: On Hope III: Terms of (Dis)engagement—Critique and Solidarity After October 7

November, 2023

Hagar Kotef, PhD, is Professor of Political Theory at SOAS, University of London. She is the author of *The Colonizing Self: Home and Homelessness in Israel/Palestine* (2020) and *Movement and the Ordering of Freedom* (2015), both published by Duke University Press.
Merav Amir, PhD, is Senior Lecturer (Associate Professor) in Political Geography at Queen's University Belfast. Her recent publications include "Post-occupation Gaza: Israel's war on Palestinian futures" (*Geografiska Annaler*, 2021), "Unfastening Israel's future from the occupation: Israeli plans for partial annexation of West Bank territory" (*Antipode*, 2023), and "Cartographic ignorance and the 1967 redrawing of the Israeli map" (*Environment and Planning F*, 2024).

A/symmetry

As Jewish Israelis who write critically about Palestine/Israel, we inhabit a world that has always been divided. Our sense of belonging, our attachments, our loved ones, are split across the "/" of Palestine/Israel. Residing in this split space and sustaining political alliances and affective attachments across the divide never implied that "the two sides" were symmetric or equivalent in any meaningful way, but it always meant there were two sides.

Over the years, one of these sides rarely emerged in our writing and activism as an object of concern and care. Given the radical imbalance in power, in means, capacities, and degrees of violence, and given the relations of domination between occupier and occupied, Israel was, above all, the *object of our critique*. While we never saw Israel purely and merely as a settler-colonial state (even though it is undoubtedly a state that is based on settler-colonial practices and upholds a settler-colonial structure); while we always assumed Jews should have some form of a safe haven in that territory (even though our critique did not stop at the occupation of 1967, and encompassed the injustice committed in and following 1948 as well, and as such called for a critical account of precisely such notions); while we never saw all Jewish Israelis as equally culpable (although we did see them as complicit and implicated in the project of dispossession), the gravity of our critical engagement—both theoretically and politically—has always been focused on what we saw as the most urgent violence and oppression to be addressed: the violence of the Israeli state. Our political critique of Israel thus allowed, perhaps, the fact that we sustain alliances across the divide to fade into the background. But on October 7, when Israeli civilians[1] were butchered,[2] molested,[3] tortured,[4] burned alive in their homes,[5] kidnapped,[6] and raped,[7] our duality, the "two sides" in us,

---

[1] Roughly 70% of those killed in the assault on October 7, 1266 in total, were civilians. The full list is available at: https://www.ynet.co.il/news/category/51693. Human Rights Watch (2023) documented and verified several of these incidents, classifying them as war crimes.

[2] Some of those who were murdered on that day were only identified months after the fact, often by teams of archeologists and anthropologists who had to sift through the rubble, since some of the bodies were severely dismembered and scattered (Shuster 2023, Boxerman 2023).

[3] Evidence has been found for many cases of genital mutilation, including castration, cutting vaginas and breasts, shooting at genitals, and stuffing genitals with objects. See for example Graham-Harrison (2023) and Williamson (2023).

[4] Reuters (2023), NBC (2023).

[5] The militants systematically set fire to houses to either burn the residents trapped inside or to force them to come out and surrender. See Kingsley et al. (2023).

[6] Overall, approximately 240 Israelis were taken hostage. The majority were captured by Hamas, but some were also taken by the Islamic Jihad and by unaffiliated groups. The vast majority of the hostages, around 220, were civilians, including elderly people, women, children, and babies. The youngest of them, Kefir Bibas, was nine months old at the time of his kidnapping; the oldest were eighty-five years old. According to testimonies given by some of those who were released, the conditions under which they were kept varied significantly, but almost all were deprived of access to basic necessities. Some of those conditions were a result of the harsh scarcities which the Israeli assault on the Strip has caused, such as food scarcity, poor water quality, and lack of medical provisions. But some of the conditions in captivity were evidently deliberate, such as depriving the hostages of regular access to toilets and separating children from their parents. There is also evidence that hostages have been tortured physically and mentally, and that some have been subjected to ongoing sexual violence. None of the captives were allowed visits by Red Cross representatives while being held captive. At the time of writing, 32 of the hostages have been pronounced dead, and 129 are still in captivity (BBC 2023).

[7] The substantial amount of evidence gathered thus far shows that sexual violence was used systematically and extensively by Hamas on October 7. The collection of forensic evidence was hampered due to several factors, predominantly the fact that most of the bodies were evacuated under fire while battles between the IDF and Hamas combatants were still ongoing. Moreover, many of the bodies were burned, blown to pieces, or dismembered to the degree that identifying them became an arduous task. Initially, the Israeli authorities also treated these areas as battlefields rather than as crime scenes, and the chaos characterizing the treatment of the collected bodies in the first hours and days further contaminated much of the forensic evidence. Still, the evidence gathered from witness testimonies, videos streamed in real time by Hamas militants, CCTV footage, and bodycam videos of first responders tells a decisive story of multiple instances of gang rape, genital mutilation, cutting of intimate body parts, and the parading of naked women who were taken into Gaza. Physicians for Human Rights Israel published one of the first systematic reports (Physicians for Human Rights Israel 2023). For an account of this report and its methods see Chotiner (2023). For some of the testimonies see Kottasová (2023). "We've collected by now 1,500 terrible testimo-

came to the fore. Our sense of devastation over what happened to our community has rendered our "other side" more visible, more vocal. It should be emphasized that our insistence on the facts of that day in no way implies that we justify the Israeli response, or that we vindicate Israel's brutal and vengeful attacks on Gaza. Indeed, this insistence and our critique of the war both emerge from the same political principles: we object to the massacring of civilians, to the bombardment or burning of homes on those residing in them, to the violent targeting of an entire population based on their identity. The scale is incomparable but the principle is similar. Moreover, to mark the events of the day for their particular brutality is to create a gap between what we see and always saw as legitimate resistance whose principle we can share, and the particularities of that specific attack; is to say why this time it was different from everything we saw before; why this time we were so deeply devastated.

What we knew to be the truth about that day, and this sense of devastation, however, were unfamiliar to many of our friends and colleagues on the left. The "two sides" in us—of us, which are us—were taken as asserting some imagined symmetry.
– How can you compare?

We did not compare. There is no comparison; how can one compare one sense of devastation to another? How can one bottomless pain, one infinite darkness, be equated to anything else—even to another bottomless pain, another infinite darkness? Relating to the "two sides" of these attacks and the war that followed did not reflect a shift in our alliances or a change in our political commitments. It reflected who we are, the duality we inhabit—our sense of belonging, our attachments, the people we love and communities we care about. What became clear is that each expression of this pain, any movement between the two sides, was seen as questioning our politics, the sincerity of our commitments. In other words, it violated, in some way, the unwritten terms of engagement.

Terms of Dis/engagement

Political action, Hannah Arendt argued, is a way in which the many act in concert. Part of its conditions are therefore inhabiting a shared world. For Arendt, this was

---

nies that the mind cannot digest" (Hottest Place in Hell 2023). For one of the few and bravest Palestinian accounts of this violence see Natour (2023).

almost literally a mode of inhabiting a single, defined space—her ultimate model of political activity was the citizens coming together to the agora, and collectively agreeing on the terms of their own rule. But even if such a concrete space is not possible when we consider politics in mass societies, working together politically (as a solidarity movement, as an academic community) requires that we understand our lives as defined by shared conditions, and share some sense about how we would like to shape them. We will later return to what happened to this shared world. For now, we want to focus on a different condition of possibility for action.

For Arendt, collective action is based on fundamental equality. But following feminist and queer theory, critical race theory, and the combined work of activism and critical thought, the understanding of what a joint struggle means, and how we create its conditions of possibility, shifted. Once we understand that the basic political conditions from which we operate, those we seek to overturn, are those of radical inequities, joint struggles and a politics of solidarity must be based on recognizing one's privileges, and acknowledging these inequalities. More privileged bodies—of white people, of those who inhabit able bodies, of cisgender activists, or, as in the case at hand, of Jewish Israelis in the context of Palestine/Israel—are called on to engage in protective presence of the more vulnerable; those in positions of (relative) power are called on to follow the path defined by the oppressed rather than determining the course of action themselves. Recognizing privilege does not necessarily entail liberal guilt, but rather committing oneself to a politics of listening and stepping back, of using privilege (which is not within our power to relinquish) against the logic which sustains it. Positionality is thus integral to how we calculate political action. We do not inhabit a world of abstract equality, and thus we cannot engage in efforts to facilitate more just societies while presuming that we can leave such inequalities behind.

There were, therefore, always terms of engagement. Some words had to be said; other words were never to be said; some commitments had to be declared; there were always limitations on how. Whereas this was true for all, for those of us belonging to the side of the oppressor it was all the more required. Our positionality has meant that our solidarity with the Palestinian cause needed to be reaffirmed anew time and again, and that the terms of such solidarity-work needed to be attuned to a changing landscape which was not of our own shaping. We accepted those terms of engagement willingly; we understood that we need to confirm our commitment time and again to create the coalitions necessary for a collective fight for a joint future. Amidst the ongoing Israeli violence and its long history, the efforts of ethnic cleansing, of systematic attempts by Israel to erase Palestinian presence and histories, our Palestinian partners needed to know we are not part of this project; that we stand with them, that we fight against it.

But after October 7 it soon became apparent that there was another term, perhaps a new one, or perhaps one that was there all along but was never voiced: that there was an expectation that we would completely renounce our Israeli side, that we were supposed to abandon our identifications with it, that any expression of grief for our Israeli friends and families, any recognition that there are "two sides," no matter how unequal, asymmetrical, steeped in power imbalance they may be, is already a violation of these terms and questions the sincerity of our political alliances.

– *Can you clarify your position? How do your words align with your politics?*

As we saw it, we still fought the same fight, still held the same values and ethical principles, even if this time some of the victims were Israeli. In essence, this has meant that these terms, which always implied a certain level of stepping back, were now translated into an expectation, sometimes even a demand, that we would acquiesce, or at the very least remain silent, when facing violence oriented towards our elimination.

It may seem strange, even inappropriate, to talk about "elimination" of Israelis as Israel is conducting a genocidal war in Gaza. This is even more so if one cannot appreciate that October 7 was not akin to any other attack, and sees it as yet another round of violence, only more extensive and "successful" perhaps, in the ongoing cycles of fighting between Israel and the Palestinians (more on that below). But in this carefully planned attack, of highly trained and well-organized combat units that raided the Israeli south, going from house to house with a clear determination to kill or kidnap every civilian they could capture[8]—and not just Jews, but everyone on that land (Hamas, Islamic Jihad, and those who followed likewise murdered and kidnapped migrant workers and tourists who could not be mistaken for Jewish Israelis, as well as Palestinian citizens and residents of Israel, who clearly identified themselves as Palestinians to the attackers and were nevertheless murdered[9])—the logic of elimination cannot be denied.

Self/Elimination

One of us wrote once:

> How can a critique be formulated when its material conditions are the object of critique? One can criticize one's state, to be sure—its violence, its wars. But how can one question the le-

---

8 Kingsley et al. (2023).
9 See, for instance, Goldman and Koplewitz (2023).

gitimacy of one's own home; how can one point to the wrongs that are embedded into the very nature of her or his political existence? ... What would it mean for her or him to recognize that her or his attachment to this place is founded upon a history—not such a distant history—of violence and conditioned, at least to some extent, on the perpetuation of this violence? ... The I itself becomes the object of critique and her or his voice—the place from which she or he speaks, her or his language, the dialogues available for her or him—can no longer pretend to assume a position which is simply and clearly oppositional to injustice.[10]

To engage in a critique that seeks to undo the conditions which form and substantiate the "I" rests on the possibility that this "I" still exists, albeit transformed (even if radically so) in the post-critique world. For us, this was part of the terms of engagement. Our writing, our activism, our participation in networks of solidarity were based on the assumption that the joint struggle will get us closer to bringing into life the political community we saw as just and to which we aspired to belong, a community whose ultimate goal is to transcend identitarian (or national) politics. We saw this struggle as guided by an aspiration to bring into being a deeply democratic polity. We still believe that it was such a struggle, that for some of the Palestinian Solidarity Movement it still is, and that for the rest it can still be. To be sure, in the weeks and months following October 7 the grounds have been shifting rapidly, and what dominated the discourse at one moment completely disappeared in another. At the beginning, the eliminatory logic of Hamas's attacks was quite openly adopted, with the circulation of open letters which clearly stated that under no conditions would it be justified for Israel to protect its citizens, with those who clearly pronounced that decolonizing struggles have no bounds and no ethical limits, with some who kept referring to texts that not merely justify the violence of the oppressed, but further talk about decolonization as the full and complete elimination of the settlers.[11] Even if later this explicit eliminatory logic has been largely replaced by denying the very eliminatory character of Hamas' actions, this later erasure also follows a similar logic.

Within these shifting grounds, the horizon is still open. If our political horizon is indeed radically democratic, critique can adopt some form of self-effacement, some version of self-negation, since the political future it steers toward is inclusive, no matter what form it may take. But if the horizon of politics is based on identities and remains confined to a zero-sum game of "sides," if it endorses violence whose logic does not just call for but implements in reality acts predicated on the physical elimination of one's "side," "self-negation" ceases to be a form of engagement. It becomes an existential question.

---

10 Kotef (2018), p. 343.
11 E.g. Tuck and Yang (2012), Fanon (1963).

This point calls for some clarifications lest it be interpreted as subscribing to utopian naivety. First, in these claims, too, there is no symmetry. Israel has been carrying out acts of eradication, to various degrees, of Palestinians as individuals, of Palestinian communities, their histories, their political identity,[12] at least since its establishment. The war on Gaza, worse even from the 1948 Nakba in its acts of elimination—of peoples, of homes, of the means of existence, of the physical environment—is in this sense the most brutal, most direct and effective incarnation of its logic. Indeed, Israel's capacity to execute such violence has no match on the Palestinian side. There is no comparison. But this does not mean that the violence of October 7—the date on which the largest number of people were killed in a single day during the long history of that conflict—is inconsequential, and that its logic can be ignored. It has to be contended with. The sheer refusal to do so by many of our colleagues implicitly accepted its logic of elimination—the logic in which only one side can win, only one side can be recognized.

Second, this is not to say that Israel should be vindicated from its responsibility for laying the ground for the October 7 attack. This does not only entail its long history of violence, oppression, dispossession, and expropriation against and of the Palestinians. As Israel proved itself immune to countless strategies of Palestinian resistance over the years, violent and nonviolent alike, it fostered adopting more extreme means. Israel has further been classifying *all* forms of Palestinian nonviolent resistance as forms of terror ("diplomatic terror," "economic terror," "legal terror," etc.), rendering armed struggle indistinguishable from other tactics. Yet seeing Palestinian resistance as fully dictated by the terms set by Israel, as nothing but a reaction to these terms, empties it of its meaning. It similarly deprives Palestinians of their political agency as expressed in the specific tactics and strategies of resistance they choose to deploy, and in the political horizons such resistance endorses. Whereas decolonization is essentially reactive, whereas it is largely constrained by the means of oppression and domination set by the colonizer, it can nevertheless take various forms.

Finally, we fully recognize that Palestinian resistance cannot be confined to nonviolence alone and this is not the first time that Palestinian violence has deliberately targeted civilians. To stand in solidarity with the Palestinian struggle is also to accept this. Yet solidarity work does not mean suspending all moral judgment, or even a political evaluation of the efficacy of resistance. Recognizing the legitimacy of violent resistance in principle does not mean that there should be no limits to what is accepted as legitimate violence. Where that limit is, how it should be determined and by whom are not questions that we can discuss now, but for us, it

---

12 Amir (2017).

is clear that a line was crossed on October 7. And to say this *does not mean a sudden objection to Palestinians' rights to freedom and justice*. In fact, as we read the political map in both Israel and Palestine, to accept Hamas's path, as it was set on October 7, as the path for this liberation is to make any just future in that land impossible.

Beyond all this we should add that there is also a crucial difference between understanding violence within a context, and accepting it as morally permissible, politically worthy, or even desirable on the one hand, and, on the other, determining that the outcomes of this violence are not grievable or mournable—because the question in our circles has been not just what is right or wrong, desirable or not, but also which kind of grief one is allowed to express publicly. Lives which are ungrievable, Butler argues, are the lives that never counted as lives at all.[13] And even if we do accept the legitimacy of the violence that took those lives, *to deem the death of some ungrievable, as many of our colleagues and even friends indeed did when they referred to (or refused to even mention) those who were killed on October 7, is to go much further than supporting this violence; it is to refuse to recognize those victims as human to begin with, irrespective of how or why their lives were lost. This refusal to recognize lives as grievable must therefore be understood as a different issue to that concerning the legitimacy of violence.*

This refusal was often asserted to be a response to the much more widespread refusal to recognize Palestinians' lives as grievable—to the long history and present in which the killing of Palestinians by Israel has been accepted with overwhelming indifference by the West and actively supported by it. But should this hierarchical value of life, this disposability or ungrievability of Palestinians' lives, be countered by a reversal? And even if this reversal, this refusal to grieve Israelis' lives is a tactical choice and not an ethical one, a way of trying to avoid feeding the Israeli war, shouldn't we ask what the effects of this tactic are? What if it proves to be counterproductive? What if this reversal which denies the value of lives becomes the grounds for Israel justifying this war as an existential one as it further feeds the logic of elimination?

If grieving for the lives lost on October 7 violates the terms of engagement, then what does that tell us about these terms?

---

13 Butler (2004).

World/s

Part of the problem was that we no longer shared a world. October 7 has created a split in the reality inhabited by the left. It is not that we no longer agreed on the meanings we ascribe to the facts or that we assigned different values to them. What we witnessed was a split regarding the facts themselves, an ontological fracture in the very world we inhabit. In this fractured world, two incommensurable narrations of the events solidified right in front of our eyes. In the world we inhabited, the cruelty of the violence carried out by Hamas militants was irrefutable. We knew for a fact, from firsthand accounts, from those who lived through it, from our networks of activists, researchers, and independent journalists we know we can trust, that Hamas militants did not only sow indiscriminate death and destruction in the kibbutzim, towns, and festival sites they stormed, but that they tormented many of those they captured, that they tortured them and dismembered their bodies. We also now know, through verified and cross-checked sources, that they committed rape and other forms of sexual and gender-based violence, while deploying an extraordinary level of brutality. But very quickly we found that many of our friends, our comrades, the people in our academic and activist networks, were living in a completely different reality, a reality in which these atrocious acts never happened or if they happened it was only in the margins, and likely not by Hamas, and certainly not as part of the execution of a premeditated doctrine. The very facts we know to be true were questioned, and then denied, cast as fake, or in some versions "merely" rendered insignificant, irrelevant, nothing more than a by-product of "decolonization," or simply too disruptive to the Palestinian cause to be considered.

 This split has not been created *ex nihilo* or out of callousness. Indeed, in the chaos of the attack's aftermath, many unsubstantiated rumors were circulating, only to be debunked later on, as the facts revealed themselves.[14] The denial was also a response to a reality of bloodshed, in which the recognition of Israelis' deaths and suffering became the grounds to justify the brutal attacks on Palestinians (in Gaza but also in the West Bank and to a lesser extent, but still in significant ways, within Israel). It was additionally influenced by previous years in which the Israeli army and other Israeli official sources have proven, time and again, that the

---

[14] For some insights into how this dynamic unfolded, see Hasson and Rozovsky (2023). We should note that some of the information which was first circulated and was later debunked came from first responders who were exposed to highly atrocious scenes over days. A few have later been shown as suffering from trauma due to this exposure. This trauma may have compromised some of the testimonies they provided early on.

information they provide cannot be trusted.[15] Finally, at least partially, it emerged from an inability of many Palestinians, who have lived to see Israel as an omnipresent and unwavering violent power with an unrivalled military superiority, to imagine a reality in which the Israeli military is simply not there, where civilians are being massacred for hours and almost no one comes to the rescue. For them, Israel is an almighty military power; for us it is a collapsing, corrupt, and fractured state, whose government is all too willing to completely neglect and sacrifice its citizens. It is a government which had effectively abandoned its citizens long before October 7, in a systematic weakening and destruction of all state institutions by consecutive Netanyahu governments. This became all too apparent not only on October 7, with the ineffective response of the Israeli army and the other security forces, but also in the following weeks and months—in the government's abandonment of the kidnapped in the hands of Hamas, its neglect of the people evicted due to the war from the south and north, and its prioritizing narrow sectorial interests over the welfare and security of its citizens, including its soldiers.[16] Many of our Palestinian partners who have a very different image of that state found it easier to believe that those who were killed that day were mostly soldiers, or that it was the Israeli army which killed the majority of Israeli civilians as part of the infamous "Hannibal Procedure."[17]

---

[15] The attempts to cover up the killing of the journalist Shireen Abu Akleh is perhaps the case which attracted most attention in recent years. For further details see TOI Staff (2023).

[16] On the government's failures following the October 7 attack, see Nessman and Teibel (2023).

[17] The Hannibal Procedure is the name originally given to an IDF order which applies when enemy forces are attempting to kidnap Israeli soldiers. The order authorizes the use of disproportionate force to stop the kidnapping without seeking prior approval, even if that firepower might put the lives of those Israeli soldiers at risk. It should be noted that it was introduced to obstruct the kidnapping, and whereas it allows for the risking of the captured soldiers' lives, it does not prioritize the killing of the captured over their being captured. It further distinguishes between putting the lives of these soldiers at risk, which the order permits, and killing them, which it does not (even if this distinction may be blurry). It also solely applies to attempts to capture soldiers, and is not applicable when civilians are involved. The procedure has been heavily criticized and in 2017 it was replaced with a set of more detailed orders, but it may nevertheless still affect decision-making processes in some instances. In an effort to downplay the scale of the Hamas attack, and to question its deliberate targeting of civilians, some have argued that a wide deployment of the Hannibal Procedure has led to the killing of many, if not most Israeli civilians. Such accounts rely on two to three incidents which may be interpreted as complying with the Hannibal Procedure.

The first is a questionable case in which an Israeli helicopter may have (and more likely have not) shot at civilians at the Nova music festival. The case is interesting as it is also indicative of how fake news circulates. On November 18 the Israeli newspaper *Haaretz* reported that according to a police investigation, "a helicopter of the IDF which arrived at the scene ... shot at the terrorists and

In Israel and significant parts of the West, this split had a mirror image (albeit not a symmetrical one). The vast majority of Israelis, and many others worldwide, refused to see or listen to the news and stories arriving from Gaza. They refused to see the horrendous outcomes of the massive Israeli bombing, the unprecedented death, displacement, and the inhumane conditions that ensued, the suffering that resulted from Israel preventing humanitarian aid from entering Gaza, the starvation, diseases, the lack of basic medical equipment. They refuse to see the quick death and the cruelty of the slow death that will probably continue for decades to come. They refused to see the growing cruelty towards Palestinians in Israeli prisons, including the alarming instances of sexual violence and humiliation, the increased violence of settlers, paramilitary organizations, and soldiers in the

---

may have also hit a few of the party attendees" (our translation; for the original report in Hebrew see Breiner 2023). Following further investigation, it appeared that it was a police and not a military helicopter, and was thus not equipped with ammunition. Either way, the way those reports circulated in the Arab-speaking world is indicative. The *Haaretz* piece was falsely translated as stating that "an Israeli helicopter killed settlers at the 'Nature Festival,' not Hamas" (e.g. here: https://twitter.com/bodkim2022/status/1726009177665904734). On November 19, the Palestinian Authority (PA) issued a statement saying that Israeli helicopters bombed the site of the Nova Music Festival during the Hamas attack. According to the statement, the Israeli civilians who were killed there were casualties of this bombing. (The statement was released officially by the PA and then deleted following American pressure. The original statement is available at: https://ynet-pic1.yit.co.il/cdn-cgi/image/format=auto/picserver5/crop_images/2023/11/19/BkVOLiDNa/BkVOLiDNa_0_9_946_1269_0_x-large.jpg.) Even if there was a helicopter, and even if it did kill some civilians as the original *Haaretz* report stated, the police records show that the helicopter only arrived at the scene at 11:15 a.m., more than four hours after the massacre commenced. By then, most of the 364 attendees of the festival who were killed that day were already dead. The fake news cycle, however, had already begun on October 9. Social media accounts shared some footage, which was claimed to be leaked, showing an Israeli helicopter shooting at people on the ground. These accounts claimed that this footage shows the IDF shooting at people at the Nova festival. Yet this video was, in fact, officially released by the IDF and shows a helicopter attacking Hamas militants in Gaza on October 9. For an analysis of the footage, see Marchant de Abreu (2023).

The second incident took place in Kibbutz Be'eri. When IDF forces finally arrived at the scene, a hostage situation developed in which fourteen civilians were held in a house by Hamas militants. After a lengthy standoff, and some negotiation attempts, the militants opened fire at the soldiers. The military commander at the scene ordered a tank to fire at the house despite knowing that there were civilians in it. All but two of the hostages died. See Kingsley et al. (2023). This was a clear case in which the IDF has knowingly killed hostages.

Finally, there may have been incidents in which abducted civilians were killed by IDF forces as they were taken to Gaza. There is no available data on this, and as far as we know no orders were given to kill civilians to prevent their capturing, but there are some indications that some civilians may have been killed while the IDF was targeting militants returning to Gaza. See for example Gal (2023).

West Bank, the rising racism toward Palestinians within Israel.[18] And they refused to acknowledge that the widespread support for Hamas's violence can only be explained by decades of oppression and denial of rights or that this support did not amount to the support of their actions on October 7.[19]

The disregard for Palestinian lives is the bigger geopolitical story here. It is what allows, for example, for the massive support, including in military aid, that enables the Israeli war. The disregard to Israeli lives is a more limited story, which is mostly prevalent on some segments of the left. Yet even though this is a minute story amidst the unprecedented disaster unfolding, it is nevertheless not merely, or even mainly, a personal one (a story of lost friendships, networks of activists and academic communities, and compromised working environments). It is also a political story. Sharing a world, agreeing on basic facts, is a precondition for joint political action, even if the people and groups across our political alliances inhabit the bottomless pain of the fall and winter of 2023 differently, and even if some of these losses touch closer to our exposed nerves than others. A refusal to see the facts, to recognize what happened, is a refusal to inhabit the same world, a world in which some things occurred, and these things are part of what we now need to work to overcome. Basically, at stake here are the conditions of possibility at the heart of solidarity.

Solidarity

To inhabit the duality we insist on is to fight the imperative to choose between the two sides. It is to try to insist against the logic of sides, even if it may not be completely possible in a moment in which the violence of extermination is carried out.

To be forced to pick a side is to be torn. Yet in order to move beyond the logic of sides, both sides—their losses, their pain—must be recognized. Again, and we cannot emphasize this enough: such recognition is not part of an attempt to justify the war Israel is waging against the people of Gaza—and the Palestinian people more generally—and its brutality (indeed, since what is at stake is *mutual* recognition, it *cannot* be). It is also not a demand to partake in some performative pol-

---

[18] For information about the surge in violence against Palestinian prisoners see Addameer (2023); for the increase in settler violence in the West Bank see B'Tselem (2023b); for violence aimed at the Palestinian citizens of Israel see Adalah (2023a).
[19] According to a survey conducted by the Palestinian Center for Policy and Survey Research (PSR) carried out between 22 November and 2 December 2023, 72% of the adult Palestinian population in the OPT said they supported the attack carried out by Hamas (82% in the West Bank and 57% in the Gaza Strip). See: https://www.pcpsr.org/en/node/961.

itics of "condemnation." It is a call to take a moment to see the other as a human being rather than a tool in some struggle about "the narrative."

In the spaces we inhabit, such recognition was for the most part refused. Our pain as Israelis has been disregarded, dismissed, seen as an obstacle ("it serves to justify..." etc.), in some moments celebrated (as the fruits of resistance), and in other moments even became a joke. Of course, this does not apply to "the left" in general, only to a segment of it, even if it seems to be an increasingly dominant segment. There are other efforts—efforts to keep a shared space possible, to have conversations, even if they are difficult, to maintain or rebuild bridges. There are people who agree, with love and solidarity and care for each other, to disagree for now, to resume the shared political project when the wounds are less open.[20]

Like many, we have been broken into pieces; pieces so small, many of which will never be found as we try to recompose ourselves. And it is often difficult to keep the pieces that remained open to others. The polarization we identified here is undoubtedly also a function of this difficulty. If we could keep more of our hearts open, as much as possible, and also recognize that we may fail—indeed, that one cannot but fail at times when trying to climb out of this darkness—then maybe, just maybe, there is hope.

---

[20] See, for instance, Dominus (2023).

V. Epilogue

Ali Al-Awar
Chapter 26: A View from Gaza

November 4, 2023

> **Ali Al-Awar**, PhD, is a research associate at the Forum for Regional Thinking. He is a prolific writer addressing Israeli affairs in the Palestinian media and is a member of the Palestinian Outreach Committee for Interaction with Israeli Society. He has taught and lectured at various institutions including Tel Aviv University, Ankara University, the Truman Institute for the Advancement of Peace at the Hebrew University, and many others.

As a Palestinian born in Deir al-Balah in Gaza, I have witnessed the destruction and suffering caused by years of conflict, and by this war. I lost my older sister during the 2014 war when an Israeli Apache helicopter bombed her house and she became a martyr, leaving behind three sons, two daughters, and her husband. In the current 2023 war, Israeli planes bombed my uncle's house, killing his wife and four children; it is a tragedy that knows no consolation. I cannot understand why Israel targeted my uncle's house [update: on February 4, 2024 Ali's niece and her husband were also killed in an IDF bombing, leaving their one-year old and three-year-old orphaned]. We are a peaceful family—we value peace, we have social relationships with Israelis, we have Jewish friends in Israeli universities. I am a member of the "Women Waging Peace" organization, and of the "Rihla" organization that works to bring Arab and Jewish students together for co-existence between Israelis and Palestinians.

Everything is lost, I feel, and our connection has been severed. The war has destroyed social relationships between Israelis and Palestinians. But I have hope that we can start anew, make peace, and return to the days when my Israeli friends and I enjoyed coffee and ate Palestinian hummus at the Bab al-Amoud restaurant in East Jerusalem. I hope that the war ends soon, that Palestinian children will no longer be killed by American weapons. I want to see President Biden pressure Benjamin Netanyahu to achieve a ceasefire, instead of giving him a green light to indiscriminately kill Palestinians, most of them women and children.

Truly, my family and I are living through dark days, filled with sorrow for the loss of my uncle's wife and their children in this war. I pray for peace, and I continue to pray for the war to come to an end so that I can be reunited with my family and loved ones in Gaza.

To understand how we got to this moment, which is a crucial and painful turning point in the history of the Palestinian–Israeli conflict, we need to understand Hamas's calculations. The mounting marginalization of Hamas by most of the Arab world and by the Fatah-controlled Palestinian Authority has put the movement on high alert. A few recent developments exemplify this sidelining of Hamas: on August 14, 2023, at the Al-Alamein summit in Egypt, which included Egyptian president Abdel Fatah al-Sisi, King Abdullah II of Jordan, and Palestinian Authority president Mahmoud Abbas, Abbas received full legitimacy from Sisi and King Abdullah to lead the Palestinian people. Hamas's leadership interpreted this as complete disregard for their position and role in the Palestinian polity, where they enjoy the support of about 50 % of the population. Concurrently, normalization negotiations between Saudi Arabia and Tel Aviv under the auspices of the White House caused concern within Hamas about future developments that will compound the organization's marginalized position. Abbas sent a Palestinian delegation to Riyadh to coordinate with Saudi Arabia on the normalization issue between Saudi Arabia and Israel, in essence providing the normalization efforts with an aura of legitimacy while ignoring Hamas.

Hamas was determined to reclaim a central and critical role on the Middle East map and to push its political agenda, aiming to undermine normalization agreements between the UAE and Israel, and halt normalization negotiations between Saudi Arabia and Israel. This very likely explains the timing of Hamas's October 7 operation, named "Operation Al-Aqsa Flood"—the name referring to Al-Aqsa Mosque, which has been under constant attack by radical Jewish settler groups accompanied and protected by the Israeli police. These factors likely prompted Hamas to carry out their military operation against Israeli settlements neighboring the Gaza Strip. I feel regret and sorrow for the killing of innocent Israeli civilians during this operation.

Subsequently, Israeli prime minister Netanyahu declared war on Hamas, aiming to eliminate it. Israeli planes began bombing and destroying residential towers and houses, causing casualties among Palestinian children, women, and the elderly. To date, 9,500 Palestinians, including children, women, and the elderly, have been killed by Israeli air strikes. Air strikes continue on schools, hospitals, Jabaliya camp, Shati camp, and other cities in the Gaza Strip. Israel has not allowed a humanitarian ceasefire or the cessation of war. The Israeli military initiated a ground operation and was met by Palestinian resistance-factions' fire, which continues to exact a heavy price from the army, with a rising death toll of Israeli soldiers.

The images from Gaza are painful, showing the bodies of children and adults lying in the streets and under the rubble. Israeli air strikes and ground efforts have targeted hospitals, churches, mosques, and homes, killing Palestinian children. Israel continues to kill even those moving from northern to southern Gaza, bombing in the north, center, and south. The official spokesperson of the Israeli military claims that Hamas leadership is hiding at Al-Shifa Hospital, but this narrative is false. Hamas has stated that its leadership remains in tunnels underground.

Again, a majority of the targets bombed by Netanyahu's government are civilian targets, with these strikes killing Gaza's children and women. But the disregard that has been shown to civilian lives is not limited to the lives of Palestinians, it also extends to Israeli civilians. Hamas holds Israeli captives underground, and the ongoing Israeli air strikes could potentially result in the deaths of these captives inside the tunnels.

I urgently send a message to the families of Israeli hostages: for your children and grandchildren to return home, Netanyahu must stop the fighting and refrain from bombing houses and tunnels. Your children and grandchildren are in Hamas's hands in the tunnels, and they surely are suffering a harsh and painful reality. Netanyahu must stop the war and the air strikes. Do not allow Netanyahu to continue the war for even a minute—every minute that passes, your children and grandchildren may die. You must know that Hamas members and members of Hamas's Al-Qassam Brigades subscribe to an ideology of martyrdom, and they will not surrender Israeli captives to Netanyahu alive unless there is a prisoners exchange deal. I fear for the Israeli captives' lives; they may die in the tunnels with members of the Al-Qassam Brigades.

Finally, I hope the war stops for peace to return, and for the occupation and settlements to end. I hope the Palestinian–Israeli conflict concludes according to legitimate international parameters, set by UN and UN Security Council resolutions, based on the two-state solution—a Palestinian state with its capital in East Jerusalem alongside the state of Israel.

Nicholas Kristof
Chapter 27: Do We Treat Palestinians as Lesser Victims?

October 21, 2023

> **Nicholas D. Kristof** is an American journalist and political commentator. A winner of two Pulitzer Prizes, and an op-ed columnist for the *New York Times*, he is the co-author of several books, among them *Half the Sky* (2009), *A Path Appears: Transforming Lives, Creating Opportunity* (2014), and *Tightrope: Americans Reaching for Hope* (2020).

The crisis in the Middle East is a knotty test of our humanity, asking us how to respond to a grotesque provocation for which there is no good remedy. And in this test, we in the West are not doing well.

The acceptance of large-scale bombing of Gaza and of a ground invasion likely to begin soon suggests that Palestinian children are lesser victims, devalued by their association with Hamas and its history of terrorism. Consider that more than 1,500 children in Gaza have been killed, according to the Gaza Ministry of Health, and around one-third of Gazan homes have been destroyed or damaged in just two weeks—and this is merely the softening-up before what is expected to be a much bloodier ground invasion.

I've flown into beautiful, sun-washed Tel Aviv, where the graffiti reads "Destroy Hamas." Israelis have been shattered by the Hamas terrorism and kidnappings, an attack that felt existential and explains the determination to dismantle Hamas whatever the cost. The anxiety in Tel Aviv is palpable, peaceful though it seems, while Gaza is an inner ring of hell and probably on a path to something much worse.

The United States speaks a good deal about principles, but I fear that President Biden has embedded a hierarchy of human life in official American policy. He expressed outrage at the massacres of Jews by Hamas, as he should have, but he has struggled to be equally clear about valuing Gazan lives. And it's not always evident whether he is standing foursquare with Israel as a country or with its failed prime minister, Benjamin Netanyahu, a longtime obstacle to peace.

What are we to make of the Biden administration's call for an additional $14 billion in assistance for Israel, and its simultaneous call for humanitarian aid for Gazans? Defensive weapons for Israel's Iron Dome system would make sense, but

---

(From The New York Times. © [2023] The New York Times Company. All rights reserved. Used under license.)

https://doi.org/10.1515/9783111435046-028

in practice, is the idea that we will help pay for humanitarians to mop up the blood caused in part by our weapons?

What are we to tell Dr. Iyad Abu Karsh, a Gazan physician who lost his wife and son in a bombing and then had to treat his injured two-year-old daughter? He didn't even have time to care for his niece or sister, for he had to deal with the bodies of his loved ones. "I have no time to talk now," he told a *Times* colleague, his voice trembling over the phone. "I want to go bury them."

In his speech on Thursday, Biden called for America to stand firmly behind Ukraine and Israel,[1] two nations attacked by forces aiming to destroy them. Fair enough. But suppose Ukraine responded to Russian war crimes by laying siege to a Russian city, bombing it into dust and cutting off water and electricity while killing thousands and obliging doctors to operate on patients without anesthetic.

I doubt we Americans would shrug and say: "Well, Putin started it. Too bad about those Russian children, but they should have chosen somewhere else to be born."

Here in Israel, because the Hamas attacks were so brutal and fit into a history of pogroms and Holocaust, they led to a resolve to wipe out Hamas even if this means a large human toll. "Gaza will become a place where no human being can exist," declared Giora Eiland, a former head of the Israeli National Security Council. "There is no other option for ensuring the security of the State of Israel."[2]

I think that view reflects a practical and moral miscalculation. While I would love to see the end of Hamas, it's not feasible to eliminate radicalism in Gaza, and a ground invasion is more likely to feed extremism than to squelch it—at an unbearable cost in civilian lives.

I particularly want to challenge the suggestion, more implicit than explicit, that Gazan lives matter less because many Palestinians sympathize with Hamas. People do not lose their right to life because they have odious views, and in any case, almost half of Gazans are children. Those kids in Gaza, infants included, are among the more than 2 million people enduring a siege and collective punishment.

Israel has suffered a horrifying terrorist attack and deserves the world's sympathy and support, but it should not receive a blank check to slaughter civilians or to deprive them of food, water, and medicine. Bravo to Biden for trying to negotiate some humanitarian access to Gaza, but the challenge will be not just getting aid into Gaza but also distributing it where it's needed.

---

1 White House (2023b).
2 Eiland (2023a).

A prolonged ground invasion seems to me a particularly risky course, likely to kill large numbers of Israeli soldiers, hostages, and especially Gazan civilians. We are better than that, and Israel is better than that. Leveling cities is what the Syrian government did in Aleppo and Russia did in Grozny; it should not be an American-backed undertaking by Israel in Gaza.

The best answer to this test is to try even in the face of provocation to cling to our values. That means that despite our biases, we try to uphold all lives as having equal value. If your ethics see some children as invaluable and others as disposable, that's not moral clarity but moral myopia. We must not kill Gazan children to try to protect Israeli ones.

References

Abu Iyad. 1981. *My Home My Land: A Narrative of the Palestinian Struggle* (with Eric Rouleau). New York Times Books.
Achitov, Neta. 2023. "How to rehabilitate the soul of an entire society?" *Haaretz*, October 18, https://www.haaretz.co.il/magazine/2023-10-18/ty-article-magazine/.highlight/0000018b-4244-df22-a5eb-4b7dbd4f0000.
ACLU. 2011. "Surveillance under the Patriot Act." American Civil Liberties Union. https://www.aclu.org/issues/national-security/privacy-and-surveillance/surveillance-under-patriot-act. (last accessed: February 2, 2024).
Adalah. 2023a. "Interrogations, arrests, and indictments of Palestinian citizens of Israel since 7 October." November 15, https://www.adalah.org/en/content/view/10959.
Adalah. 2023b. "Israeli Knesset passes draconian amendment to the counter-terrorism law criminalizing 'consumption of terrorist publications'." November 8, https://www.adalah.org/en/content/view/10951.
Adalah. 2023c. "Crackdown on freedom of speech of Palestinian citizens of Israel." November 16, https://www.adalah.org/en/content/view/10925.
Addameer. 2023. "Addameer reviews the most recent developments inside the occupation's prisons and the ongoing arrest campaigns in the West Bank and occupied Jerusalem." https://www.addameer.org/media/5240.
Aderet, Ofer. 2023. "Rabin before Oslo: there are few commitments from the Palestinian side." *Haaretz*, August 29, https://www.haaretz.co.il/news/politics/2023-08-29/ty-article/.premium/0000018a-417c-d435-a59e-cffeae870000.
Aichner, Itamar. 2023. "Netanyahu: 'Gaza will turn into a heap of rubble, we will destroy Hamas's capabilities'." *Calcalist*, October 7, https://www.calcalist.co.il/local_news/article/hkcgvnyz6.
Amar, Dvir. 2023. "Dozens of rabbis: There should be no consideration for the civilian population of the enemy." Artutz Sheva, October 12, https://www.inn.co.il/news/616515.
Amir, Merav. 2017. "Revisiting politicide: state annihilation in Israel/Palestine." *Territory, Politics, Governance*, vol. 5, no. 4: 368–387.
Andrejevic, Mark. 2005. "The work of watching one another: lateral surveillance, risk, and governance." *Surveillance & Society*, vol. 2, no. 4: 479–497.
Arab48. 2023. "48 عرب موقع". غزة بـ تتعلق مضامين نشر بادعاء كابول من طه مهند اعتقال تمديد. October 12, https://www.arab48.com/ة-بغزة-تتعلق-مضامين-نشر-بشبهة-كابول-من-طه-مهند-اعتقال-تمديد/2023/10/12/محلية-أخبار/محليات.
Arendt, Hannah. 1971. "Thinking and moral considerations: a lecture." *Social Research*, vol. 38, no. 3: 417–446.
Arendt, Hannah. 1973. *The Origins of Totalitarianism.* Harvest Books.
Arendt, Hannah. 2013 [1958]. *The Human Condition.* University of Chicago Press.
Abraham, Yuval. 2023. "'A mass assassination factory': inside Israel's calculated bombing of Gaza." *+972 Magazine*, November 30, https://www.972mag.com/mass-assassination-factory-israel-calculated-bombing-gaza/.
Baruch, Hizki. 2023. "MK Tzvi Sukkot opened a parliamentary office at the site of the attack in Hawara." Arutz Sheva, October 5, https://www.inn.co.il/news/615786.
Baruch, Uzi. 2023. "Minister Struck to Channel 7: Unfortunately, returning to the Gaza Strip will involve many casualties, but a day will come when we return to it." Arutz Sheva, March 21, 2023. https://www.inn.co.il/news/596073.

B'Tselem. 2023a. "Revenge policy in motion; Israel is committing war crimes in Gaza." October 10, https://www.btselem.org/press_releases/20231010_revenge_policy_in_motion_israel_committing_war_crimes_in_gaza.

B'Tselem. 2023b. "Under cover of Gaza war, settlers working to fulfil state goal of Judaizing Area C." October 19, http://www.btselem.org/press_releases/20231019_under_cover_of_gaza_fighting_settlers_working_to_fulfil_state_goal_of_judaizing_area_c.

Baker, Abeer. 2023. "Position paper on the Israeli law prohibiting the consumption of terrorist publications." 7amleh—Arab Center for the Advancement of Social Media. November 20, https://7amleh.org/2023/11/20/7amleh-releases-a-position-paper-on-the-israeli-law-prohibiting-the-consumption-of-terrorist-publications.

Bar'el, Zvi. 2023. "Israel has adopted a new paradigm in place of the previous one, but it too will fail." Haaretz, Octobber 13, https://www.haaretz.co.il/news/politics/2023-10-13/ty-article/.premium/0000018b-24ce-d3fc-a3bf-bfef39d80000.

BBC. 2023. "Hamas hostages: stories of the people taken from Israel." https://www.bbc.co.uk/news/world-middle-east-67053011. (last accessed: Feb 2, 2024).

Ben-Gurion, David. 1971. Knesset Minutes, October 25.

Ben Hurin, Yitzhak. 2009. "Rice pressures: Israel must proceed toward a ceasefire." Ynet, January 8, https://www.ynet.co.il/articles/0,7340,L-3652543,00.html.

Bender, Arik. 2015. "MK Yogev to Gaza Envelop resident: 'You supported the disengagement, tough luck'" Maariv January 20, 2015 https://www.maariv.co.il/news/elections-2015/Article-460498.

Bloomberg. 2023. "Israeli Defense Minister Warns Hamas 'Will Regret' Deadly Attacks" Bloomberg Quicktake, YouTube, October 10, https://www.youtube.com/watch?v=vtjHcnNB0E8.

Blumenthal, Paul. 2023. "Israeli President Suggests That Civilians In Gaza Are Legitimate Targets." October 16, Huffpost, https://news.yahoo.com/israeli-president-says-no-innocent-154330724.html.

Bokra. 2023. "موقع بكرا". اطلاق سراح د. عامر الهزيل بعد اعتقاله لأيام بسبب منشور في فيسبوك. October 19, https://bokra.net/Article-1528320.

Borger, Julian. 2023. "'An atmosphere of fear': free speech under threat in Israel, activists say." Guardian, October 22, https://www.theguardian.com/world/2023/oct/22/an-atmosphere-of-fear-free-speech-under-threat-in-israel-activists-say.

Boxerman, Aaron. 2023. "What we know about the death toll in Israel from the Hamas-led attacks." New York Times, November 12, https://www.nytimes.com/2023/11/12/world/middleeast/israel-death-toll-hamas-attack.html.

Breiner, Joshua. 2023. "Assessment by the security system: Hamas didn't know of the Nova Festival ahead of time, they recognized it from the air." Haaretz, November 18, https://www.haaretz.co.il/news/politics/2023-11-18/ty-article/0000018b-e1a5-d168-a3ef-f5ff4d070000.

Butler, Judith. 2004. Precarious Life: The Powers of Mourning and Violence. Verso.

Bwaret, Amir Ali. 2023. "48 موقع عرب". تمديد اعتقال المرشح لبلدية رهط عامر الهزيل حتى الإثنين المقبل. October 14, https://www.arab48.com/محليات/أخبار-محلية/2023/10/14/تمديد-اعتقال-المرشح-لبلدية-رهط-عامر-الهزيل-حتى-الإثنين-المقبل.

Channel 4. 2023. X Post, October 13, https://x.com/Channel4News/status/1712822560407097379?s=20.

Chotiner, Issac. 2023. "How Hamas used sexual violence on October 7th." New Yorker, December 10, https://www.newyorker.com/news/q-and-a/how-hamas-used-sexual-violence-on-october-7th.

Cohen, Ido David. 2023. "Hamas's massacre is part of the divine plan." Haaretz, October 13, https://www.haaretz.co.il/gallery/media/2023-10-13/ty-article/.premium/0000018b-29aa-d628-a3af-fdab105b0000.

References

Cohen, Raphael. 2023. "Why the Oct. 7 attack wasn't Israel's 9/11 | Rand." Rand Corporation, November 13, https://www.rand.org/pubs/commentary/2023/11/why-the-oct-7-attack-wasnt-israels-9-11.html.

Cohen, Gilad and Halabi, Einav 2023. "Hundreds ascended to the Temple Mount, Gaza threatens to breach agreements: 'Returning to confrontations at the fence.'" Ynet, October 1, https://www.ynet.co.il/news/article/bkbtl68la.

Dayan, Moshe. 1956. "Moshe Dayan's eulogy for Roi Rutenberg." *Jewish Virtual Library*, April 19, https://www.jewishvirtuallibrary.org/moshe-dayan-s-eulogy-for-roi-rutenberg-april-19-1956.

Diaz, Jaclyn, and Lauren Frayer. 2023. "Palestinians in Israel cite threats, firings and discrimination after Oct. 7." NPR, November 21, https://www.npr.org/2023/11/21/1213892449/palestinians-israel-war-discrimination-censorship.

Dominus, Susan. 2023. "It destroyed my heart." *New York Times*, December 14, https://www.nytimes.com/2023/12/14/magazine/israelis-palestinians-peace-forum.html.

Dubnov, Arie M. 2024. "The Gates of Gaza." *Hazman Haze*, https://hazmanhazeh.org.il/the_gates_of_gazza/?_atscid=1_137_148123909_15116754_0_Tzeazx3jztdwudsa8dh.

Eiland, Giora. 2023a. "It's not a revenge, it's us or them." *Yediot Ahronot*, October 10, https://www.ynet.co.il/yedioth/article/yokra13625377.

Eiland, Giora. 2023b. "It's time to rip off the Hamas band-aid." *Ynet*, October 12.

Eldar, Shlomi. 2023 "Restrain ourselves before we conquer Gaza." Haaretz, October 9, https://www.haaretz.co.il/opinions/2023-10-09/ty-article-opinion/.premium/0000018b-1443-d2fc-a59f-d55bc66a0000.

Fabian, Emanual. 2023. "Defense minister announces 'complete siege' of Gaza: no power, food or fuel." *Times of Israel*, October 9, https://www.timesofisrael.com/liveblog_entry/defense-minister-announces-complete-siege-of-gaza-no-power-food-or-fuel/.

Fanon, Frantz. 2004 [1963]. *The Wretched of the Earth.* Translated by Richard Philcox. New York: Grove Press.

Fishman, Alex. 2021. "Robots instead of Rabatim" Yedioth Ahronot. March 25, https://www.yediot.co.il/articles/0,7340,L-5904317,00.html.

Gal, Shai. 2023. "'Save us': the Apache pilots who arrived first speak." *Mako*, November 21, https://www.mako.co.il/news-military/6361323ddea5a810/Article-02cfdbceafc4b81027.htm.

Galant, Yoav. 2023. Twitter Post. October 9, https://twitter.com/yoavgallant/status/1711335592942875097.

Gandy, Oscar H. 1993. *The Panoptic Sort: A Political Economy of Personal Information.* Westview.

Gil-Shuster, Corey. 2019. "From the river to the sea, Palestine will be free: Palestinians, what does that mean?" Ask Project, *YouTube*, March 27, https://www.youtube.com/watch?v=hgwtQlwK-hA.

Goichman, Rafaela, "An 'Inside Job': right wing activists and Iranian actors spread conspiracy theories and fake news." The Marker. October 8, 2023. https://www.themarker.com/captain-internet/2023-10-08/ty-article/0000018b-0ecd-d8fc-adff-6fedb90c0000?_ga=2.267518286.1105494879.1697298053-1865821451.1694532844.

Goldman, Adam, and Gal Koplewitz. 2023. "Israel's hidden victims, Arab Bedouins, were attacked by Hamas too." *New York Times*, October 29, https://www.nytimes.com/2023/10/29/world/middleeast/israel-hamas-arab-bedouins.html.

Gorali, Moshe. 2023. "The connection between this bad government and the gates of hell that opened from Gaza." Calcalist, October 7, https://www.calcalist.co.il/local_news/article/hjyj1cal6.

Graham-Harrison, Emma. 2023. "UN hears accounts of sexual violence during 7 October attacks by Hamas." *Guardian*, December 6, https://www.theguardian.com/world/2023/dec/05/un-hears-accounts-of-sexual-violence-during-7-october-attacks-by-hamas.

Grossman, David. 2023. "How to talk of hope when reality brings so much despair." *Haaretz*, October 31, https://www.haaretz.com/israel-news/2020-10-31/ty-article-magazine/.premium/how-to-talk-of-hope-when-reality-brings-so-much-despair/0000017f-e30e-d38f-a57f-e75eea1c0000.

Haaretz Editorial. 2023. "Hostages and kidnapped first." *Haaretz*, October 9, https://www.haaretz.co.il/opinions/editorial-articles/2023-10-09/ty-article/0000018b-102b-dfff-a7eb-b3fbc0bb0000.

Haaretz Podcast. 2023. "Yitzhak Barik: The conception of a small and smart army failed, right now the citizens have to defend themselves." October 10, https://open.spotify.com/episode/7JZi5GqQKm4YyIvNgcLzg8?si=2bde181e111840ec.

Haaretz Update. 2023. "Hanegbi: We failed the mission: there will not be negotiation with an enemy we want to eradicate." *Haaretz*, October 14, https://www.haaretz.co.il/news/politics/2023-10-14/ty-article/.premium/0000018b-2f19-d450-a3af-6f1d9f4b0000.

Halabi, Einav, Gilad Cohen and Moran Azulai. 2023."Thousands ascended to the Temple Mount during khol hamo'ed, Jordan protested to Israel." Ynet, October 4, https://www.ynet.co.il/news/article/sjhgtr9ga.

Haleve, Michal. 2023. Facebook post, October 16, https://www.facebook.com/watch/?v=869235201393916.

Hashmonai, Adi. 2023. "'Her posts will lead to terror': Arab Israeli actress charged with incitement." *Haaretz*, October 29, https://www.haaretz.com/israel-news/2023-10-30/ty-article/.premium/arab-israeli-actress-charged-with-incitement-over-october-7-posts/0000018b-7d00-d0f6-afeb-7f950a3b0000.

Harel Amos, et al. 2013. "The IDF cancels security in communities on the northern and southern borders. Security for settlements in the West Bank will continue as usual." Haaretz, September 17, https://www.haaretz.co.il/news/politics/2013-09-17/ty-article/0000017f-f0d4-d487-abff-f3fe9d670000.

Harel, Amos. 2023. "The triangle of the IDF, Smotrich, and the Palestinians leads in one direction: Escalation." Haaretz, October 8, https://www.haaretz.co.il/news/politics/2023-10-06/ty-article/.highlight/0000018b-0147-d037-a9af-51dfe9b50000.

Harkabi, Yehoshafat. 1983. *The Bar Kokhba syndrome: Risk and realism in international politics*. NY: Rossel Books, 1983.

Hason, Nir. 2023a. "Five arrested on suspicion of spitting on Christians and churches in the Old City of Jerusalem." October 4, https://www.haaretz.co.il/news/law/2023-10-04/ty-article/0000018a-f9a5-d12f-afbf-f9f507550000.

Hason, Nir. 2023b. "Beyond the festive images from Jerusalem, there is a volatile reality that could flare up at any moment." Haaretz, October 2, https://www.haaretz.co.il/news/politics/2023-10-02/ty-article/.premium/0000018a-f109-dfa2-a99e-f96b8dd40000.

Hason, Nir. 2023c. "Policewomen were filmed throwing Palestinian women to the ground in the Old City, Ben Gvir praised them." Haaretz, October 2, https://www.haaretz.co.il/news/politics/2023-10-02/ty-article/.premium/0000018a-f001-d12f-afbf-f1553c990000.

Hasson, Nir, and Liza Rozovsky. 2023. "Hamas committed documented atrocities. But a few false stories feed the deniers." *Haaretz*, December 4, https://www.haaretz.com/israel-news/2023-12-04/ty-article-magazine/.premium/hamas-committed-documented-atrocities-but-a-few-false-stories-feed-the-deniers/0000018c-34f3-da74-afce-b5fbe24f0000.

Heller, Or. 2021. "Manager of Erez crossing: Open Gaza—regardless of the hostages." Channel 13, July 1, https://13tv.co.il/item/news/politics/security/director-erez-crossing-1275118/.

Hidaboroot. 2023. "Amidror: There's no choice, we have to conquer Gaza again." October 8, https://www.hidabroot.org/article/1186653.

Hitbonenut. 2010. "What could be worse than the Holocaust?" May 9, https://hitbonenut.net/archives/952.

Hochman, Guy. 2023. "From reserve duty to the maternity ward." *YouTube*, October 14, https://youtu.be/OaVVYtjHI_k?si=QebS3k3IbAWMGVFa.

Hottest Place in Hell. 2023. "We've collected by now 1,500 terrible testimonies that the mind cannot digest." December 1, https://www.ha-makom.co.il/post-women-abuse-byhammas.

Human Rights Watch. 2023. "Israel/Palestine: videos of Hamas-led attacks verified." October 18, https://www.hrw.org/news/2023/10/18/israel/palestine-videos-hamas-led-attacks-verified.

Inon, Maoz. 2023. "Hamas killed my parents, but Israel's war is not the answer." Al Jazeera, October 19, https://www.aljazeera.com/opinions/2023/10/19/hamas-killed-my-parents-but-israels-war-is-not-the-answer.

Israel Ministry of Foreign Affairs. 2023a. "Hamas–Israel conflict 2023: key legal aspects." December 3, https://www.gov.il/en/departments/news/hamas-israel-conflict2023-key-legal-aspects.

Israel Ministry of Foreign Affairs. 2023b. "Hamas–Israel conflict 2023: frequently asked questions." December 6, https://www.gov.il/en/Departments/General/swords-of-iron-faq-6-dec-2023.

Kan Reshet Bet. 2023. X post, October 11, https://twitter.com/ReshetBet/status/1712073712269176932.

Kaplan Sommer, Allison. 2023. "Rabbi at Israeli military training base says 'whole country' is 'ours,' including Gaza and Lebanon." *Haaretz*, November 5, https://www.haaretz.com/israel-news/2023-11-05/ty-article/rabbi-at-israeli-military-base-says-whole-country-is-ours-including-gaza-and-lebanon/0000018b-a031-d42c-a9ef-ad772cdc0000.

Khoury Jacky, et al. 2023. "A Palestinian was killed in Nablus during the entry of thousands of Jewish worshippers, including the Police Commissioner, to Joseph's Tomb." July 20, Haaretz, https://www.haaretz.co.il/news/politics/2023-07-20/ty-article/.premium/00000189-706f-d09f-a3a9-f7ef03990000?utm_source=App_Share&utm_medium=iOS_Native.

Kingsley, Patrick, et al. 2023. "The day Hamas came." *New York Times*, December 22, https://www.nytimes.com/interactive/2023/12/22/world/europe/beeri-massacre.html.

Klein, Naomi (2023) *Doppelganger: A Trip into the Mirror World*. Knopf Canada.

Kook, Ẓevi Judah ben Abraham Isaac. 1981. *Erets ha-Tsevi: Rabenu ha-Rav Tsevi Yehudah ha-Kohen Kuḳ, zatsal ba-maʻarakhah ʻal shelemut artsenu*. Netivei Or.

Kottasová, Ivana, Kareem Khadder, Richard Allen Greene. 2024. "One in 100 people in Gaza has been killed since October 7." CNN, January 8, https://www.cnn.com/2024/01/08/middleeast/gaza-death-toll-population-intl/index.html.

Kotef, Hagar. 2018. "Fragments." *Critical Inquiry*, vol. 44, no. 2: 343–349.

Kottasová, Ivana. 2023. "What we know about rape and sexual violence inflicted by Hamas during its terror attack on Israel." CNN, December 7, https://edition.cnn.com/2023/12/06/middleeast/rape-sexual-violence-hamas-israel-what-we-know-intl/index.html.

Kupchan, Charles A. 2023. "Israel's 9/11 moment: by Charles A. Kupchan." Project Syndicate, November 2, https://www.project-syndicate.org/commentary/israel-must-learn-from-us-strategic-mistakes-in-middle-east-by-charles-a-kupchan-2023-10?barrier=accesspaylog.

Langutzki, Yosi. 2023. "15 years I've been warning about the obstacle in Gaza, no one listened." *Haaretz*, October 8, https://www.haaretz.co.il/opinions/2023-10-08/ty-article-opinion/.premium/0000018b-0b2d-dc5d-a39f-9f6deac60000.

Lattimer, Mark. 2023. "Assessing Israel's Approach to Proportionality in the Conduct of Hostilities in Gaza" Lawfare, November 16, https://www.lawfaremedia.org/article/assessing-israel-s-approach-to-proportionality-in-the-conduct-of-hostilities-in-gaza.

Lepkovitch, Israel. 2023. "Over 3,000 worshippers tonight at Joseph's Tomb in Nablus." Kol Rega October 5, https://www.kore.co.il/viewArticle/141562.

Lis, Jonathan. 2023. "Netanyahu: First goal is to purge Israel from enemies, then exact huge price." Haaretz, October 7, https://www.haaretz.com/israel-news/2023-10-07/ty-article/.premium/israeli-prime-minister-netanyahu-we-are-at-war-we-will-win/0000018b-0978-dc5d-a39f-9f7cb7ee0000.

Lyon, David (ed.) 2003. *Surveillance as Social Sorting: Privacy, Risk, and Digital Discrimination.* Psychology Press.

Lyon, David. 2017. "Digital citizenship and surveillance| Surveillance culture: engagement, exposure, and ethics in digital modernity." *International Journal of Communication*, vol. 11:824–842.

Mada al-Carmel. 2023. "Position paper: The war on Gaza: policies of silencing, intimidation, and persecution against Palestinians in Israel." November 30, https://mada-research.org/storage/PDF/%D8%AA%D9%82%D8%AF%D9%8A%D8%B1%20%D9%85%D9%88%D9%82%D9%81%202023/eng/PositionPaper-March-2023-ENGAA.pdf.

Marchant de Abreu, Catalina. 2023. "Israeli army did not fire on own civilians at Nova music festival." France 24, November 3, https://www.france24.com/en/tv-shows/truth-or-fake/20231113-disproving-claims-that-israeli-helicopter-fired-on-their-own-civilians-at-nova-music-festival.

McCloskey, Stephen, 2020. "UN's warning that Gaza will not be a "liveable place" by 2020 has been realized." Open Democracy, January 15, https://www.opendemocracy.net/en/north-africa-west-asia/uns-warning-that-gaza-will-not-be-a-liveable-place-by-2020-has-been-realised/.

McKernan, Bethan and Kierszenbaum, Quique. 2023."'We're focused on maximum damage': ground offensive into Gaza seems imminent." Guardian, October 10, https://www.theguardian.com/world/2023/oct/10/right-now-it-is-one-day-at-a-time-life-on-israels-frontline-with-gaza.

Mechazkim. 2023. Facebook post, October 15, https://www.facebook.com/story.php?story_fbid=pfbid02SMrqRG77N7JkEoHvwZc66tEP7ft2Y3nGVvUJCNxpVNMgd1jkLfD3wPjN4GbzWPSwl&id=100068869359344&mibextid=Nif5oz&paipv=0&eav=AfZlTcsRHMypY1f9h_dCgwBk0tOIZq34genPx1Zc20RoSI5EECWsBlUyzzvDyyKyFEw&_rdr&utm_source=972%20Magazine%20Newsletter&utm_campaign=62351e6f78-EMAIL_CAMPAIGN_9_12_2022_11_20_COPY_01&utm_medium=email&utm_term=0_f1fe821d25-62351e6f78-318931876.

MEMRI. 2023. "Interview by Ygal Karmon with Channel 13." *YouTube*, https://www.youtube.com/watch?v=Q5UBg5-PwY4. (last accessed: Feb. 2, 2024).

Monetta, Sara. 2023. "Israeli Arabs arrested over Gaza social media posts." BBC News, October 21, https://www.bbc.com/news/world-middle-east-67181582.

More, Dror. 2013. "There is a leadership crisis, complete disregard for the public." *Ynet*, January 5, https://www.ynet.co.il/articles/0,7340,L-4328581,00.html.

Moshe, Eliram. 2023. "Bereaved father from Ashkelon to defense minister: Allow Palestinians to participate in joint memorial ceremony." Kan Darom, April 15.

Natour, Rajaa. 2023. "Our national liberation will never be through Israeli blood." November 19, https:/politicallycorret.co.il/not-my-freedom-ar/?fbclid=IwAR2BC3eAk3cpO5klE3YRvazI9606gje_-ExFOtDk9fez8tWrKuaJMVnBzZs.

NBC. 2023. "Dashcam footage shows Hamas terrorists beating Arab man at kibbutz." October 13, https://www.nbcnews.com/video/dashcam-footage-shows-hamas-terrorists-beating-arab-man-at-kibbutz-195176517537.

Netanyahu, Benjamin. 2023. "Remember Amalek," Twitter, November 3.

Nessman, Ravi, and Amy Teibel. 2023. "Many Israelis are furious at their government's chaotic recovery efforts after Hamas attack." AP News, October 26, https://apnews.com/article/netanyahu-israel-government-hamas-war-anger-failure-0e8712cb539b84befb95a4a061813b79.

NPR. 2023. "Netanyahu's references to violent biblical passages raise alarm among critics." November 7, https://www.npr.org/2023/11/07/1211133201/netanyahus-references-to-violent-biblical-passages-raise-alarm-among-critics.

Oren, Amir. 2014. "The operation in Gaza: Bring the head of the snake – and we'll talk to him." Haaretz, July 8, https://www.haaretz.co.il/news/politics/2014-07-08/ty-article/.premium/0000017f-e7af-df2c-a1ff-fffff2b80000.

Pacchiani, Gianluca. 2023. "COGAT chief addresses Gazans: 'You wanted hell, you will get hell'." *Times of Israel*, October 10, https://www.timesofisrael.com/liveblog_entry/cogat-chief-addresses-gazans-you-wanted-hell-you-will-get-hell/.

Peri, Smadar. 2023. "The Egyptians insist: We passed a warning to Israel – pay attention to Gaza." Ynet, October 9, https://www.ynet.co.il/news/article/bkx2odbba.

Physicians for Human Rights Israel. 2023. *Sexual & Gender-based Violence as a Weapon of War.* https://www.phr.org.il/wp-content/uploads/2023/11/5771_Sexual_Violence_paper_Eng-final.pdf.

Rabinovich, Itamar. 2023. *Middle Eastern Maze: Israel, the Arabs, and the Region 1948–2022.* Brookings Institution Press.

Ravid, Barak. 2014. "Netanyahu's hour glass is running out." Haaretz, July 13, https://www.haaretz.co.il/news/politics/2014-07-13/ty-article/.premium/0000017f-e990-d62c-a1ff-fdfbde4b0000.

Reuters. 2023. "Israeli forensic teams describe signs of torture, abuse." December 15, https://www.reuters.com/world/middle-east/israeli-forensic-teams-describe-signs-torture-abuse-2023-10-15/.

Reuveni, Tamar. 2023. Facebook post, October 12, https://www.facebook.com/story.php?story_fbid=pfbid02ALUukZK2wQXCeg4S5LbXyjQo79BhccqoXhZJ85FYJdjG2aERniujgWisnWWGAMzwl&id=1059125323&mibextid=Nif5oz&paipv=0&eav=AfZtLIfe2b1kZf_hD-qbz2vg08NQwFDIeENRftKmto6YggL4_oLeZG3oaR_iQqq8vNw&_rdr&utm_source=972%20Magazine%20Newsletter&utm_campaign=62351e6f78-EMAIL_CAMPAIGN_9_12_2022_11_20_COPY_01&utm_medium=email&utm_term=0_f1fe821d25-62351e6f78-318931876.

Sacks, Jonathan. 2007. *To Heal a Fractured World: The Ethics of Responsibility.* Schocken.

Segal, Arnon. 2023. "This is how we will return to Gaza." *Olam Katan*, October 11, https://olam-katan.co.il/archives/11458.

Segal, Arnon. 2023a. "A new record: 5,323 Jews ascended to the Temple Mount on Sukkot" Makor Rishon, October 6, https://www.makorrishon.co.il/opinion/675831/.

Segal, Arnon. 2023b. This is how we will return to Gaza." Olam Katan, October 11, https://olam-katan.co.il/archives/11458.

Segal, Raz. 2023. "A Textbook Case of Genocide." Jewish Current, October 13, https://jewishcurrents.org/a-textbook-case-of-genocide.

Shapiro, Fred R. 2006. *The Yale Book of Quotations.* Yale University Press, New Haven.

Sheizaf, Hagar and Haj Yehya, Diya. 2023. "The night journey to Joseph;s Tomb illustrates how the settlers realize their vision." Haaretz, April 13, https://www.haaretz.co.il/news/politics/2023-04-13/ty-article-magazine/.premium/00000186-ea57-d8c1-a3be-eb5751df0000.

Shtekerman, Rotem and Lutzky, Dafna. 2014. "Partial information, neglect and disregard: the making of the crisis of trust between the IDF and the residents of the Gaza Envelop." The Marker, August 8, https://www.themarker.com/markerweek/2014-08-08/ty-article/0000017f-df2d-df7c-a5ff-df7fc4d00000.

Shuster, Ruth. 2023. "Israeli archaeologists help identify human remains in Gaza border communities." *Haaretz*, October 30, https://www.haaretz.com/israel-news/2023-10-30/ty-article/.premium/israeli-archaeologists-help-identify-human-remains-in-gaza-communities/0000018b-80c6-d4a8-a3cf-bcef30330000.

Sidler, Shirly. 2014. "The IDF will discontinue military security in Envelop communities that are not adjacent to the fence." Haaretz, December 29, https://www.haaretz.co.il/news/politics/2014-12-29/ty-article/.premium/0000017f-e168-d75c-a7ff-fdeddadf0000.

Sidler, Shirly. 2015. "Despite residents' protest, IDF forces leave Gaza Envelop communities." January 4, https://www.haaretz.co.il/news/politics/2015-01-04/ty-article/0000017f-e3fd-d7b2-a77f-e3ff42140000.

Stal, Ziv. 2023. "I was there. In Kfar Azza. Indiscriminate bombing of Gaza is not the solution." *Haaretz*, October 17, https://www.haaretz.com/opinion/2023-10-17/ty-article-opinion/.premium/i-was-there-in-kfar-azza-indiscriminate-bombing-of-gaza-is-not-the-solution/0000018b-3990-d0ac-a39f-b9921c5a0000.

Stinberg, Mati. 2021. "On blindness: The latest confrontation with Hamas as an expression of a conceptual breakdown." June 8. The Forum for Regional Thinking. https://www.regthink.org/on-the-blindness/.

Tamari, Dov. 2018. "Since 1967 there's no deterrence." Haaretz. Novermber 27, https://www.haaretz.co.il/opinions/2018-11-27/ty-article-opinion/.premium/0000017f-f724-d460-afff-ff66de6e0000.

Teibel, Amy. 2023. "An Israeli ministry, in a 'concept paper,' proposes transferring Gaza civilians to Egypt's Sinai." AP News, October 30, https://apnews.com/article/israel-gaza-population-transfer-hamas-egypt-palestinians-refugees-5f99378c0af6aca183a90c631fa4da5a.

TOI Staff. 2023. "On anniversary, IDF spokesman apologizes for Shireen Abu Akleh's death for 1st time." *Times of Israel*, May 12, https://www.timesofisrael.com/on-anniversary-idf-spokesman-apologizes-for-shireen-abu-aklehs-death-for-1st-time.

Tuck, Eve and K. Wayne Yang. 2012. "Decolonization is not a Metaphor." *Decolonization: Indigeneity, Education & Society* 1:1 pp. 1–40.

Tusing, David. 2023. "Palestinian singer Dalal Abu Amneh under house arrest following social media post." *The National*, October 22, https://www.thenationalnews.com/arts-culture/music-stage/2023/10/22/dalal-abu-amneh-israel-gaza/.

Tzuri, Matan. 2015a. "IDF stops Gaza Envelop community's protest march." Ynet, January 2, 2015 https://www.ynet.co.il/articles/0,7340,L-4610687,00.html.

Tzuri, Matan (2015b). "Listen to the commander of the Gaza Brigade – It is arrogance to try to deter anyone in Shujaiya" Ynet January 4, 2023 https://www.ynet.co.il/articles/0,7340,L-4611002,00.html.

UNRWA. 2024. "UNRWA situation report #61 on the situation in the Gaza Strip and the West Bank, including east Jerusalem." January 7, https://www.unrwa.org/resources/reports/unrwa-situation-report-61-situation-gaza-strip-and-west-bank-including-east-Jerusalem#:~:text=Since%207%20October%202023%2C%20up,repeatedly%20in%20search%20of%20safety.

Wall Street Journal. 2023. "'This is Israel's 9/11', says Israeli ambassador to the United Nations." Dow Jones & Company, October 9, https://www.wsj.com/video/this-is-israel-911-says-israeli-ambassador-to-the-united-nations/EEB7D0D5-81CF-480D-A3E3-7B2FE666EE29.

Weitz, Gidi. 2023. Another conception collapses an indicted man cannot lead the country." Haaretz October 9, https://www.haaretz.co.il/news/politi/2023-10-09/ty-article/.highlight/0000018b-10f0-d2fb-a3df-d1f5ac2a0000.

White House. 2023a. "Remarks by President Biden on the October 7th terrorist attacks and the resilience of the State of Israel and its people." October 18, https://www.whitehouse.gov/briefing-room/speeches-remarks/2023/10/18/remarks-by-president-biden-on-the-october-7th-terrorist-attacks-and-the-resilience-of-the-state-of-israel-and-its-people-tel-aviv-israel/.

White House. 2023b. "Full transcript: Biden's speech on Israel–Hamas and Russia–Ukraine wars." October 19, https://www.nytimes.com/2023/10/19/us/politics/transcript-biden-speech-israel-ukraine.html?mwgrp=a-dbar&smid=url-share.

Williamson, Lucy. 2023. "Israel Gaza: Hamas raped and mutilated women on 7 October, BBC hears." BBC, December 5, https://www.bbc.co.uk/news/world-middle-east-67629181.

Woolf, Virginia. 1938 [1966]. *Three Guineas.* Houghton Mifflin Harcourt.

Zaken, Danny. 2021. "Bennet on Netanyahu and Iran: I was shocked by the gap between rhetoric and action." *Globes*, November 23, https://www.globes.co.il/news/article.aspx?did=1001391840.

Zaytun, Yoav. 2023. "Galant: I order a complete siege of Gaza." *Ynet*, October 9, https://www.ynet.co.il/news/article/rjjzuhbzp.

Zipperstein, Steven J. 2018. *Pogrom: Kishinev and the Tilt of History.* Stanford University Press.